194

52149

CONTINENTAL PHILOSOPHY II

CONTINENTAL PHILOSOPHY II

Derrida and Deconstruction

EDITED BY HUGH J. SILVERMAN

ROUTLEDGE
New York and London

52149

First published in 1989 by
Routledge
29 West 35th Street, New York, NY 10001
11 New Fetter Lane, London EC4P 4EE

Library of Congress Cataloging in Publication Data

(Continental philosophy; 2)
Bibliography: p.
Includes index.
1. Derrida, Jacques—Criticism and interpretation.
2. Deconstruction. I. Silverman, Hugh J. II. Series.
PN98.D43D46 1989 194 88—26403

British Library Cataloguing in Publication Data

Derrida and deconstruction.—(Continental
philosophy; II).
1. French philosophy. Derrida, Jacques,
1930–. Critical studies
I. Silverman, Hugh J. II. Series
194

ISBN 0–415–03093–5
ISBN 0–415–03094–3 Pbk

CONTENTS

CONTENTS

5 Hegel

6 Nietzsche

7 Freud

8 Husserl

9 Heidegger

10 Sartre

CONTENTS

INTRODUCTION

Continental Philosophy-I addressed the major developments in the continental mode of philosophizing from the time of Merleau-Ponty's last lectures on 'philosophy and non-philosophy' in 1961. It provided a rather comprehensive account of directions and practices in continental philosophy in the past quarter of a century. *CP-II* focuses on one of those major aspects of continental thought, namely, 'deconstruction' and the corresponding philosophical practice of Jacques Derrida. In contrast to *CP-I* in which the task was to explore major figures and their practices in the contemporary context, *CP-II* takes up the methods and orientations of deconstruction with respect to some of the most important names in the history of philosophy. Each of the essays in this volume assesses Derridean deconstruction as a *philosophical* practice in relation to dominant historical figures in the western tradition. This list of names is brought up to the contemporary era and even into the past several decades in terms of Heidegger, Sartre, Levinas, and Foucault. And while Levinas (who had studied with both Husserl and Heidegger) is the only one of those considered who continues to write, his study of Husserl, published in the early 1930s, introduced Sartre to Husserlian phenomenology long before Levinas's own philosophy was at all known.

Naturally, the set of philosophers presented in *CP-II* is selective.[1] Yet it is representative of those many significant periods and orientations in the history of philosophy that preoccupy continental thinking as it is understood today. Even with this limitation, there will be other names that ought to have been included here. However, our task has been to demonstrate aspects of Derridean deconstruction in relation to the history of

1

philosophy and its highlights. Comprehensiveness and exhaustiveness has not been our concern. We wanted to offer a general account, not a total account (as Foucault would have said). Given limitations of space, we opted for in-depth studies of those figures considered rather than a superficial overview.

For many years Jacques Derrida taught the history of philosophy at the École Normale Supérieure in Paris. Recently appointed *Directeur d'Études* at the École des Hautes Études en Sciences Sociales, Derrida's teaching is no longer officially limited to lectures in the history of philosophy. Indeed, only since he began teaching at Yale (and now at the University of California at Irvine) for a portion of the academic year has he taken up interdisciplinary contemporary topics in an institutional capacity. Thus many of his formative essays were devoted to readings of important figures in the history of philosophy. This second volume of *Continental Philosophy* captures the spirit as well as the content of those historical studies by following a more or less chronological–diachronic accounting of Derrida's relation to Plato, Meister Eckhart, Descartes, Kant, Hegel, Nietzsche, Freud, Husserl, Heidegger, Sartre, Levinas, and Foucault.

While we have set out to present facets of Derridean deconstruction in relation to these major figures in the history of philosophy, our task has also been to demonstrate the principal aspects of deconstruction as philosophy. While other studies of deconstruction bring out the dominant features of the strategy and method,[2] this volume explores not only what Derrida has said about figures in the history of philosophy but also how his practice both draws upon and rereads the tradition itself. The contributors to this volume examine what Derrida has written about the various philosophers in question, studying and developing the character, features, and implications of the relation itself. At the same time, they demonstrate their own manner of philosophizing in the continental tradition and bring out aspects of Derridean readings that have import for contemporary philosophical understanding. The contributors themselves are philosophers who have already written not only on Derrida and deconstruction but also on the corresponding philosopher whom they discuss. Hence they are each particularly well qualified to treat the conjunction of Derrida and the figure in question. Furthermore, the bibliography offered at the end of this volume provides not only a full listing of Derrida's publications in French and in English but also a broad spectrum of writings on Derrida and deconstruction available in English. Along with the essays themselves, this bibliography should provide a substantial reference tool for anyone interested in exploring this topic further.

Jacques Derrida was born in 1930. While his philosophical training was done at the École Normale Supérieure, where he subsequently taught until quite recently, his writings have had an impact upon a broad spectrum of thinking in the human sciences and cultural criticism. Although he received his *doctorat d'État* in Paris only recently (1980) and on the basis of his many publications, Derrida's writings have had an even more significant effect outside France than at home. This element of alterity at the center is important for understanding continental philosophy in general. The term itself was introduced by British philosophers who referred to the philosophy practiced on the European continent as other than that which they themselves did. At first, and in its original version, continental philosophy was characterized almost exclusively as some type of phenomenology (transcendental, existential, or hermeneutic). Analytic philosophy (positivist, linguistic, or ordinary language) set itself off against these accounts of phenomenology. Gradually, even in Britain, continental philosophy came to characterize an aspect of philosophy (a legitimate 'area' of philosophy) that could be taught as part of the philosophy course offerings. With the burgeoning of interest in continental thought, this 'area' became a mode of philosophizing in its own right – even one that could be practiced by British and American philosophers irrespective of what was happening on the continent itself. Indeed, often some of the most adventuresome and significant work in continental philosophy has been occurring outside the European continent (though still owing its debt to certain traditions and modes of thinking prevalent there in this century). Hermeneutics, semiotics, critical and dialectical theory, structuralism, post-structuralism, 'French' feminism, deconstruction, and post-modernism all came to operate as continental thought whether in Europe or elsewhere. That Jacques Derrida often lectures and teaches in the United States (and on occasion in Britain) intensifies the non-geographical location of what is now known as continental philosophy.

Deconstruction itself has extended far beyond the limits of philosophical gates. Although first developed as philosophy, it has spread not only into literary, art, and film criticism and theory, but also into psychoanalytic, pedagogical, and social theory. To return deconstruction here to the history of philosophy is to revert to its place of formation as textual reading. Indeed, to put it in a nutshell, deconstruction is the reading of texts in terms of their marks, traces, or indecidable features, in terms of their margins, limits, or frameworks, and in terms of their self-circumscriptions or self-delimitations as texts. But what does this mean? It means that deconstruction is concerned with offering an account of what is going on in a text – not by seeking out its meaning, or its component parts, or its systematic implications – but rather by marking off its relations to other texts, its contexts, its sub-texts. It means that deconstruction accounts for how a text's explicit formulations undermine its implicit or non-explicit aspects. It brings out what the text excludes by showing what it includes. It highlights what remains indecidable and what operates as an indecidable in the text itself. The essays in this volume bring out these elements of marginality, supplementarity, and indecidability as they operate in the reading of texts in the western philosophical tradition. They mutually illuminate aspects of deconstruction and of the philosophical texts in question. They will be valuable to those interested in understanding deconstruction via the history of philosophy, and even the history of philosophy via deconstruction.

The making of *Continental Philosophy* is no simple task in itself. Essays are referred to a reader competent in the topic and evaluated for their cogency, effectiveness of expression, and ultimate importance. The *CP* staff also reads these essays carefully and helps to edit the contributions down to a polished piece of work. Without the energy and diligence of the Assistant Editorial Staff, *CP* would not meet the standards of high quality and philosophical significance that we set for these volumes. The many hours and continuous efforts which Barry, James

Clarke, Jim Hatley, and Brian Seitz give to making *CP* a success are most extraordinary. This project takes shape, moves into place, and reaches its completion through their devoted and generous contribution. We are correspondingly grateful for the help and concern of our editors Stratford Caldecott in London and Maureen MacGrogan in New York. Their own efforts on our behalf and in developing the *Continental Philosophy* series at all of its various stages has our special thanks and appreciation. Furthermore, we are pleased to acknowledge the significance of these volumes now appearing under the aegis of the new Routledge.[3]

Hugh J. Silverman, *Editor*

Chapter 1

PLATO'S *PHARMAKON*: BETWEEN TWO REPETITIONS

Walter Brogan

Yes, there is much of the
ancients in what I have
said. Everything perhaps.[1]

In the first part of *Dissemination*, Derrida offers a deconstructive
reading of Plato. His discussion reveals a complex network
of significations associated with the word *pharmakon* in and
surrounding Plato's texts. The unraveling of this hardly noticed
and variously translated word, which does service for Plato in
some of his most striking passages, reveals it to have an oper-
ational force that both sustains Plato's discourse within the
closure of metaphysical oppositions and hierarchical valuations
and, in instituting these dichotomies, differs from the systematic structures that it produces. The word *pharmakon* has for
Plato, as 'supplement,' '*hama*,' 'hymen,' and other such 'words'
have for other writers, a supplementary power and indecidable
meaning that disrupts, in an 'originary' manner, the pristine
purity and unadulterated presence that Plato ostensibly aspires
to as the aim and final guarantee of philosophical discourse.

In this paper I follow three strands of Derrida's intricate and
often oscillating investigation of Plato's texts: (1) One reading
of Plato that Derrida gives follows Plato's suppression of writing
and traces the effects of this decision which produces the
Platonic system of metaphysical oppositions and the effacement
of an 'originary' or arche-writing in Plato's texts. (2) In another
reading, Derrida strategically pursues the various meanings of
the Greek word *pharmakon* in and surrounding Plato's texts.
Here some of the facets of Derrida's deconstructive reading of
Plato are exposed. This reading discovers another text in Plato,

7

one that has been read out to some extent in the history of Platonic interpretations, in part because of a proliferation of translations of the term *pharmakon* that cover over the contradictory force of this term in Plato and in part due to a certain necessity rooted in the metaphysical assumptions about language with which philosophy has operated. (3) But Derrida also recognizes within Plato's own writings deconstructive strategies that themselves demand a 'double reading' and disrupt the univocity of Platonism. I follow Derrida in allowing these three strands to play on each other and do not attempt to deal with each of them in isolation.

I Writing on Derrida

Before entering these phases I would like to make some prefatory remarks about the difficulty of offering a reading of Derrida's discussion of Plato's *pharmakon*. The word *pharmakon* in Greek has multiple and contradictory meanings. Among these are included: a drug, a healing remedy or medicine, an enchanted potion or philter, a charm or spell, a poison, a means of producing something, a dye or paint. Although, as Derrida points out, Plato never uses the word, *pharmakon* is related to the word *pharmakos* which means a scapegoat sacrificed for atonement and purification. It is also related to the word *pharmakeia* which means pharmacy or sorcery and is also the name of the maiden with whom Orithyia was playing in the myth of Boreas that Plato relates in the *Phaedrus*.

Derrida insists that even when Plato contextualizes this word in such a way as to lead its meaning in one of these directions rather than another, the multivalence of the word remains in effect in the Greek text. A persistent element of Derrida's discussion in the 'Pharmakon' essay involves the often legitimate and even necessary neutralization, as a result of translation decisions, of the playful force of the different functions of the same word, the neutralization of what Derrida calls Plato's 'anagrammatic writing'.[2] Every translation is *a* reading which runs the risk of closing off as much as it opens up. For Derrida this is not so much an indication of the difficulty or impossibility of translating as a symptom of a more general problematic with regard to writing. The effect of the necessary substitution of various words to translate *pharmakon* in various contexts is to obliterate and make almost unreadable the 'malleable unity' that allows this word to function.

> All translations into languages that are the heirs and depositories of Western metaphysics thus produce on the *pharmakon* an *effect of analysis* that violently destroys it, reduces it to one of its simple elements by interpreting it, paradoxically enough, in the light of the ulterior developments it itself has made possible. Such an interpretative translation is thus as violent as it is impotent: it destroys the *pharmakon* but at the same time forbids itself access to it, leaving it untouched in its reserve. (*D*, p. 99)

The logic of Western philosophy requires the dismemberment and separation of the contradictory force of the word *pharmakon* into two opposing terms in order that the contradiction be exposed. The problems of translation and interpretation are bound up, therefore, with the metaphysical character of the language to which a text is being transferred and the language from which it is transformed. A remedy is the opposite of a poison and therefore not a poison. The one excludes the other. The resolution of this contradiction in the framework of speculative dialectics, for example, requires a decision that one term be valued over the other and the contradiction be sublated in yet a third term. In contrast, deconstruction attempts to subvert this dialectical logic that would reincorporate whatever operated outside its system by virtue of its being in charge of the opposition between the inside and outside. To do so, it employs the logic of neither/nor and both/and against that of binary opposition.[3]

Yet another difficulty in writing a commentary on Derrida's commentary on Plato's *pharmakon* involves the nature of commentary. What Derrida is after in his reading of Plato is not available to the traditional commentator:

> To come to an understanding with Plato, as it is sketched out in this text, is already to slip away from the recognized models of commentary, from the genealogical or structural reconstitution of a system, whether this reconstitution tries to corroborate or refute, confirm or 'overturn,' mark a

return-to-Plato or give him a 'send-off' in the quite Platonic manner of the *khairein*. What is going on here is something altogether different. That too, of course, but still completely other. (*D*, p. 104)

What Derrida, one might say, is after is that excess, that fold, which cannot be comprehended and identified within the system that a traditional commentary would pretend to comment on. The kind of repetition such a commentary proffers belongs already within the Platonic system that Plato effected. The commentator subjects the value of his or her writing to the authentic meaning of the text that is being commented on. As a substitute, such a commentary defers to the original in its attempt to uncover it. In contrast, Derrida seeks to displace the assumption of authorial privilege. As we will see, this is also characteristic of Plato's style of writing and the kind of repetition at work here implicates the very issue of writing in general for both Plato and Derrida.

Derrida offers his 'commentary' on Plato as a kind of post-script addended to an already stated position. He begins by saying: 'To a considerable degree, we have already said all we *meant to say*' (*D*, p. 65). This indicates that the text which follows is not governed by intentional structures that unfold a preplanned point of view about the meaning of the writings under examination in *Dissemination*. But if Derrida has already said all he meant to say, then we might expect to find laid out beforehand, in a pre-text to this lengthy epilogue, what he means to say. Instead, we find only another hors d'oeuvre, an 'outwork,' that begins: 'This (therefore) will not have been a book. . . . These texts are assembled otherwise; it is not my intention here to *present* them (*D*, p. 3).

So we are faced in this 'book' with a preface and appendix, a preface that postpones its task of prefacing and an epigraph that extends 'by force of play' this circling of the question of what is taking place in his work. *Dissemination* deconstructs the difference between the inside and the outside and is itself written around the edges of this opposition – neither inside nor outside, both interior and exterior, to the kind of writing that tries to contain itself within the defined contours of a book:

There is nothing but text, there is nothing but extratext, in sum an 'unceasing preface' that undoes the philosophical representation of the text, the received opposition between the text and what exceeds it. The space of dissemination does not merely place the *plural* in effervescence, it shakes up an endless contradiction, marked out by the undecidable syntax of 'more.' (*D*, p. 43)

Derrida's non-book is not written in the traditional style of a commentary. It does not flow from preface to main body to conclusion in the manner to which we have become accustomed. It does not accept Plato's insistence that 'good' writing, like a living body, is properly organized with head and feet. *Dissemination*, although containing a lengthy essay on Plato and constant allusions to him, disrupts by its literary style Plato's apparent thesis about writing. Moreover, it does not pretend to make present a 'thesis' about Plato. Derrida, like Socrates, risks the accusation that he turns everything upside down and makes the lower appear to be the higher. Like Socrates, he risks the charge that he never says anything and refuses to be pinned down.

Derrida's style of writing in his Pharmakon essay is performative rather than informative. It doesn't so much inform us about what Plato says as actively repeat the activity of writing the text by incisively cutting into the Platonic text at a point where the text is open to a moment of alterity and from which divergent paths through the texts can be pursued. In the case of Plato, it is the *pharmakon* that functions in this manner. The *pharmakon* is that double-edged word in Plato's text that causes the metaphysical oppositions to waver and oscillate. But in wavering and oscillating, these oppositions are neither disbanded nor overcome. Rather their formative power is once again surfaced; they begin again to play out their games, they are enabled again to trace their own origins. Derrida tries to attend to this movement of the text. It is a movement that cannot be experienced if one understands the structure of a text to be emanating from a fixed center or origin. Every origin is always already displaced in the activity of writing. Writing poses signs as substitutes for the intrinsically absent and nonlocatable origin, an origin, therefore, that is always other and different – an origin that is perpetually deferred by writing. But this origin is itself writing, a 'protowriting' that produces difference, and within this productive, doubling repetition opens up an interval in which a dialogue can take place.

According to Derrida, no text is fixed, stable, and completely circumscribed by its predetermined standpoint. Derrida's deconstructive writing actively disrupts the insistence that a text be read in a prescribed manner. But his writing is not for this reason a willful countertext that forces its interpretation onto the text. Rather, deconstruction is an approach to reading a text that grows out of a contemporary 'epoch' of post-metaphysical thinking that aligns itself in various ways with the work of Nietzsche, Bataille, Freud, Saussure, Levinas, Heidegger, and others who attempt to think the absence of a center out of the closure of metaphysics: 'It is a question of explicitly and systematically posing the problem of the status of a discourse which borrows from a heritage the resources necessary for the deconstruction of that heritage itself. A problem of *economy* and *strategy'* (*WD*, p. 282). Derrida is concerned to radicalize a discourse and movement which already has a certain heritage and necessity in our age. This radicalization involves the recognition that being post-metaphysical or writing after Platonism is always already caught up in relationships between the inside and the outside, the within and the beyond, etc., relationships that, if taken for granted, only reaffirm the metaphysical bonds that one is attempting to overcome. The 'strategy' of deconstruction seeks to break up and disseminate the economy of the text by drawing out the excess and subtracting the remainder that is both inside and outside the text and refuses to yield its power to slide between these categories. The *pharmakon* is one of Plato's words that resists confinement and lends itself to dissemination.

One of Derrida's favorite 'metaphors' for deconstruction is weaving, a metaphor that is also prominent in Plato's dialogues.[4] The web of writing is not constructed along the lines of simple hierarchies that interrelate fixed points that we call concepts and words. The woven text has a texture that stretches and shrinks, can expand, can be grafted onto, can fold, warp, and unravel. To follow the patterns and interlacing of the composition requires the weaver's art of looping and knotting. The surface of the woven cloth dissimulates its complex and intricate networking:

There is always a surprise in store for the anatomy or
physiology of any criticism that might think it had
mastered the game, surveyed all the threads at once,
deluding itself, too, in wanting to look at the text without
touching it, without laying a hand on the 'object,' without
risking – which is the only chance of entering into the
game, by getting a few fingers caught – the addition of some
new thread. Adding, here, is nothing other than giving to
read. (D, p. 63)

II The derivative status of writing

The dialogue that thematizes Plato's ambivalent relationship to
the written word is of course the *Phaedrus*. In the *Phaedrus*,
Socrates makes the point that the written speech of Lysias, like
the epitaph on the tomb of Midas, has interchangeable parts
that have no organizational or compositional integrity. The
speech seemed to Socrates to say 'the same thing several times
over.'[5] Like the epitaph, it is infinitely repeatable. It has no
beginning or end, is not organized like a living being with head
and tail. It is a dead discourse – mere repetition. Phaedrus,
in contrast, considers the speech to have 'not overlooked any
important aspect of the subject' (*Phaedrus*, 235b). Having a
complete grasp of the subject, nothing more can be added to
it. Thus the only task that remains is to memorize it so that one
will always have it available to repeat randomly and at will. The
two positions with regard to Lysias's speech are ironically not
far apart.[6]

What Socrates does in his first speech, his repetition of
Lysias's position, is to control the speech, arrange it on the
basis of definition, subject it to the laws of dialectic. This
decision about the style of writing that befits philosophical
discourse sets the stage for the confrontation between sophistry
and philosophy. The philosopher places his discourse at the
service of a definition of the matter to be investigated.His
discourse manifests the truth that this definition reveals and
unfolds this truth in distinction from its opposite. In contrast,
the sophists' speech is capricious and without foundation. It
does not hold itself responsible to the truth: 'There is, they
maintain, absolutely no need for the budding orator to concern

himself with the truth' (*Phaedrus*, 272d). Philosophical writing has something beyond itself to report. It can only repeat this message which has been inscribed elsewhere. Thus Derrida concludes: 'The philosophical text, although it is in fact always written, includes, precisely as its philosophical specificity, the project of effacing itself in the face of the signified content which it transports and in general teaches.'[7] Philosophical writing is, by virtue of its willingness to efface itself in the face of truth, to be considered superior, according to Plato, to that other kind of writing which tries to take a stand on its own and solidify its position without regard for truth. Philosophical writing is the good servant that remains silent in the presence of the master and that merely marks a place for this presence in the master's absence. This 'good' writing remains the servant of that whose precursor it is, but which it cannot directly address or present.

For Plato, even philosophical writing is tertiary and derivative. It gives way to the *logos* that is written in the soul which in turn responds to that excess beyond being – the good – which engenders the ideas in *logos*. The philosophical word can never of itself accomplish or fulfill the philosophical project. Thus Socrates's first speech in the *Phaedrus*, his reorganization of Lysias's speech, remains incomplete, as Phaedrus points out to Socrates. This is perhaps why so many of Plato's dialogues end without a resolution of the matter at issue. Thus Cratylus says at the end of his dialogue with Socrates: 'Very good, Socrates. I hope, however, that you will continue to think about these things yourself' (*Cratylus*, 440e). And in the *Euthyphro* Socrates's last statement is: 'And so we must go back again and start from the beginning to find out what the holy is' (*Euthyphro*, 15c). And lest we think this trait is abandoned after Plato's early work, we should note, as an example, the irony of Socrates's statement at the end of the *Theaetetus*: 'Our midwife's skill pronounces all of our utterances to be mere wind eggs and not worth the rearing' (*Theaetetus*, 210b). In the *Seventh Letter*, Plato makes a surprising claim: 'I certainly have not written any work in regard to the matter for thinking, nor shall I do so in the future, for there is no way of putting it into words like other studies' (*Letter VII*, 341c). For Plato, neither the philosopher's written words, nor his *logos*, his own presence as a guarantee of the accurate interpretation of his words, is sufficient since no discourse is capable of capturing the truth.

Plato's insistence on the subservience of the written word is not merely a position he takes but a conviction that affects the way he writes. In the *Phaedrus*, during Socrates's speech of atonement to *eros* – his homage to the excess and madness that the first two speeches attempted to exclude – Socrates finds himself unable to report directly on the nature of the soul: 'What manner of thing it is would be a long tale to tell, and most assuredly a god alone could tell it, but what it resembles, that a man might tell in briefer compass' (*Phaedrus*, 246a). And in the *Republic*, Socrates responds to the request of his interlocutors for a direct account of the good by saying that he can only offer an image. Socrates calls himself one who is greedy for images. In fact, the whole center of the *Republic* operates out of images, analogies, and allegories.[8] This is ironic from a philosopher who has set the tone for western philosophy by banning myth, imaging, and art from the philosophical community because of their distance from the truth and their relation to non-truth.[9]

Plato's lack of desire to be an author who reports the truth to us can be seen in the *Symposium* through the way he has Socrates distance himself from any claim to authority about the subject of *eros* of which he is speaking. He does not present his own speech on *eros* but recalls a speech he has heard from Diotima. In fact, the entire dialogue of the *Symposium* is cast in the form of a remembrance of a previous account of the banquet by someone who remembered, to some extent, what had taken place. Socrates is not the reporter of the dialogue, and his speech is not his own. Often at the most crucial point in a dialogue, Socrates indicates that he is speaking under divine inspiration or under the influence of the daimonic voice that prohibits a certain course of action. In the *Phaedrus*, Socrates attributes his speeches first to some forgotten author, then to the local deities, then to the nymphs and Pan, then to the cicadas who are chirping about, and finally even to Phaedrus. This decentering of Socrates is carried even further in Plato's later dialogues. This may indicate Plato's sensitivity to the transformation of philosophy into a written legend. Perhaps the matter of philosophy had already been absorbed into philosophical scholarship of a secondary sort. Perhaps philosophy had already become a matter of fidelity to the master. Had Plato already been accused of inaccurate record-keeping? At any rate, a primary indication for Plato of the difference between sophistry and philosophy is found in the philosopher's recognition that he is not the author of his own discourse. This is, perhaps, the reason why Plato never says anything in his dialogues. The question, directed solely toward discovering what Plato said – what he meant to say – is naive and misguided. Plato's strategies completely undermine such an approach to his text. Thus, Derrida comments on the chain of significations in which the word *pharmakon* is caught:

> The system here is not simply that of the intentions of the author by the name of Plato. . . . Finely regulated communications or corridors of meaning can sometimes be declared or clarified by Plato when he plays upon them 'voluntarily,' a word we put in quotation marks because what it designates, to content ourselves with remaining within the closure of these oppositions, is only a mode of 'submission' to the necessities of a given 'language.' (*D*, p. 95)

In the final part of the *Phaedrus*, Plato explicitly takes up the issue of writing. As Derrida points out, this discussion of writing has been considered an embarrassment to the structural integrity of the dialogue. It appears as an appendix to an already completed discussion of speech, dialectic, and the soul. Apparently few of these critics considered the appropriateness of presenting as an afterthought this discussion of writing as a reminder for those who are forgetful. But in fact the issue of writing is pervasive in the dialogue. The dialogue begins after all with the hidden written speech of Lysias that Phaedrus is carrying with him outside the city. At the end of the dialogue, writing is condemned by Thamus as a *pharmakon* (a poison?) that will poison people's memory and increase forgetfulness. And at the beginning of the dialogue, as Phaedrus is about to read the text of Lysias, Socrates tells Phaedrus that he has discovered the *pharmakon* (recipe? philter? allurement?) that alone would tempt him to leave the city as they have done. Writing, like the madness of *eros*, is dangerous, seductive, and ambivalent:

16

Only the *logoi en bibliois*, only words that are deferred, reserved, enveloped, rolled up, words that force one to wait for them in the form and under the cover of a solid object, letting themselves be desired for the space of a walk, only hidden letters can thus get Socrates moving. If a speech could be purely present, unveiled, naked, offered up in person in its truth, without the detours of a signifier foreign to it, if at the limit an undeferred *logos* were possible, it would not seduce anyone. It would not draw Socrates, as if under the effects of a *pharmakon*, out of his way. (*D*, p. 71)

It is the written speech that is erotic to Socrates, that lures him as a *pharmakon* from the city. It is the sight of the written speech under Phaedrus's cloak that arouses Socrates – much as the opening in Charmides's cloak when Charmides comes over to Socrates to write down Socrates's prescription (*pharmakon*) for relief of his headache (*Charmides*, 155d–e). It is clear that Plato's condemnation of writing is not as straightforward as it might appear. Despite its derivative status, or perhaps because of it, writing has an almost irresistible appeal.

Plato's erotic relationship to writing is as ambiguous as the evaluation of *eros* in the speeches delivered in the *Phaedrus*. There Socrates distinguishes between erotic madness that comes from the gods and the base madness that had been the subject of the previous addresses (*Phaedrus*, 244a). In the *Symposium*, Diotima relates *eros* to death and says love is a desire not to die, a longing for immortality (*athanasia*). She also says *eros* is a *pharmakeus*, a pharmacist (one adept at sorcery?) (*Symposium*, 203d). In the *Phaedrus*, as previously noted, Pharmacy is the maiden who, in the myth of Boreas, is playing with Orithyia when Boreas sweeps Orithyia to her seduction and death. But Socrates tells us he is too preoccupied with the search for self-knowledge to bother about myth. Both myth and writing give way to the truth that is discovered through self-presence. Socrates and Phaedrus conclude that authors of written compositions are worthy of reproach if they regard it as containing important truth of permanent validity. For ignorance of what is a waking vision and what is a mere dream image of justice and injustice, good and evil, cannot truly be acquitted of involving reproach, even if the mass of men extol it (*Phaedrus*, 277e).

Plato's suspicion of writing and myth turns on the question of morality. As Derrida notes: 'It is truly *morality* that is at stake, both in the sense of the opposition between good and evil, or good and bad, and in the sense of mores, public morals and social conventions' (*D*, p. 74). The trial of writing at the end of the *Phaedrus* is a discussion of the conditions that make it proper or improper. Writing has a precarious moral status. So, of course, do the poetic myths of Homer for which philosophy is said to provide a countercharm (*alexipharmakon*) to their spellbinding allurement (*Republic* X, 608a). The argument for the kinship between the case of writing and that of myth is reinforced not only by the fact that both are frequently called *pharmakon* by Plato but also by the fact that Plato cloaks the attack on writing in a myth, even after having claimed to leave myths aside. All writing and myth are repetitions of the truth and not themselves the bearers of truth. But there are two kinds of repetition, the one good and the other bad. Good writing is 'written in the soul' (*Phaedrus*, 278a). But Derrida warns:

> One must here take care: at the moment Plato seems to be raising writing up by turning live speech into a sort of psychic *graphe*, he maintains this movement within a problematic of *truth*. Writing *en tei psuchei* is not pathbreaking writing, but only a writing of transmission, of education, of demonstration, or at best, of dis-covering, a writing of *aletheia*. Its order is didactic, maieuthic, or at any rate elocutionary. Dialectical. This type of writing must be capable of sustaining itself in living dialogue, capable most of all of properly teaching the true, as it is *already* constituted. (*D*, p. 154)

Socratic discourse submits itself to this dependency. The Socratic art is the art of midwifery. Its erotic longing for immortality cannot be fulfilled by itself. Its signifiers can only engender when they are united with the signified from which they originate. They have no offspring on their own. Diotima tells Socrates:

> Remember that it is only when he discerns beauty itself

through what makes it visible that a man will be quickened with the true, and not the seeming, virtue – for it is virtue's self that quickens him, not virtue's semblance. And when he has brought forth and reared this true virtue, he shall be called the friend of god, and *if* ever it is given to man to put on immortality, it shall be given to him. (*Symposium*, 212a)

Bad writing, in contrast, is 'a seed scattered wastefully outside: at the risk of *dissemination*' (*D*, p. 149). This is perhaps why *Dissemination* is not written as a book. Were it subject to the Platonic laws of writing, it would be bad writing. But Derrida's dissemination breaks loose these moral dichotomies. Were bad writing indeed simply on the outside and purely external, Plato would not have found it erotic nor would he have considered it to be a dangerous supplement. Plato had to expurgate this *pharmakos* (scapegoat) by establishing its otherness in relation to and in opposition to good writing.[10] Derrida suggests that philosophy since Plato is played out in the play between these two kinds of writing, these two kinds of repetition.

III Patriarchal writing and patricide

In Plato's mythical account in the *Phaedrus* of the origin of writing, Theuth brings his 'invention' to Thamus as a gift to assist the people of Egypt to become wiser and to improve their memory (*Phaedrus*, 274e). But King Thamus rejects Theuth's claim that his 'offspring' will be a *pharmakon* for memory (*mneme*). Writing is only good for reminding (*hypomnesis*). It will not produce wisdom but only its semblance. It will teach the people to rely on alien, external marks and to forget the true interior knowledge that is written in the soul. Theuth is reprimanded for usurping the prerogative of the king to be the judge of the worth of writing. Derrida addresses the issue of hierarchical systematization and patriarchal thinking to which Plato subjects writing: 'Writing will have no value, unless and to the extent that god-the-king [Theuth is Ammon, the father of the gods and sun king in Egyptian mythology] approves of it' (*D*, p. 76). Writing has no intrinsic value, no essence of its own. Only that kind of writing that can stand in the presence

19

of the father and receive its meaning from him is worthy of serious pursuit. To do so, writing would have to be natural, living discourse – *logos*. Artificial, invented writing can never replace *logos*. Writing is a miserable substitute, a simulacrum, of worthy discourse. It is offered as a supplement to compensate for the loss of memory, for the absence of a present relationship to truth. But it also tries to make the presence of the father unnecessary, to supplant the authority of the king with its own remarks. It can serve, Plato tells us, as a playful reminder for those who already know and as a geriatric pastime for those no longer capable of engendering (*Phaedrus*, 276d). But it also carries with it the danger of deception and misuse because it is incapable of recognizing and responding to its own true origin. Theuth, the loyal servant of Thamus, has only produced a dead son with his *techne*. In contrast, the living word that is generated by Thamus has the power to repay its debt to its creator. This is the 'legitimate son' as opposed to its 'orphan' brother whose claim to represent the father is always in question (*Phaedrus*, 276a–b) and who is constantly in need of outside parental intervention to keep him from going astray. Derrida makes the following comment about this Platonic myth which, as he shows, can be inserted into a web of other related myths and references to the origin of writing in transcultural mythologies:

> Plato had to make his tale conform to structural laws. The most general of these [are] those that govern and articulate the oppositions speech/writing, life/death, father/son, master/servant, legitimate son/orphan–bastard, soul/body, inside/outside, good/evil, seriousness/play, day/night, sun/moon.[11]

Later on (*D*, p. 103), Derrida adds good/evil, true/false and essence/appearance to this matrix of opposition.

Both writing and speech are products of the father. Yet the father as such can only appear in his offspring as repeated. The repetition is never identical with the father. Speech and writing stand in the space that the father opens up through his creations, the space of differences. The interior space of *logos* written in the soul remains submissive and responsive. For living discourse, this space is the relationships of the ideas that are the multifaceted progeny of the good. In the *Phaedo*, Socrates says he sought truth in the world of *idea*, lest he be blinded by the eclipse of the sun (*Phaedo*, 99d). *Logos* represents and keeps in memory the effects of the good since it cannot look directly at the good. As Derrida says: 'The true is the presence of the *eidos* signified' (*D*, p. 111). In contrast, writing, *graphe* as opposed to *logos*, is also a repetition, but:

> What is repeated is the repeater, the imitator, the signifier, the representative, in the absence, as it happens, of *the thing itself*, which these appear to reedit, and without psychic or mnesic animation, without the living tension of dialectics. (*D*, p. 111)

Writing is the orphan child whose activity takes place in the radical absence, the death of the father. It reduplicates the father's progeny as they are there on their own without recourse to their animate nature which only their father can sustain. It is interesting to take note in this regard of a passage in the *Phaedo* that indicates a moment of doubt in Socrates, as he faces his death, concerning his rejection of the art of writing. On his deathbed, Socrates has been composing lyrics and his companions ask him what has induced him to write for the first time. He responds that he had always interpreted the daimonic voice in his dreams that commanded him to practice and culti- vate the arts as meaning philosophy. But since his trial he was not so sure and thought it best to write poetry in order to obey the voice (*Phaedo*, 61a–b). The rest of the dialogue is a discussion of philosophy as the art of dying and of the ambiguity as to whether the poison (*pharmakon*) he is about to take is a great good or an evil. Only in the *Phaedo* – within the horizon of the death of Socrates and thus at the advent of Plato's need to reincorporate and reinscribe the Socratic gesture that began philosophy – is there any indication that Socrates ever wrote anything. If writing for Plato is an ill-begotten and dangerous *pharmakon*, it is nevertheless the case that Plato writes. He writes after and in the face of the death of Socrates. Derrida writes:

> One could cite here both the writing *and* the pederasty of a young man named Plato. And his ambiguous relation to the paternal supplement: in order to make up for the father's

death, he transgressed the law. He repeated the father's death. (*D*, p. 153)

But Socrates is a strange father figure since he himself never produced anything of his own and offered his philosophical activity as a surrogate for the immortal presence of the true father. Can Plato write in such a way as to defer and postpone the loss of Socrates's daimonic power to elicit the effects of the father's presence? Or is his writing a mere mimicry, a violent patricidal repetition that both re-enacts and renounces Socratic discourse?

IV The double reading/writing

In examining speech and writing in Plato, Derrida acknowledges Plato's persistent and tenacious systematization of the meaning and value of each in terms of their proximity to truth. In Plato, and throughout the tradition, this takes the form of a decision that establishes differences, opposes one to the other and excludes one in favor of the other. One moment of Derrida's deconstructive reading of Plato is certainly to reverse the hierarchical preference for speech over writing and to show that this reversal is already at play in Plato's text. Evidence of this was mounted in Derrida's analysis of the metaphor of 'writing in the soul' for speech, in his persuasive argument that even dialectic and dialogue are imitations (*mimesis*) and repetitions of the *eidos* and that truth is itself for Plato the *eidos* signified in *logos*, in his analysis of Plato's recourse to writing myths, to recollection and to the displacement of authorial privilege as a substitute for a direct and immediate access to the good beyond being, and in his recovery of Plato's ambivalent relationship to the *pharmakon* of writing.

But Derrida is not so much concerned merely to reverse the hierarchy within the schema of opposition. His concern is rather with the movement that initiates these oppositions and their reversal:

The old opposition between speech and writing no longer has any pertinence as a way of testing a text that deliberately deconstructs that opposition. Such a text is no more 'spoken' than it is 'written,' no more *against* speech than *for* writing, in the metaphysical senses of these words. Nor is it *for* any third force, particularly any radicalism of the origin or of the center. (*D*, p. 181, note 8)

Derrida complicates the play of reflexivity in which the two concepts of original and image mirror each other in Plato's text. Living *logos* duplicates nature (*physis*) which in turn exists as repetition by repeating itself and coming after itself. Writing doubles this repetition but endangers it by intensifying the gap and slippage between 'original' and copy, between the thing and its disguise.

What announces itself here is an internal division within *mimesis*, a self-duplication of repetition itself; *ad infinitum*, since this movement feeds its own proliferation. Perhaps, then, there is always more than one kind of *mimesis*; and perhaps it is in the strange mirror that reflects but also displaces and distorts one *mimesis* into the other, as though it were itself destined to mime or mask *itself*, that history – the history of literature – is lodged. (*D*, p. 191)

Plato attempts to contain the force of this play under the yoke of truth. He lays down the rules under which this play is forbidden and prohibited. He turns play into a game. It is a game of opposition, of the law of contradiction. These laws mark the alternatives within the closure of metaphysics. At the borders and around the edges of this closure, in *Dissemination* and other writings, Derrida attends to the excess within this closure and between the alternatives provided by metaphysics. He does so by looking for and analyzing those words like *pharmakon* that 'admit into their games both contradiction and noncontradiction (and the contradiction and noncontradiction *between* contradiction and noncontradiction)' (*D*, p. 221). To do so, he employs a different syntax, a syntax that 'both marks and goes back over its mark with an undecidable stroke' (*D*, p. 193). Derrida's double reading/writing of Plato's *pharmakon* affirms the indecidability of the meaning of this word and reinscribes its play in Plato's text.

Chapter 2

MYSTICISM AND TRANSGRESSION: DERRIDA AND MEISTER ECKHART

John D. Caputo

Derrida himself has warned us that it is a mistake to confuse what he says about *différance* with some kind of negative theology – in particular with that of Meister Eckhart whom he mentions by name. I begin by endorsing and underlining that point which I take to be but the beginning, not the end, of the question about deconstruction and negative theology. I set out from there to defend what I call (borrowing an expression from Kierkegaard) the 'armed neutrality' of *différance*. Neutrality: it does not imply or exclude the existence or non-existence of any entity (it is ontically neutral). Armed: it is not particularly hospitable to existence claims but holds them all suspect. Because it is not a substantive position on its own but rather a parasitic practice, deconstruction has no ontological commitments. Thus while it would be comical to find a negative theology in deconstruction, it would not be at all surprising to find deconstruction in negative theology – as a practice, as a strategy, as a way that negative theologians have found to hold the claims of cataphatic theology at bay.

In the second part of the essay I turn to Meister Eckhart himself and I demonstrate the way he called upon a certain deconstructive practice in order to make medieval onto-theo-logic tremble. Then, in the third part, I argue that one finds in Eckhart a great disseminative energy aimed at promoting and enhancing the life of the spirit, a grammatological exuberance and joyful wisdom whose political subversiveness did not go unnoticed by the guardians of onto-theo-logic.

I Negative theology and the armed neutrality of différance

Différance is not God, not even a hidden God, not even the innermost concealed Godhead of negative theology, although sometimes, in the flush of Derrida's more famous accounts of *différance*, it begins to sound a little like a *deus absconditus*. For example, Derrida says in a well-known text that *différance* is not an entity, that it makes no appearance (is not a *phainomenon*), and has no truth. Still *différance* is nothing to be taken lightly, for it makes possible what is present, and while it has no truth or manifestness itself (indeed has no 'itself'), *différance* enables what is manifest to make a show. That sounds a lot like the hidden God Who withdraws behind the veil of the very world which He has created. Sometimes *différance* sounds like that ultimate un-knowable, the un-knowing of which constitutes the most learned wisdom of all (*docta ignorantia*).

Now it is just this suggestive proximity to negative theology which is likely to lead us astray. For *différance* has nothing to do with even 'the most negative of all negative theologies' and this for the very good reason that such theologies:

> are always concerned with disengaging a superessentiality beyond the finite categories of essence and existence, that is, of presence, and always hastening to recall that God is refused the predicate of existence, only in order to acknowledge his superior, inconceivable, and ineffable mode of being. (*MdP*, p. 6 *MoP*, p. 6)[1]

Negative theologies are always just detours on the way to even higher, more sublime affirmations. They are ways of saying in even stronger terms that an entity, namely God, exists: He exists so deeply, so thoroughly, so purely, so perfectly, that we even have to take the word 'is' back if and when we say it. Negative theologies are modified onto-theo-logies, variations on the philosophy of presence which always turn out to be philosophies of super-presence.

And so if we find ourselves saying that *différance* is neither a word nor a concept, that there is no name for what we mean to say when we say *différance*, that is not because we have stumbled upon, or been overtaken by, a being of such supereminence that words fail us. It is because we have in mind the conditions under which words are formed in the first place, and the 'word' for that is a kind of a non-word, anterior to words, the general condition or rule of formation for words. Hence *différance* is not a mystical *nomen innominabile* but a grammatological one. *Différance* is older than the name of Being, older than any name, is not itself a name, in the French language or any other. But this, Derrida says, is to be understood not in all its mystical depth but rather in all its grammatological platitude:

> The unnameable is not an ineffable Being which no name could approach: God, for example. This unnameable is the play which makes possible nominal effects, the relatively unitary and atomic structures that are called names, the chains of or substitutions of names in which, for example, the nominal effect *différance* is itself enmeshed. (*MdP*, p. 28; *MdP*, pp. 26–7)

The namelessness of *différance* does not consist in being an unnameable being but in pointing to the differential matrix which generates names and concepts, in which they are produced as effects. Of course, as soon as it is coined, uttered, repeated, and entered into the lexicon of 'post-structuralist' thinkers, *différance* becomes itself another nominal unity, one more effect of the differential matrix of which it means to be no more than indicator. But it would be a serious misunderstanding to think that it is some master name or kerygmatic announcement of a Being beyond Being, or of a presence which is so pure that it cannot itself appear and be present except by means of the finite and imperfect traces of itself which it leaves behind. Lacking all ontological profundity and mystical depth, *différance* stretches out laterally over the surface as the chain of substitutability, as the coded tracing, within which are generated all names, all the relatively stable nominal unities, including the name of God, including even the name *différance*.

And in a commentary on Levinas and Heidegger, Derrida warns us against confusing *différance* with any of the sayings of Meister Eckhart in particular. Eckhart himself is perfectly clear about the upshot of his negative theology: 'When I said that God was not a Being and was above Being, I did not thereby contest his Being, but on the contrary attributed to him a *more elevated Being'* (*Q, 196*, 25–28).[2] And upon this Derrida comments: 'This negative theology is still a theology and, *in its literality at least*, it is concerned with liberating and acknowledging the ineffable transcendence of an infinite existent' (*ED,* p. 217; *WD,* p. 146).

Negative theology is engaged in the business of establishing ontic transcendence, that is to say, the super-eminent existence of an entity, of a being whose Being is so pure – Eckhart calls it the *puritas essendi,* the purity of Being – that it is best affirmed by being denied, that is, affirmed to be *beyond* Being. And that is why Eckhart was able to write, to the puzzlement of his commentators and to the consternation of the Inquisition, both that God is *esse* while creatures are a pure nothing (not even a little bit), *and* that God is an absolute nothing, a naked desert, while being is the first of all creatures. He wanted to establish the Being of God in so pure a region that the affirmation of His Being had to be continually purified by a denial of Being. Eckhart's orthodoxy on this point is unmistakable, but he had a way of saying things which made his inquisitors nervous.

Now that leads me to the next point I want to make about *différance,* that it has no ontic import, that it carries no ontological weight. In this same remark on Eckhart, Derrida continues:

> *In its literality at least,* but the difference between
> metaphysical ontotheology, on the one hand, and the
> thought of Being (of difference) on the other, signifies the
> essential importance of the *letter. . . .* That is why, here,
> when the thought of Being goes beyond ontic
> determinations it is not a negative theology, or even a
> negative ontology. (*ED,* p. 217; *WD,* p. 146)

The thought of the ontological difference or, for Derrida, of the letter, of *différance* – on this point, I take it, and Derrida too seems to take it, we have to do with parallel thoughts – 'goes beyond ontic determinations.' This is *not* because it affirms a super-ontic entity, but because it has an altogether different, non-ontic function. Difference/*différance* is not itself something ontic, nor does it establish the existence, or higher existence, or non-existence, of anything ontic. Difference/*différance* does not affirm a hidden God (deferring himself behind the chain

27

of signifiers), but neither does it deny God. What then is its function?

> 'Ontological' anticipation, transcendence towards Being, permits, then, an understanding of the word God, for example, even if this understanding is but the ether in which dissonance can resonate. This transcendence inhabits and founds language. (*ED*, p. 217; *WD*, p. 146)

The role of difference/*différance* is to establish the conditions within which discourse functions. It founds (and un-founds, undermines) languages, vocabularies, showing how they are both possible and impossible, that is, incapable of a closure which would give them self-sufficiency and a feeling of success in nailing things down. So difference/*différance* establishes the possibility (and impossibility) of a language which addresses God, even of one which invokes the dissonances of negative theology – even as it establishes the possibility (and impossibility) of a discourse in which God is denied. It does not settle the God-question one way or another. In fact, it *un*settles it, by showing that any debate about the existence of God is beset by the difficulties which typically inhabit such debates, by their inevitable recourse to binary pairs which cannot be made to stick. That is why Nietzsche says that atheism, too, represents the ascetic ideal, the desire to pin things firmly in place (*Genealogy of Morals*, III, section 27).

That, too, is why I am unhappy with Mark Taylor's recent and otherwise quite innovative adaptation of Derrida to 'death of God' theology.[3] Taylor starts out on the right foot by saying that he wants to write an 'a/theology', that is, one that stays on the slash, that writes in between theism and a-theism. He situates himself within the crucial Derridean gesture of indecidability – for *différance* does not show that there either is or is not a God. The problem I have with Taylor is that he proceeds to assimilate Derrida into the familiar death of God story – by which the transcendent God of Christianity becomes the immanent spirit of Hegel, which becomes in turn the divine Man of Feuerbach. If the first round of death-of-God thinking ended up with the birth of Man, with a humanistic atheism, then the role of Derridean deconstruction is to provide us with an even more radically non-humanistic atheism by stamping

28

out that last remnant of metaphysics: Man himself. At the end of his story, God has become *écriture* (with nothing left over). The sacred scripture has become all there is of the sacred itself: God as glyph, as hieroglyph. Now that is not to stay on the slash of indecidability but to make a reductionist decision against God, to reduce the ambiguity of a genuine a/theology and to turn *différance* against God.

The armed neutrality of *différance* means that it is even-handedly antagonistic to all claims of existence or non-existence. It plays no favorites when existence claims are afoot, but gives all parties to the dispute an equally hard time. It shows the limits under which our discourse labors when 'someone says something about something to someone' (*hermeneuein*). *Différance* is neutral by being uniformly nasty about letting vocabularies establish their credentials and get set in place, as if they really were making good in some strong sense on their claims. Its neutrality lies in its unremitting and unbiased antagonism which does not single out theologians for particular abuse but is equally hostile to ontological claims made across the board. It is, for example, just as inhospitable to empiricists and phenomenologists who talk about the 'perceptual' world. Such armed neutrality is, however, not aimed at locking us inside a play of signs but at making us think twice about claiming that our discourse has accomplished what it sets out to do. It throws a scare into our discourse, destroys a bit of the prestige and self-importance of 'reference,' and ends up creating a salutary distrust in the power of language to do what it sets out to do (along with providing an account of how language accomplishes what it does manage to do).[4]

II   Deconstruction and negative theology in Meister Eckhart

Now I would say that Meister Eckhart is a salient example of this recognition that language is caught up in a self-defeating enterprise, that the very terms we employ to assert that something is are caught up in complicity with their opposites, so that language keeps on saying what it says, undoing what it does, and in general failing again and again to make good on its claims. It will of course be objected that I have come back to square one because Eckhart did all of this in the name of a super-essential being, that his confession of the failure of language had an ontological agenda, viz., to establish the super-existence of God beyond the frailties of language.

I have never denied that there is some truth to that.[5] Nor, as we have seen, does Eckhart. When the theologians of the Curia swept down upon him, he hastened to assure them that he spoke with 'brother Thomas' (Aquinas), that he believed in the living God, and that his more extreme formulations were mostly intended to show the existential clout of the truths of the Christian faith.[6] The Christian religion, he insisted, is filled with teachings which should swell our hearts and stir our being instead of just sitting helplessly on the shelves of the monastery library. Eckhart had a faith, a commitment, to the God of Abraham and Moses and to the God Whom Jesus dared call *abba*, father. (Nowadays, the dare is to call God 'mother.')

Now, I started out by saying that I endorse the notion that deconstruction is a parasitic practice. For deconstruction can make a living only inasmuch as there is already someone who wants to say something about something to someone. Deconstruction requires a prior hermeneutics, the anterior work of addressing one another about the matter at hand. Deconstruction lies in wait for 'discourse' to stake its claims and then it pounces on it, showing how much trouble this discourse has bought for itself by its boldness. Were no one bold enough to launch the hermeneutic project, were no one willing to make such claims in the first place, then deconstruction would never get off the ground. This is another way of saying that deconstruction itself has nothing to say, or better that there is no deconstruction 'itself,' that it is a parasitic practice, not a substantive position. In classical terms, the Being of deconstruction always exists *in alio*, by inhabiting the discourse of others, never *in se*, as something present in itself, as some form of *ousia*.

In short, deconstruction is first of all a practice – it is what it does – not a body of theories, and secondly a parasitic practice – what it does is to inhabit the discourse of those who have something to say and to make trouble for them. It needles its way into the discourse of others and shows them how much trouble they have brought upon themselves. Deconstruction does not want to deny that something exists, but only to show the difficulty we have getting that said. That is what it means to say that nothing exists outside the text – viz., that existence claims cannot be disentangled from the web of discourse which make them possible to begin with. Existential assertions cannot break out into the open with atomistic independence, seize upon the things themselves, and then vaporize, leaving us in naked contact with *die Sache selbst*. Deconstruction requires a prior project which it then inhabits and disrupts, not by scattering it to the four winds, but by heightening its appreciation for its own difficulty.

That is why I find in Meister Eckhart a great medieval deconstructive practice, one keenly appreciative of all the trouble that medieval onto-theo-logic has brought down on its head. He understands quite well that the terms 'Being' and 'Nothing' are functions of each other, that each is inscribed in the other, marked and traced by the other, and that neither gets the job done, alone or together. Neither alone seizes upon the living God, nor do both together in a Hegelian synthesis. As a professional theologian at Paris he showed his colleagues the complicity in which binary schemes like Being/Nothing or creator/creature are caught up. He argued that if you start out with the 'being of creatures' then that makes God a nullity, not even a little bit. On the other hand, if you concede the nullity of creatures, then you have perforce admitted, not only that God has being, or is being, but more strongly still that being is God (*esse est deus*). And he did not just make these claims off the cuff, in vernacular sermons to an uneducated audience which could not give him an argument, but he made them in Latin at Paris, to the most sophisticated audience of the day, and he used the most refined arguments of medieval onto-theo-logic to back them up.[7]

Eckhart had an acute sense of what we nowadays call the 'textuality,' the interdependence and differential structure, of the terms of scholastic discourse. That is why he had no great confidence in any particular name we sent God's way. He argued emphatically that to call God 'creator' was just to mark Him off in terms of 'creatures'; to call Him 'cause' was to mark Him off from 'effects'; to call Him 'good' was to name Him in reference to the will; and to call Him 'true' was to give Him a name relative to the intellect (*C-M*, pp. 200–3). Every one of these 'absolute' attributes was 'relative' to something else in the discursive chain. Every time the intentional arrow was aimed at God, it came up with 'God,' which sends us skidding back to something else in the chain of signifiers. The divine names just keep referring back to other names in the chain. We never get a name which is really God's own name, which really seizes upon God, and then, having done its duty, having delivered us into the inner chambers of the Godhead, quietly dissipates into thin air. Eckhart kept warning us about the contingency of the signifiers we deploy. This warning reached its shrillest and most startling moment when, faced with the difficulty of getting something said about God, he openly preached one day to what must have been a very startled congregation, 'Therefore I pray God that he may make me free of God' (*C-M*, p. 202).

Now we may hear in this a prayer for presence, for the transcendental signified which puts the play of signifiers to rest ar d makes us one with the One. I do not deny that there is a wide streak of this in Eckhart, a streak of Neoplatonic, henological metaphysics, in which everything gets centered on the 'Godhead' beyond 'God,' on the One beyond multiplicity, on the silent unity of soul with God beyond time and place. This notion of mystical unity does not contradict onto-theo-logic but crowns and perfects it. It fulfills the metaphysical desire for presence in a way of which metaphysics itself was incapable, with a surge of intuitive unity which surpasses the wildest dreams of conceptual reason. Having discovered the complicity and play of terms in medieval onto-theo-logic, Eckhart was not above trying to arrest that play and calm the storm he had stirred up, by bringing the onto-theo-logical system with which he was wrestling into a higher, mystical closure.

But I say that to reduce Eckhart to such a gesture is to cut him off at the knees, to repress everything *else* which is astir in his text, and to miss the good that deconstruction does for religious thinkers, and which Eckhart was putting into practice. For if Eckhart was not above pushing for closure he was at the same time acutely aware of the impossibility of closure, of the wide-open uncompletability and unstabilizability of onto-theological discourse. When he prayed aloud for God to rid him of

God he was blowing the whistle on metaphysical theology – plain and simple.

Now it is my claim that if he thought (as he certainly did) that there was a higher, unitative way beyond language, he was at the same time – whether he liked it or not, whatever his *vouloir-dire* – putting such a way into question. For once *he* has recourse to the stabilizing discourse of the Neoplatonic One beyond multiplicity, to the 'Godhead' beyond God, to the timeless unity of the soul's ground with God's ground, *we* today recognize that that *too* is just another creature, another signifier which belongs to an historical vocabulary. Neoplatonism did not drop from the sky, did not emanate from the One. 'Godhead' too is another effect of *différance*, a differential effect achieved by a discourse which deploys a God/Godhead distinction. 'Godhead' sends us skidding back to 'God' from which (by being distinguished from which) 'Godhead' derives its sense and impact. To reach out for the 'Godhead' beyond God is but to name Him relative to 'God,' to remain within the chain of mundane predicates. 'Godhead', too, drags a chain of signifiers behind it. The Godhead beyond God is also a creature, what a religious person would call an idol, what Derrida would call an effect of *différance*, or Heidegger an issue of the Difference.

We do not get anywhere if we let our frustration and impatience with the play of signifiers lure us into invoking another domain of signifiers in which the reigning truth is that we have here to do with the transcendental signified beyond all signifiers. The only headway to be made is to confess that we never escape the chain of signifiers, to concede that the trouble we are in is permanent, and to press ahead anyway. The prayer to rid us of 'God' has to be kept permanently in place. It demands a constant vigil, watching and praying always that we do not fall down to graven images, including that most alluring image of all, the image that we are beyond images. The prayer to rid us of God is a prayer to keep the play of images in play, to give it no rest, to be unattached to any creature, no matter how sublime and fine, even if it be the mystical Godhead itself, or the *Seelenfünklein*, even if it be the most exquisite reaches of Eckhart's dazzling mystical speculations.

The only headway is to 'awaken' to the fix we are in, we who believe in something – and who does not? – to raise our level of vigilance, to watch and pray, to be permanently on the alert against mistaking graven images for the living God, mistaking the effects of *différance* for the things themselves (be they perceptual, scientific, or theological). 'I pray God that he may make me free of God' is an ongoing prayer which keeps the discourse open. This is a prayer against closure, against turning the latest and best creations of discourse into idols. It arises from an ongoing distrust of our ineradicable desire for presence, of our insidious tendency to arrest the play and build an altar to a produced effect. I pray God – that is, He Who is everything and none of the things which this signifier names, *nomen omninominabile et nomen innominabile* – to rid me of 'God,' that is to say, of all of those nominal effects which try to cow us into submission, all of those historico-cultural–linguistic effects which are collected together by the word 'God.'

I am arguing that if we pressed these considerations upon Eckhart it would show quite clearly that he had very little invested in the metaphysics of presence, in Neoplatonic henology, and that everything he had to say revolved around seeing the failure of signifiers to catch God in their net.[8] I am arguing that it belongs to the innermost tendencies of his thought to let go of the Godhead too, of the henology, of the *Seelengrund* and *Gottesgrund*, for they too are nominal effects. The dynamics of his own teachings are to rid us of all idols, of every 'God,' of every signifier which gets too important and asserts its authority, even if that be 'Godhead' itself. I pray God to rid me of 'Godhead,' that is, to keep me free of attachment to any signifier.

III   Eckhart's joyful wisdom

At this point it may be objected that I am trying to turn Eckhartian mysticism into a despairing and faithless agnosticism, a dispirited silence about an infinitely distant God. But exactly the opposite is the case. For, by resisting any closure of Eckhart's discourse I am defending its open-endedness and its enormous affirmative energy. Eckhart's sermons celebrate God's enveloping action in the world and in his own life. His writing explodes in an extravaganza of images, in a play of mystical signifiers, in a profusion of discourse which aims at keeping the life of the soul with God alive. There is no better example, to my knowledge, of a certain mystical dissemination and a religiously joyful wisdom than the brilliant, playful virtuosity of Eckhart's German sermons and Latin treatises. He rewrites the words of Scripture, turns and twists the most familiar sacred stories, reinterprets the oldest teachings in the most innovative and shocking ways. Derrida's dichotomy between rabbinic and poetic hermeneutics (*ED*, pp. 102–3; *WD*, p. 67) has nothing to do with the Sacred Scriptures, for Eckhart's commentaries on the Scriptures stir with a poetic energy which exploits all of the associative and rhythmic power of his Latin and Middle High German tongues.

And always with the same effect: to prod the life of the spirit, to promote its vitality, to raise its pitch, to enhance its energy. Like a religious answer to Nietzsche six centuries before the fact, Eckhart engages with Dionysian productivity in a multiplication of religious fictions which serve the interests of a 'life' which lives out of its own superabundance, without why or wherefore, for the sake of life itself:

> If anyone went on for a thousand years asking of life: 'Why are you living?' life, if it could answer, would only say: 'I live so that I may live.' That is because life lives out of its own ground and springs from its own source, and so it lives without asking why it is itself living. If anyone asked a truthful man who works out of his own ground: 'Why are you performing your works'? and if he were to give a straight answer, he would only say, 'I work so that I may work.' (*Q*, 180, 23–31; *C-M*, p. 184)

There is a grammatological exuberance, a transgressive energy, in Eckhart which suggests a kind of medieval analogate of Mallarmé and Joyce. He had a way about him of making the whole tremble, of soliciting the foundations of onto-theo-logic. The papal bull which condemned him said that even when his sayings were not in error they were still dangerous (*C-M*, p. 80). On this point, at least, the Pope was right. The powers that be, the guardians of orthodoxy, always have a fine ear for disruptive discourse. For the life of him, Eckhart could not see what they were exercised about. That is because Eckhart was concerned with the dynamics of the soul's life with the living

God, not with defending the political power base of the magisterium. The Inquisitors understood that texts outlive good intentions, that they would retain their disruptive power long after the reassuring voice of this humble Dominican friar was silenced – by everyone's account, the Pope's included (*C-M*, p. 81), a loyal son of the Church.

This master of silence and of the silent unity of the soul with God was an eloquent preacher – by profession and vocation – and a prolific writer who produced a massive corpus, only a fragment of which has come down to us today. His defense of silence was carried out by a multiplication of discourse. He is a master of life (*Lebemeister*) *and* a master of the letter (*Lesemeister*) who plays with the syntax and semantics of the scriptural texts and the texts of the masters before him in order to tease out of them ever new senses. He is a master of repetition who knew well that his *commentarium* was not to be a simple reproduction but a new production, a new rendering which made the old text speak anew and say what had not been heard.

He was constantly altering the syntax of a text, rewriting it so that it said something new. He would fuss with trivial features of texts to which no attention at all had been paid and make everything turn on them, even to the point of reversing their traditional meaning. He would even play with the letters in a word. When he was defending his notion that *esse est deus*, he said that *esse* is the tetragrammaton, that ESSE and YHWH constitute the same sacred four-letter word, the four-letter word of the Sacred itself.[9] His grammatology included a tetragrammatology. He would invert sayings to see what fruit they would yield. When brother Thomas soberly taught, in a carefully nuanced way, that *deus est suum esse*, Eckhart boldly announced that *esse est deus* and creatures are a pure nothing. And that did not prevent him from also teaching that God is above being and being is the first of all creatures. When Jesus said that Mary had chosen the better part (the *vita contemplativa*) by invoking Martha's name twice ('Martha, Martha, you worry and fret about so many things'), Eckhart explained that the repetition of Martha's name meant that she had two gifts (the *vita contemplativa* and the *vita activa*) and hence that Martha had chosen the better part (*Q*, 280–9)!

A recent study offers an interesting catalogue of the ways

he played with the phonic and graphic substance of the two languages he spoke.[10] He reads *mutuo* (reciprocal) as *meo tuo et tuo meo* (mine yours and yours mine). He asked us to hear in the angel's *ave* to Mary the Middle German *ane we* (without pain) which is what Mary experienced once she consented to God's demands. He plays with the proper name of his own religious order (*ordo praedicatorum*, order of preachers) which he said meant order of praisers, those who offer divine predicates. He even tinkered with the word 'eagle,' hearing in the Middle High German *adeler* (eagle) not Hegel, to be sure, but *edeler*, the noble man. He said that true thankfulness (*dankbaerkeit*) is, not thoughtfulness, but fruitfulness (*vruhtbaerkeit*), that is, to be made fruitful by the gift one receives, and that means to give birth (*gebern*) from it in return (*in der widerbernden dankbaerkeit*). In the Vulgate version of Rom. 6:22, *Nun vero liberati a peccato* ('Now, however, you have been liberated from sin'), Eckhart finds eight different grammatical functions in *vero*, including: 'truly' (*vere*) delivered from sin; 'delivered from sin by truth' (*vero*, the dative of *verum*, 'by truth'), and so on. In the opening line of John's Gospel, '*In principio erat verbum*' ('In the beginning was the Word'), the words *principium*, *erat*, and *verbum* are submitted to similar multiple readings, disseminating and multiplying their senses. He even changes the opening lines of the Pater Noster, according to Christian belief the only prayer to come from the lips of Jesus himself, so that 'thy will be done' becomes 'will, become thine [i.e. God's],' because he taught that willing to do God's will is not as high as getting beyond willing altogether.

The only test to which Eckhart seems to put his innovations is their ability to generate new spiritual vitality, to keep the life of the soul with God in motion. He was a pragmatist of the spiritual life with a taste for multiplying and inventing discourses aimed at promoting and enhancing spiritual life. He was a *Lesemeister* (master of readings, of letters) because he was a *Lebemeister* (master of life, spiritual master).

Moreover, his emancipatory words put the powers that be on the spot and tended to break open the rigid hierarchy and exclusionary order of the political system which accompanies onto-theo-logic. He produced a significant deconstructive effect upon the prevailing onto-theo-logical power structure, upon let us say the onto-theo-politic of his day – for which he was made personally to pay.[11] In Eckhart everything turns on *Gelassenheit* (a mainstay of Heidegger's vocabulary) which means letting-be and which includes everything which liberates and sets free. *Gelassenheit* means letting God be God, letting Him be – in yourself, in others, in everything, which is obviously a very non-exclusionary idea. *Gelassenheit* is a principle of love (*caritas*) with some teeth in it, a *caritas* put forward by a Christian which had a deconstructive kick to it.

As I have recently written:[12]

Eckhart saw the life and love of God to be ubiquitous, not confined to just a few privileged souls, not just to priests, e.g., which made the *church*men of his day uneasy, or to males (he preached to women and told them that they all had the divine spark, the *Seelenfünklein*), which made these same church*men* uneasy, or even just to Christians, which made nearly all Christendom uneasy. Furthermore, he did not think that the presence of God was confined to *churches* at all, or that God necessarily prefers the Latin language, but that the German vernacular in which he preached would do just fine. And that is why the Reformation took a liking to him and why the Papal Inquisitors gave him a hard time. Although a high-level Dominican administrator himself, Eckhart set about disseminating power-clusters in medieval Christendom, disrupting the political power of onto-theo-logic, and for that he earned the wrath of the Curia and felt the blows of its institutional power.

We can write Eckhart's writing off as negative theology, as a closet metaphysics of presence, or we can let it be. My claim is that if we press Eckhart about his Neoplatonic henology, his metaphysics of the one, he has to give *that* up, too, as so much idolatry, so much onto-theo-logic. What Eckhart was doing and saying, preaching and teaching, had nothing to do with onto-theo-logic or henology. Nothing turns for him on calling God Being or presence, even a super-essential Being, a super-essential presence. That is just a way of making the prevailing onto-theo-logic tremble.

At the end of the sermon on poverty he says 'Whoever does not understand what I have said, let him not burden his heart with it' (C-M, p. 203). This discourse on mystical poverty does not defend some onto-theo-logical theory about God or the soul. And it can be well understood without understanding any of the subtleties in which the sermon engages. The sermon means only to lead us to the point where we will try to be (existentially) the poverty of which it speaks. We cannot understand his talk, Eckhart says, unless we make ourselves like what he is talking about. And if we are like this poverty, then we do not need to burden ourselves with this talk about God and Godhead.

What Eckhart taught had little to do with a Neoplatonic One or a super-essential presence. Rather he taught with irrepressible exuberance the joyful wisdom of a life graced by God and in the process shattered with loving joy the most prized graven images of onto-theo-logic. Nothing is more typical of Eckhart than the argument he pursues with mystical perversity that the better part belongs not to Mary, languishing dreamily at the feet of Jesus, trying to be one with the One, but to Martha, who rushed about making the preparations for Jesus's visit, with all of the energy and robustness of life.[13]

Chapter 3

DERRIDA AND DESCARTES: ECONOMIZING THOUGHT

Dalia Judovitz

> Archimedes, in order that he might
> draw the terrestrial globe out of his
> place, and transport it elsewhere,
> demanded only that one point should
> be fixed and immoveable.
>
> Descartes, *Meditations*

A discussion of Derrida's critique of Descartes in 'Cogito and the History of Madness,' is inseparable from the context of its debate, the exchange between Derrida and Foucault. The fact that a critique of Descartes provides the groundwork for the elaboration of the debate between structuralism and post-structuralism (as represented by the respective positions of Foucault and Derrida), is by no means accidental. At issue is far more than the question of interpretation of the Cartesian text. Rather, the Cartesian text functions for both as the crucial site of articulation of a moment that qualifies the essential shape of modernity, a turning-point towards metaphysics and the emergence of history.[1] If, for Foucault, Descartes's exclusion of madness is instrumental in the foundation of reason, for Derrida, madness and dreams are merely stages for the introduction of hyperbolic doubt, which through its figurative function generates an excess that comes to define subjectivity in terms of a rational economy. Whereas for Foucault subjectivity is defined through a gesture of exclusion, the constitution of an exteriority, that founds through its muted silence the possibility of reason, for Derrida, reason is constituted obversely through the production of an excess whose totality engenders the reflexive play of reason and its liminal definition as economy.

Each of these interpretations of the Cartesian text presents a different scenario of the foundation of Cartesian subjectivity and its legacy to modernity. While, for Foucault, the origin of reason is grounded in the historical exclusion of madness, for Derrida on the contrary, reason is constructed through the totalizing gesture of hyperbolic doubt, whose inclusive character extends the boundaries of reason and redefines its character as a rational economy. At issue in both is the centrality of reason as an originary point whose strategic role determines concepts both of economy and of history, concepts that since Saussure have been seminal to the structuralist debate and the elaboration of a post-structuralist critique. Through a critical reading of Derrida's interpretation of the Cartesian text and his debate with Foucault, this study hopes to provide a new understanding of the questions posed by the Cartesian text, as well as to determine the legacy of its heritage to structuralism and to its post-structuralist critique.

We will now turn to an examination of the Derridian reading of Descartes's *Meditations*, which is already itself an answer to and in conversation with Foucault's reading of the same text. Instead of limiting this analysis to a mere commentary on the terms of the debate outlined above, the scope of this discussion will be expanded in order to consider the relation of Descartes's argument of doubt to fiction. By focusing on the use of doubt and fiction in the *Discourse on the Method*, and the redefinition of their relation in the hyperbolic doubt argument in the *Meditations*, this study will demonstrate how questions of doubt are resolved through the strategic use of fiction.[2] My contention is that fiction defined either in terms of feint in the *Discourse* or explicitly figured through the persona of the evil genius in the *Meditations*, constitutes the ground of the debate both in the Cartesian text and the Foucault–Derrida debate.[3]

In the analysis that follows, the seminal terms of the argument of doubt in the *Meditations*, those of madness, dreams, hyperbolic doubt, and the fiction of the evil genius will be examined not merely as stages that document the passage from doubt to total doubt, but also as literary and rhetorical topics. By focusing on the rhetorical and figurative structure of this constellation of terms, this study will address one of the major paradoxes of Cartesian philosophy as a discourse that attains certitude through the use of fiction, in order to posit truth as an entity beyond fiction. By examining Descartes's interpretation of doubt in different contexts and by means of specific literary devices, this analysis will demonstrate the extent to which the very meaning of the Cartesian philosophical arguments is determined by literary and rhetorical practices.

I

Let us now turn to the passage in the *First Meditation*, so heatedly debated between Derrida and Foucault.[4] The context of the passage is the leading *topos* of the Cartesian text, that of the effort to destroy all his previous beliefs in the effort to start all over again on firm ground, that is, certitude. However, this effort to make a *tabula rasa* of all his former opinions does not entail for Descartes the same problems that he has already dealt with in the *Discourse*. He no longer needs to reject as *absolutely false* everything in which he finds (*imaginer*) the least doubt (*HR* I, p. 101). Rather, it now suffices to examine the principles, that is the founding premises that will bring about the ruin of the total edifice. The question of authority and legitimization that haunts the *Discourse* Part 2, involving Descartes's right to reform the edifice of philosophy by questioning the foundations of knowledge and his relation to the philosophical tradition, has now been displaced by Descartes's personal inquiry into the structure of his own beliefs.

If the *Meditations* no longer demand a provisional moral (*morale provisoire*), that is because the question of legitimization and reform that haunts the *Discourse* has shifted from an external examination to an internal one. The speaking subject of the *Meditations* will now authorize and define his own legitimacy as the founder of a philosophy that seeks absolute certitude, and hence must define itself as capable of attaining it and maintaining it. The *First Meditation* opens by considering the problem of doubt engendered by the senses, since they have proven *sometimes* to be deceptive:

> All that up to the present time I have accepted as most true
> and certain, I have learned either from the senses or
> through the senses; but it is sometimes proved to me that

these senses are deceptive, and it is wiser not to trust
entirely to any thing by which we have once been deceived.
(*HR* I, p. 145)

The fact that the senses are sometimes deceptive leads Descartes
to their *total* denunciation, so that their evidence will henceforth
be deemed absolutely false. However, as Descartes
subsequently admits, the deception engendered by the senses
is not as radical as the deceptions interior to the mind as experienced passively either in sleep or in madness. Descartes goes
on to explore the far more radical doubt that now involves
questions regarding the interiority of the mind, as opposed to
the exterior, sensorial and bodily doubt experienced in relation
to the world.

The problem is not only that we may be deceived by the
senses, but also that we may be deceived and not even know
it or be able to recognize it as such, as in the case of dreams
and madness:

But it may be that although the senses sometimes deceive
us concerning things which are hardly perceptible, or very
far away, there are yet many others to be met with as to
which we cannot reasonably have any doubt, although we
recognise them by their means. For example, there is the
fact that I am here seated by the fire, attired in a dressing
gown, having this paper in my hands and other similar
matters. And how could I deny that these hands and this
body are mine, were it not perhaps that I compare myself
to certain persons devoid of sense, whose cerebella are so
troubled and clouded by the violent vapours of black bile,
that they constantly assure us that they think that they are
kings when they are really quite poor, or that they are
clothed in purple when they are really without covering,
or who imagine that they have an earthenware head or are
nothing but pumpkins or are made of glass. But they are
mad and I should not be any less insane were I to follow
examples so extravagant. (*HR* I, p. 145)

Foucault analyzes this passage in order to claim a fundamental
imbalance in what he calls the 'economy of doubt' between
madness and dreams and error. He claims that 'dreams or

illusions are surmounted within the structure of truth; but madness is inadmissible for the doubting subject' (*HF*, p. 57). Derrida responds to Foucault's claims about the exclusion of madness by pointing out that in doing so Foucault goes against the philosophical tradition of interpreting madness in the context of the argument of doubt in general. For him, Foucault is the first to have isolated madness from sensation and dreams, in order to explore its methodological function independently. For Foucault, however, the exclusion of madness is constitutive of 'the advent of a *ratio*,' whose purpose is to inter madness and silence its speech. This new way of defining thought is decisive for Foucault, in so far as its normative character, established at the expense of madness, outlines the very possibility of history, as a 'meaningful language that is transmitted and consummated in time' (*HF*, p. 34). Thus for Foucault, the necessity of madness defines the possibility of history – its 'historicity,' a question to which we shall return when we consider the relation between concepts of economy and history.

However, as Derrida observes, and as I shall demonstrate through my own reading of the passage above, Descartes is not concerned here with determining the notion of insanity, but rather to ask questions regarding the general truth of ideas (*WD*, p. 51). As Derrida notes echoing Guéroult: 'It is in the case of sleep, and not in that of insanity, that the *absolute totality* of ideas of sensory origin becomes suspect' (*WD*, p. 51). Derrida's claim relies not on the particular terms in which doubt is presented but on considering its function that is its economic and totalizing character. He understands madness to be merely one term, in a constellation of terms that include dreams and error, necessary to interrogate the totality of ideas of sensory origin. Descartes's reference to madness is thus framed by the larger question regarding the danger of deception that the subject experiences in dreams.

Besides considering the role of madness in this passage in philosophical terms, it is also important to consider its literary and rhetorical context. The evocation of error and madness in this passage takes place in the context of a strangely reassuring experience. The intimate representation of the author as a writing subject by the fire, holding pen and paper in his hand, reassures the reader through its objective evidence, against the very threats that the text warns to expose itself and the reader. The scene of writing is mirrored by the scene of reading, and the reliability of the self-reflexive evidence of the scene is further enhanced by the verisimilitude of the subject's own perception in the act of reading. Despite the evocation of the philosophical threat of madness, its articulation in the safety of the library and in the context of the normative communication between author and reader displaces its threatening impact.

At issue, therefore, is more than Derrida's claim that this passage presents the objections of a non-philosopher who, frightened by the totality of Cartesian doubt, must cling to and reaffirm the validity of those sensory perceptions that are immediate (*WD*, p. 50). For the immediacy in question here is not merely that of sensory evidence, but rather the simulation of sensation, that is the illusion of immediacy staged by the performative aspects of the text. Foucault analogously observes in his response to Derrida in '*Mon corps, ce papier, ce feu*,' that Derrida fails to take into account the performative aspect of the meditation as a literary genre, which for him functions as yet another index of the rationalizing dimension of the Cartesian text.[5] While I agree with Foucault that the author's representation performs before the reader the denial of the deceptions, including madness, that might subvert his reason, this performance in no way singles out the privilege and priority of madness.

If the question of madness appears in this context, it does so within a closed economic system of exchange, between the text simulating the immediacy of the authorial persona and the reader, so that its threat or exclusion cannot be experienced otherwise than by association with a rhetorical feint, with literature par excellence. In other words, at issue is not merely the Foucauldian contention that the meditation as the figure of the reasoning subject excludes madness. But rather, that madness is merely a *topos* through which the subject demonstrates agency through fiction. In so doing, Descartes is merely reiterating a baroque *topos*. Madness is but one of the numerous figures of the baroque that include dreams and artistic deception. Like them, it is the expression of the problematic character of representation: its metaphorical, deceptive, and *trompe-l'oeil* character. The question of the evocation of madness in this context thus emerges not as a problem of the interiority of thought, as Foucault claims, but rather as the expression of the excentric character of language.[6]

If Descartes reassures himself through his own representation against any actual madness, in 'the language of fiction or the fiction of language' to use Derrida's terms (WD, p. 54), this form of validation is not accounted for in his own text, since it is clear that this very language, as Derrida suggests, menaces the interiority of thought and threatens to colonize it not with the madness associated with the body and dreams, but with the far more pervasive madness of the decentering power of metaphor. If madness may appear 'quite talkative' (to use again Derridian terminology), that is because it speaks excentrically. It cannot be contained by the fiction of a language that escapes it, which exists as its negation or absence, that is to say the fiction of a language that has ceased to be metaphorical.

Descartes can no more 'decide' to exclude madness as Foucault claims, than he can constitute himself outside language and representation. It suffices to consider this issue in regard to its articulation in the *Third Meditation*, when Descartes attempts to identify his essence as a subject by feigning a set of impossible conditions. He proposes to close his eyes, shut his ears, suspend his senses, efface from his thoughts all images of corporeal things (but since this is impossible, esteem them as vain and false) and thus 'holding converse only with myself and considering my own nature' he tries to reach a better knowledge of himself (HR I, p. 157). But Descartes's effort to achieve a more familiar acquaintance with himself could only take place through an interior conversation with himself, which implies the use of representation and the exchange of signs – that is to say, the material and thus necessarily metaphorical character of language – at the very moment when he pretends to exclude from his thoughts all images of corporeal things. If madness cannot be excluded in Descartes, this is because in so doing Descartes would have to eliminate the very medium through which he comes to know himself, which is the language of the dialogue in which his thoughts are engaged and through which he can come into existence as pure subjectivity.

In order to better understand the purely rhetorical exclusion of madness in the inaugural passage of Descartes's *First Meditation*, the reader must also consider Descartes's recourse to fiction rather than madness in his initial presentation of the *cogito* argument in the *Discourse*. His effort to feign that all things are no more true than the reality of dreams, that is, that everything is false, leads to the necessary conclusion that he who thinks of these things must be something, in other words that he exists. Without even mentioning madness in the *Discourse*, Descartes goes on to make claims that are so extravagant as to even make madness appear reasonable. He goes on to feign that he has no body, that there is no world nor a place that he occupies, only to conclude that for all that he cannot feign that he does not exist and thereby establish the truth of the cogito as 'I think, therefore I am' (*HR*, I, p. 101). Thus the truth of the *cogito*'s existence is here established through the exercise of an impossible fiction, through a rhetoric of negation whose truth is based on the totalizing character of fiction and whose evidence relies on the power of representation to perform even its own negation, as if the verisimilitude of subjectivity did not require the substrate of language, even when attempting *not to speak*. As Descartes himself later admits in the *Second Meditation*, 'I am, I exist, is necessarily true each time that I pronounce it, or that I mentally conceive it' (*HR*, I, p. 150), indicating an implicit recognition of the instrumentality of language.

Going back to our analysis of the status of madness in the Cartesian text, it becomes clear that Descartes does not need to feign madness in order to 'dispossess' himself of his body, as Foucault claims, but can be through his feint in the *Discourse* more mad than madness itself, since he can represent himself as not having a body, there not being a world, and so forth. Foucault needs the hypothesis of madness in order to envisage the possibility of history itself:

The *necessity of madness*, throughout the history of the West, is linked to the deciding gesture which detaches it from the background noise, and from its continuous monotony, a meaningful language that is transmitted and consummated in time; briefly it is linked to the *possibility of history*. (*HF*, p. 34)

By attributing to Descartes the 'decision' to exclude madness, Foucault suggests that he has found through this mechanism of exclusion a model for the origins and function of history, that is, its 'historicity.' Foucault's reading of Descartes constructs through the idea of the 'decision' both a concept of agency and a mechanism of exclusion through which that agency manifests itself as a historical instance. It is exactly this notion of individual agency and subjectivity which is at issue in the Foucauldian concept of discourse and his redefinition of history as archaeology.[7] Descartes can no more decide to exclude madness than he can decide to exclude representation and language, since both are written into and are a constitutive part of the fabric of subjectivity. Rather than interpreting this *decision* as a single act which 'links and separates reason and madness,' Derrida proposes the notion of *dissension* in order to 'underline that in question is a self-dividing action, a cleavage and torment interior to meaning *in general*, interior to logos in general' (*WD*, p. 38). In other words, Derrida is suggesting that the self-dividing action of the subject is not an original act of order but rather an internal dissension within language and meaning, a differential movement within *logos* that cannot be consciously erased by positing a foundational division between the interiority of reason and the exteriority of madness.

If Derrida challenges the Foucauldian reading of Descartes, this is because at issue for him are the very dilemmas that define structuralism as a whole in its relation to history. Derrida concludes:

> Consequently, if the decision through which reason constitutes itself by excluding and objectifying the free subjectivity of madness is indeed the origin of history, if it is historicity itself, the condition of meaning and of language, the condition of the tradition of meaning, the condition of the work in general, if the structure of exclusion is the fundamental structure of historicity, then the 'classical' moment of this exclusion described by Foucault has neither absolute privilege nor archetypal exemplarity. It is an example as a sample and not as model. (*WD*, p. 42)

Derrida questions Foucault's effort to locate within history an originary moment that founds it, through a negative exclusion that comes to constitute it as a structure, as well as determine the mechanism of its structurality, that is, its 'historicity.' For Derrida, Foucault's effort raises the same questions that are involved not only in Descartes's putative exclusion of madness but also in his subsequent elaboration of hyperbolic doubt. That being, that reason as a structure, is constituted by the interplay of 'determined reason and unreason' as an originary point that escapes that very determination while setting it into motion. Derrida observes that while Foucault attempts to provide an alternative history to that of reason, he risks the repetition and the confirmation of the metaphysical viewpoint he ostensibly challenges:

The attempt to write the history of the decision, division, difference runs the risk of construing the division as an event or a structure subsequent to the unity of an original presence, thereby confirming metaphysics in its fundamental operation. (WD, p. 40)

Foucault's interpretation of history presupposes that reason constructs its symmetrical contrary, its other, only to exclude it in order to constitute itself, as if the ambiguities that already mark it as a traditional philosophical category did not already have a long established history since the Greeks. Foucault's affirmation of the division of reason from madness involves upholding its status as an event, one which reinforces an originary ahistorical interpretation of the meaning of reason as an undivided unity, whose coherence predates any oppositions.

For Derrida, on the contrary, the contradictions that mark the emergence of Cartesian reason are the *historical* expressions of determinations prefigured within reason: 'It can be proposed that the classical crisis developed from and within the elementary tradition of a logos that has no opposite but carries within itself and *says* all determined contradictions' (WD, p. 42). Derrida's concept of reason is not a virtual category that can exclude from itself madness as its other, rather for him reason carries within itself, within its language and multiple meanings, determinations that *speak* otherwise, that double and endlessly divide its unity, so that its speech can also *say* its own contradictions. Descartes's supposed 'act of force,' his internment of madness, in Foucault's words, would thus have to be reread as simply the reconfiguring of reason in relation to the very terms in which it was constituted, those of the baroque tradition that precedes it. It is within the language of the baroque, obsessed with deception and *trompe-l'oeil*, that the maddening character of madness can be perceived as already speaking its history, its destiny of unreason.[8] Once it is understood that madness is not a representative term, but merely one term in a constellation of terms that include dreams, as well as fiction and *'trompe-l'oeil'*, we can begin to understand the strategy of the Cartesian text, its necessary passage and trajectory from madness to dreams and to hyperbolic doubt.

II

Having examined the status of madness and its critique in the Cartesian text, this study will now focus on the context in which it is articulated in the *Meditations*, that of dreams and hyperbolic doubt. Descartes's subsequent analysis of dreams in the *First Meditation* becomes the medium for Descartes's passage from natural to hyperbolic doubt. Descartes pursues his inquiry by noting that the problem of deception is even more pronounced in the case of dreams than in the previous instance when he chose to doubt the reality of all things. He observes that 'there are no certain indications by which we may clearly distinguish wakefulness from sleep' (*HR* I, p. 146). The impossibility to make a distinction between these two states leads Descartes to the absurd assumption that he may in fact be asleep: 'Now let us assume that we are asleep . . .'. Derrida interprets the hypothesis of dreams as the hyperbolical exaggeration of the initial hypothesis that the senses may be sometimes deceptive: 'In dreams, the *totality* of sensory images is illusory' (*WD*, p. 48). This interpretation of the Cartesian strategy can be seen as an answer to Foucault's claim that dreams as opposed to madness are surmounted within the structure of the argument of doubt. The dream argument can thus be considered as the expansion of the rhetorical appeal to madness. But as Descartes observes, the dream as a representation may be fictitious but its substrate, in this case color by analogy with painting, is certain or real, that is to say intelligible.

This leads Descartes to conclude that two and three always form five whether he is awake or asleep (HR I, p. 147). The preservation of intelligibility, which is neither sensory nor imaginative within dreams, functions as the bridge, as the ground that mediates the transition from natural doubt to hyperbolic doubt. Without the establishment of this index of intelligibility or mark of certitude within dreams, Descartes would be unable to pursue his inquiry. However, it is important to note that this moment of certitude refers to representation and defines the character of mathematical ideas, rather than settling the actual question of their possible existence, and more importantly, any certitude that the subject may reach about itself and its own agency Although the dream as a composite fictional representation may preserve within itself the identity of other languages such as mathematics 'which only treat of things that are very simple and general,' this certitude arrived at through analysis in no way demonstrates their actual existence. Having identified even within the language of dreams a principle of intelligibility, Descartes is left to prove that this modality is operative within the modality of existence.

This bridge of intelligibility which Descartes situates within representation leads him to the search for the subject as its ultimate referent and existential support. Descartes now shifts to the third stage of the argument, that of hyperbolic doubt which involves the fiction of the evil genius:

> Nevertheless, I have long had fixed in my mind the belief that an all powerful God existed by whom I have been created such as I am. But how do I know that He has not brought it to pass that there is no earth, no heaven, no extended body, no magnitude, no place, and that nevertheless I possess the perceptions of all these things and that they seem to me to exist just exactly as I now see them? And besides, as I sometimes imagine that others deceive themselves in the things they think they know best, how do I know that I am not deceived every time that I add two and three, or count the sides of a square or judge of things yet simpler, if simpler can be imagined? (HR I, p. 147)

The certitude of mathematical truth can be maintained within the framework of natural doubt, but not within the framework of a total doubt in which the subject must question not only its own relation to representation but the theological principles that underlie it. Since Descartes's own authority cannot be found within the interiority of reason, he must do so by an appeal to a higher authority, that is to say, God as its ultimate author. Descartes is forced to conclude that although it is contrary to God's goodness that he constantly deceive himself, yet it is indubitable that he does 'permit me to be sometimes deceived' (*HR* I, p. 147). It is the indubitability of this occasional deception that leads Descartes to produce the fable of the 'double' of God – the evil genius whose role is to constantly and consistently deceive him. This fictitious being will now enact for Descartes from the outside the conditions that will allow him to prove the indubitability of his own existence.

Unlike in the *Discourse* where Descartes produced himself through the fiction of the conditions of his own existence that included the pretense of not having a body and there being no world, in the *Meditations* Descartes defines himself as the object of a fictive agency whose total deception will certify the validity of his existence. Derrida summarizes the Cartesian stratagem in the following terms:

> Now, the recourse to the fiction of the evil genius will evoke, conjure up the possibility of *total madness*, a total derangement over which I could have no control because it is inflicted upon me – hypothetically – leaving me no responsibility for it. Total derangement is the possibility of a madness that is no longer a disorder of the body. . . . This time madness, insanity, will spare nothing, neither bodily nor purely intellectual perceptions. (*WD*, p. 53)

The suggestion that the fiction of the evil genius evokes the possibility of 'total madness' is intended as an answer to his debate with Foucault. But as I have already shown in relation to the *Discourse*, Descartes *does not need madness* in order to make the rhetorical claims that Foucault associates with madness.[9] The fiction of the evil genius is no longer within the purview of madness, rather its totality is based on the figurative power of hyperbole, that is to say, the rhetorical appeal to fiction.

Thus the creation of subjectivity in the Cartesian text is

mediated by a special representation, that of the evil genius –
a representation of fiction par excellence. Its totality is not in
the order of derangement or madness, but rather in the hyperbolic leap of reason that creates itself through a self-reflective
dialogue, the mirrored fiction of itself as another. Its truth
belongs to the same order of intelligibility as mathematics: it is
self-posited and self-defined. The figurative reach of the hyperbole becomes the basis of a contract that the subject enacts with
the evil genius, its fictive counterpart, through the medium of
rhetoric in order to posit its own existence as an originary point
before all its determinations as particular modes of existence.
The totalizing power of the hyperbole as a rhetorical gesture
thus arches both beyond and before subjectivity and becomes
the index of its purely rhetorical existence. The hyperbolical
audacity of this new subject embraces in its economy – its
dialogue between infinity and finitude – the constellation of
reason, dream, and madness as its determined forms. Descartes
arrives through hyperbolic doubt at defining his existence as
that Archimedean point, the lever with which one could aspire
to move the entire world.

Through hyperbolic doubt Descartes arrives at a new definition of the *cogito* as a paradoxical point that exceeds determination and also precedes it. Produced through the economy of
hyperbolic doubt, it also emerges as the point that defines its
determined forms, that is to say, its 'history.' Derrida summarizes the philosophical function of this zero point, while
mistakenly, as this analysis will show, equating it with the
cogito:

> Invulnerable to all determined opposition between reason
> and unreason, it is the point starting from which the
> history of the determined forms of this opposition, this
> opened or broken-off dialogue, can appear as such and be
> stated. It is the impenetrable point of certainty in which the
> possibility of Foucault's narration, as well as of the
> narration of the totality, or rather of *all* determined forms of
> the exchanges between reason and madness are
> embedded. It is the point at which the project of thinking
> this totality by escaping it is embedded. (*WD*, p. 56)[10]

By insisting on the fact that hyperbolic doubt constitutes a point in excess of determination, as something that both precedes and exceeds its totality, Derrida begins to articulate via his reading of the Cartesian text his critique of Foucault and structuralism in general. The hyperbole represents an excess beyond totality, which is possible 'only in the direction of infinity and nothingness' which for Derrida means an excess in the 'direction of the nondetermined' (*WD*, pp. 56, 57). Thus the effort to reduce the hyperbolic project to a determined historical totality, as Foucault attempts to do in his *History of Madness*, risks to embed it as a term that defines economic exchange within its structure, while itself escaping economy, permutation, and transformation. The Foucauldian reading thus becomes an accomplice of the Cartesian text, since it attempts 'to conceive of structure on the basis of a full presence which is beyond play (*WD*, p. 279). The Cartesian gesture is thus mirrored in the dilemma that haunts structuralism in general. As Derrida notes in his essay 'Sign, Structure and Play in the Discourse of the Human Sciences':

> Thus it has always been thought that the center, which is by definition unique, constituted that very thing within the structure which while governing the structure, escapes structurality. This is why classical thought concerning structure could say that the center is, paradoxically, *within* the structure and *outside* it. The center is not the center. (*WD*, p. 270)

The production of subjectivity in the Cartesian text, as a center established through the decentralizing reach of the hyperbole, positions it both within the structure and outside it, since the evil genius is also the double of subjectivity, the representation of its fictive powers. This explains why subjectivity cannot be located and identified in the *Meditations* as *cogito* other than as a determination of pure existence in the context of the *sum* argument as 'I am, I exist.' This lack of specificity of the subject defined as pure existence leads Descartes to wonder whether he might mistakenly 'take some other object in place of myself' (*HR* I, p. 150). This confusion regarding the identity of subjectivity reflects its paradoxical centrality, both within and outside the structure of thought, at once present and absent.[11] If the *cogito* is no longer present in the *Meditations*, this absence can only be explained by the redefinition of its position, no longer as subject of thought but rather as the point whose centrality exceeds its historical determination as thought.

Consequently, it is not surprising that Pascal, an avid critic of Descartes in the *Pensées*, interprets this same point of indeterminacy as an argument not for the existence of the subject but rather as proof of God's existence. In the celebrated fragment 'Infinity nothing' he presents the argument for the existence of God as a wager, a bet whose character implicitly alludes to and literally parodies Descartes's metaphysical play for reason as a card game (*Des-cartes*, a pun on Descartes's name, in French).[12] For Pascal, the very ruses of reason attest to its arbitrary character in a game in which we ourselves are at stake, while we attempt to separate certitude from doubt, reason from unreason: 'Every gambler risks a certain sum to win an uncertain one, and yet, he wages finite certainty to gain finite uncertainty, without sinning against reason.'[13] By exposing the Cartesian ruse of the evil genius, its gamble with certitude in order to attain the certitude of its own finitude, Pascal reveals the paradox inherent in the Cartesian structure of reason. For Pascal, this arbitrariness at the heart of reason leads him to the affirmation of the certitude of God's existence, since he recognizes that Descartes's gamble reduced all transcendence to a finitude – the reduction of man's relation to God to a wager, an economic structure of exchange.

In the wake of the Nietzschean interpretation of Pascal, which is indebted to the Pascalian wager, Derrida proceeds to question Foucault's structuralism and his concept of history by reinterpreting in terms of free play.[14] At the end of his essay on Foucault's reading of Descartes, he concludes:

> I believe that historicity in general would be impossible
> without a history of philosophy, and I believe that the
> latter would be impossible if we possessed only hyperbole,
> on the one hand, and on the other, only determined
> historical structures, finite *Weltanschauungen*. The historicity
> proper to philosophy is located and constituted in the
> transition, the dialogue between hyperbole and the finite
> structure, between that which exceeds the totality and the
> closed totality, in the difference between history and

TOO2718

historicity; that is, in the place where, or rather at the moment when, the Cogito and all that it symbolizes here (madness, derangement, hyperbole, etc.) pronounce and reassure themselves then to fall, necessarily forgetting themselves until their reactivation, their reawakening in another statement of the excess which also later will become another decline and another crisis. (*WD*, p. 60)

The Derridian concept of historicity is posited as the difference between history and historicity, that is to say a dialogue between forms of determination, between hyperbole as the figure of excess and finite totality. In other words, Derrida seeks to establish the meaning of historicity transitively, as a differential movement, rather than as an event or crisis that comes to determine the economy of reason as a structure. The question of economy, that of the reserve and the expenditure of reason, as we saw in the case of hyperbolic doubt, is put into question by the notion of play, that is to say modalities of expenditure that are no longer determined by the economics of exchange.[15]

This is because the hyperbole is the figure of the supplemental character of representation. Derrida's critique of structuralism can be summarized in terms of the supplementary, as opposed to the purely economic interpretation of the sign, thereby re-defining Saussure's definition of the sign:

If totalization no longer has any meaning, it is not because the infiniteness of a field cannot be covered by a finite glance or a finite discourse, but because the nature of the field – that is, language and a finite language – excludes totalization. This field is the effect of that of *play*, that is to say, a field of infinite substitutions only because it is finite, that is to say, because of being an inexhaustible field, as in the classical hypothesis, instead of being too large, there is something missing from it: a center which arrests and grounds the play of substitutions. One could say . . . that this movement of play, permitted by the lack or absence of a center or origin, is the movement of *supplementarity*. One cannot determine the center and exhaust totalization because the sign which replaces the center, which supplements it, taking the center's place in its absence – this sign is added, occurs as a surplus, as a *supplement*. (WD, p. 289)

Now we can begin to understand why for Derrida everything can be reduced to a notion of historical totality, except hyperbolic doubt. The hyperbole is the rhetorical figure that makes possible the movement of supplementarity, constituting an excess in the order of the discourse of philosophy that is based on the uneconomic expenditure of representation: its metaphorical and rhetorical properties. Although hyperbolic doubt will establish in the *Meditations* the moment in the history of philosophy, which is identified with the emergence of modern 'metaphysics,' its own status cannot be defined solely within this history. Its 'historicity' is constituted otherwise, by a differential movement of philosophy and literature, that is to say, philosophy's use of the ruses of literature, feint, and the fiction of the evil genius through which Cartesian discourse founds its veracity as a metaphysical discourse.

As we have shown, the Cartesian economy of reason can only be established by virtue of fiction, whose free play is engendered by its uneconomic character. The hyperbole in the Cartesian text, itself a supplemental device, is in fact the vehicle for the attempt to foreclose and economize thought, thus gambling that the creation of its fictive limit will arrest the figurative play of language in general. The totalizing character of hyperbolic doubt thus emerges as the index of a metaphysical crisis that is but the expression of its effort to speak and economize its own finitude and thus secure philosophy as a whole. Descartes's use of hyperbolic doubt fosters the illusion that one could almost step out of philosophy, in order to provide its definition from a fictitious exteriority. The fiction of madness and of hyperbolic doubt foster the Cartesian illusion of a philosophical system that can define itself autonomously. Unable to account for the act of representation that is the mediating character of fiction and rhetoric, Descartes encloses philosophy in the closure and economy of its impossible determination as philosophy proper.

This Cartesian gesture is implicit, as Derrida suggests in his discussion of Foucault and his critique of structuralism as a whole, in all those who attempt to step out of philosophy and find themselves paradoxically secured within it, even at the moment when they seem furthest, that is 'hyperbolically' distant from it. As Derrida observes:

> The step 'outside philosophy' is much more difficult to conceive than is generally imagined by those who think they made it long ago with cavalier ease, and who in general are swallowed up in metaphysics in the entire body of discourse they claim to have disengaged from it. (WD, p. 284)

Following Nietzsche's footsteps, Derrida's critique of structuralism involves the strategic affirmation of play, a dance with philosophy that does not pretend to distance itself from literature but rather celebrates those moments when it differs from philosophy and defers its own becoming philosophy proper.

Chapter 4

DERRIDA, KANT, AND THE PERFORMANCE OF PARERGONALITY

Irene E. Harvey

I Introduction: the ornaments (*parerga*) of the third *Critique*

The *parerga*, 'what we call ornaments,' 'i.e. those things which *do not belong to the complete representation of the object internally as elements*, but *only externally* as complements',[1] in Kant's third *Critique*, in particular, have become the focus of one of Derrida's more extensive essays and instances of deconstruction in his text of the same name.[2] His investigation of Kant's usage of examples, as *parerga*, and the *parerga* of the examples themselves offers itself as an example of the following themes and issues which we intend to focus on in this essay, namely: (i) deconstruction in general, (ii) parergonality as such, (iii) Derrida's relation to Kant in general, and (iv) several possible theories of exemplarity. The question thus arises as to precisely how Derrida's essay, 'Parergon,' forms and frames these themes, exemplifies them and perhaps above all performs the parergonality which his text ostensibly offers at the same time as its theme.

Our analysis here will aim to articulate, by way of example (taking Derrida's reading of Kant as our Exemplar) the notion of exemplarity as parergonality, in particular as this is itself exemplified in Kant's third *Critique* (via Derrida's framing/deconstruction of this issue). We will also analyze the collection of scattered eruptions in Derrida's text of the notions of exemplarity and parergonality, and the twin terms of example and Exemplar as they metonymically promote not only the inflation

59

from a particular to a general or universal, but also an *economy of mimesis*[3] which is characterized *essentially* by *inversion* and displacement over the time and space of textuality (*différance*). This economy of mimesis, as a parody of an economy of the same, of the proper (indeed, even as an inversion of these metaphysical notions) will be shown here not only to entail but to rely upon a number of theories of *exemplarity as parergonality*. We will also attempt to articulate precisely what makes this inversion, via mimetic doubling and retracing (Derrida over Kant) possible and perhaps even necessary.

Our own reading here should not be pre-understood as an example of deconstruction, nor as one of critique, although it will be parallel to both in so far as our question fundamentally will be: what makes Derrida's relation to Kant possible?[4] Or, what is at stake in the deconstruction of Kant such that the conditions of the possibility of deconstruction are themselves revealed within a framework of exemplarity, however generally this term is understood? Derrida himself metonymically substitutes the following list of terms for that of "example" without apparent justification: analogy, illustration, particular, and instance.[5] Kant, also, does not thematize a theory of exemplarity despite his reliance on the same.[6] It is this unthematized yet presupposed foundation that Kant and Derrida share, albeit by inversion (and hence only via the hinge term or example) that we seek to expose here.

II Derrida's strategies

Such sharpening of the judgment is indeed one of the great *benefits* of *examples*. Correctness and precision of intellectual insight, on the other hand, they more usually somewhat *impair*. For only very seldom do they adequately fulfill the requirements of the rules (as *casus in terminis*).[7]

Derrida's reading of Kant fundamentally asks the question as to whether or not the third *Critique* can be read, seen, or analyzed as an *example of itself*. That is to say, does Kant's *Critique of Judgment* offer itself as the law of itself, the frame of itself, as both the particular and the general 'of itself'? Is the third *Critique* an instance of the sublime? of the beautiful? of aesthetic judgment? of reflective or determinant judgment? These questions are addressed by Derrida's reading as itself an example of itself; namely, Derrida's deconstructive analysis of Kant's text, of Kant's examples, in particular, is itself an example of exemplarity and a performance of parergonality. What a performative entails, according to speech act theorists,[8] is that a speech/writing act does what it says, or that it performs an action by its very expression. In Heideggerian terms, this entails the thematizing of the unthematized at the very moment of expression of the unthematized. In other words, this degree of coherence in textuality is ontologically impossible. Kant's note concerning the danger of using examples, their intrinsic tendency to be *inadequate* and even their capacity to *impair* good, appropriate, proper judgment suggests precisely this problem. Derrida notably does not cite this note in Kant's first *Critique*, but does none the less *exhibit* precisely this issue in his reading of Kant.

Not only is the *adequation* of a particular example to its 'rule' at stake here, for Derrida, but also the choice, order, function, and structure of the examples Kant uses. We shall analyze Derrida's strategies here in some detail in order to clarify precisely how the framework of exemplarity as parergonality is exemplified by this deconstruction.

In analyzing the third *Critique via* its examples, ostensibly thereby using reflective judgment, in Kant's sense, Derrida invariably begins by faithfully representing what Kant claims his own examples exemplify. That is, what he 'intends' them to mean, to illustrate, allegorize, demonstrate, or concretize. It is the *declared*[9] statements of the text that thereby take first priority in the deconstructive initiative. But this is only the beginning. Indeed, Derrida belies his own claim that this is the beginning, 'let us begin with examples,'[10] in that he has already offered us a possible law, in the form of numerous hypotheses, quasi-laws concerning the abyss, the circle, the *passe-partout*, and the parergonality which he 'may perhaps' find in/through/ behind and beneath Kant's text. Thus Derrida, in belying his own stated claim concerning what he is doing when he is doing it (that is, he claims to begin with examples – reflective judgment; yet in fact he has begun with a quasi-law – determinant judgment), is in fact performing by this very betrayal the parergonality that he will later thematize.

The initial question then for Derrida, once the explicit, intended, sanctioned functions and limits of the examples used by Kant have been thematized, is precisely *what else* do these 'same' examples do, offer, suggest, betray? In more classical terms, Derrida asks: why are they what they are? Why these particular examples? Why these here and now or those there and then? What does the order of the trilogies of examples selected several times by Kant signify? What is behind his choice? What is the law here (of his desire)? Derrida, in so framing his own analysis, has already offered explicitly and thematically the key to his strategy concerning the role of the question as 'imposing massively' on what can be found as a viable possible response. As he says, concerning questions themselves as frames: 'This questioning procedure is situated within a fundamental presupposition. It massively predetermines the system and the combination of responses.'[11]

This 'procedure' he is referring to is notably that of Hegel, and the fundamental presupposition is notably metaphysical. The system and the combination of possible responses is notably rational, or *Logos* or that of Reason. Derrida's strategy is thus analogous to that of Hegel, parallel to the discourse of Reason and yet separated from it. His strategy, as deconstruction, *uses* the discourse of Reason, uses the rhetoric of rationality, of philosophy, and of metaphysics, in order to pursue what will lead him outside of that same orbit. In this case, this is applied to Kant's text, and via Kant's examples.

The question of the surplus hidden within the examples entails a system however, for Derrida, and a system that entails what he calls, an-other *logic*. This is the logic of supplementarity,[12] in some cases, and in this, our example, it is the 'logic' of parergonality. Namely, the condition of the possibility of reading examples otherwise hinges on a certain untamed (wild, like the tulip and the ocean of the poets – indeed, sublime, as we shall see) and untameable, non-masterable excess, that although susceptible of being framed and hence made visible, cannot thereby entirely (without remainder) be brought into the light of day, of reason. In order to reveal this limit within examples and exemplarity in general (the sublime structure of exemplarity and parergonality) Derrida focuses on the example of the frame itself in Kant's text. From the frame of pictures,[13] used by Kant as an example (the first of three) of *parerga* – that extrinsic addition to the beautiful – Derrida extends the sense of frame [*cadre*] to enframing, and hence returns to the *parergon* of *parerga*. This extension is also an inflation – from the particular to its law, potentially, if not in fact – from the example to the Exemplar. In asking what frames the example, Derrida asks what frames the frame, or what is it about the frame that escapes framing? Again the thematics of betrayal arise here, and Derrida turns to the question of intrinsic and extrinsic relations, to internal and external connections, to the arbitrary and essential connections. The move then from the frame in particular, as used by Kant, is what frames the frame, and in turn what frames the frame of the frame.

Derrida answers these questions in the following manner: the frame of the picture is framed *as* (seen *as*) a *parergon*; the notion of *parergon* is itself framed via another context in which Kant also uses the term; namely, in the text, *Religion Within the Limits of Reason Alone*.[14] In turn this text is shown in precise ways to frame (at times) the third *Critique*, despite Kant's insistence upon a certain autonomy concerning the law of the law of the *Critique of Judgment*. In this respect, then, as dependent on what is outside of itself for its law, the third *Critique*, in not giving itself its own law is not an example of itself, but rather forms an example within a schema that is outside of itself. This goes *mutatis mutandis* for the relation between the third *Critique* and the first, as Derrida also indicates at a later stage.[15] Thus the frame$_1$ of the frame$_2$ of the frame$_3$ is (a) *integral* to the frame$_3$ (of the picture), (b) *constitutive*, and (c) indicates a certain *necessity* concerning the *choice* of the particular, seemingly arbitrary example – the frame of the picture. Hence, the *parerga* here are shown to be not simply, as Kant intended to show, extrinsic, external, detachable from the work of art, from the *ergon*, but rather play a central, albeit clandestine and disguised role in organizing the *ergon* itself. This duplicity as enacted by Kant's text via his examples, will be shown to characterize parergonality in general, deconstruction in general, and the discourse of philosophy in general. Kant is not alone here, despite the apparent singularity of his role, the 'good' example of 'bad' examples.

Not only does Derrida invert via the discourse of metaphysics and reason what Kant sought to establish as extrinsic and external, but he also questions the *order* of the examples when presented in a series. This occurs twice in Derrida's reading; namely concerning the trilogy of the examples of *parerga*: (i) the frame of pictures, (ii) the clothing of statues, (iii) the columns of buildings; and the trilogy of the examples of adherent (and hence impure, dependent) beauty: (i) man, (ii) the horse, (iii) buildings. Derrida asks in each case, why this order, why this sequence, what does the series indicate, and why is what is first first?[16] The critical backward step is notably analogous to Kant's own critical method concerning the conditions of the possibility of experience, metaphysics, science, and synthetic a priori judgments, to name a few examples. Derrida does not question what is given as given, but instead asks, how is this possible? According to what (logic? rule? law?) is what is given given? Analogous to Kant, but none the less not the same, as Derrida himself notes. What does the *seemingly accidental* priority of the first example actually signify? Is this a dependent or independent priority? Is it an accident? Is it instead significant with respect to some other agenda of priority and organization which the text exhibits but which is not thematized? Derrida's answer is of course, yes, to this latter question. But then what else (once again the capital question of excess and surplus lurking within the examples) is prioritized here? Namely, the frame of the choice of examples themselves. That is, the *frame* in the first trilogy organizes the choices of clothing and columns, as frames, and in addition the notion of *frame* frames *parerga*, despite Kant's intention to the contrary. In the second trilogy, we have *man* as the first example of a purposive subject/object. The place of man, Derrida suggests is not insignificant in Kant's text; it is the central theme of the third *Critique*, he argues, despite Kant's apparent reduction of its status. The framing of the examples, as humanist, as based on humanism, is revealed by Derrida in his analysis of the second example here, the 'horse.' Why (for what end) is the 'horse' necessarily an example of teleology? For what (or for whom) is the 'horse' necessarily purposive? Only for man, by man in a cosmos where man is the measure; in a humanist orientation, in short. Thus Kant's choice of 'horse' is framed not only by his explicit choice of 'man' as the first example, but by his implicit choice of man as the measure of his examples as a whole here; as the frame of the series, as the law of these examples.

Derrida's parergonal strategy of analyzing the *parerga*, the apparent ornaments, the apparent extrinsic, external marginalia of the third *Critique*, is described by him as parergonal at the same time as he exhibits parergonality inside and through the examples. He asks the hypothetical objector's question in this way:

> One might think that I am being abusive by insisting on two or three examples, perhaps gratuitous, in a secondary subchapter; and that it would be better to turn to those places less marginal in the work, closer to the center and the foundations. Certainly. [But] the objection supposes that one already knows which is the center or the foundation of the third *Critique*, that one had already taken its frame into account and the limits of its field. Now, nothing appears to be more difficult to determine. The *Critique* offers itself as a work [*ergon*] from many sides.[17]

Despite Derrida's *explicit admission* of 'not being certain where the center and where the margins are,' what 'the frame of the third *Critique* is,' and what the limits of its field are, he is *articulating* precisely these aspects of the third *Critique*, as *ergon*, and in turn setting up his own work as its frame, as the *parergon*. It is a short step to recognizing that the deconstruction of Kant's text, in this context at least, itself takes on the form of parergonality. In other words, the issue in the relation between Kant and Derrida is analogous to, indeed exemplified by, the relation between *ergon* and *parergon*, between the frame and the enframed. And it is clear that deconstruction problematizes this distinction in order to reveal that which grounds both *ergon* and *parergon* and makes this relation possible, which is evidently neither term, but rather parergonality. What parergonality entails includes the parasitic contamination of inside and outside, internal and external, interior and exterior distinctions. And this can be generalized from the merest example as an Exemplar of what cannot be exemplified.

In so far as Derrida's analysis articulates, thematizes, and gives evidence for the connections between the so-called

intrinsic and extrinsic, internal and external relations thematized by Kant, he is himself suggesting that the contamination
is itself necessary; this is, *intrinsic*. Hence, the arbitrary relations,
the chosen examples, which Kant intended as mere examples
and hence substitutable, detachable from his central argument,
are revealed as Exemplary, or as necessary, or as lawful within
a larger context or a more general economy. Ironically, the logic
of the *parergon* as *explicitly* detachable and arbitrary, yet *implicitly*
essential and necessary, indeed constitutive (but working in
effects) is indeed called a *logic*, called *parergonality*, called a *law*,
called *Exemplary*, and called above all *necessary*. Derrida's text,
however, indicates the *inverse*. It inverts its own claim in that
the logic is a so-called logic, it is like a logic, but not identical
to a logic, to *Logos* or to Reason. It is a rhetoric of logic here,
not logic as such. It is somehow parallel to logic but not identical
or subsumable within a logic.

What this so-called 'logic of parergonality' entails is the
element of what Kant called the *sublime*. It is the inadequation
of any form to content, of the frame to the framed, of framing
at all, if taken strictly, that characterizes the nature or logic of
parergonality. Hence, Derrida's claims deconstruct themselves
and perform the circle and the abyss (*which is his announced
title*),[18] and above all the 'satire of the abyss.' The abyss is the
distance between Kant and Derrida, it is the difference between
a critique and a deconstruction, between metaphysics and non-
metaphysics, between metaphysics and the rhetoric of metaphysics, between the *parergon* in Kant's sense and the same in
Derrida's sense. To ask the question of truth is not without
relevance here in the sense that one might well conclude that
Derrida has offered up the truth of Kant's example; indeed, the
truth of exemplarity as parergonality could be the last word on
the matter: framed. But of course, deconstruction does not claim
to find truth, just as critique did not claim to find knowledge,
but the condition of the possibility of the same. That one can
locate critique and deconstruction within a metaphysical framework simply displaces the real issue here since what is at stake
is prior, ontologically, to metaphysics and its claims; namely,
truth.

What is the status of exemplarity here? This question must
lead us into the conditions of the possibility of Derrida's stra-

tegies as outlined above, and in addition, what *other* other logic is at work within this performance of parergonality via the thematics of exemplarity. The central question thus entails what Derrida himself has called the *economy of mimesis*, and hence his relation to the *inflation* of examples into Exemplars. What is entailed here relates directly to the question of inversion and its conditions of possibility such that Kant's text, for example, can be inverted in order to show, expose, its 'other' logic. What allows for this inversion? What allows for Kant's step back from the given to enframe it within a system of conditions that entail totality, completeness, and, above all, closure? The sublime again arises here by its exclusion a priori and with it the logic of parergonality that can never be framed, and the structure of exemplarity which entails an intrinsic inadequation, surplus, excess, or as Kant called it, the sublime. Let us now turn to what motivates the transformation of examples into Exemplars within Derrida's Kantian analysis of Kant.

III From examples to Exemplars

The question of the inflation of examples into Exemplars is concerned with a certain transformation of *value* that inhabits this movement. It is the shift not from an example to its law, via reflective judgment, nor from a law to its example, via determinant judgment, but rather from a particular example to a particularly *good*, if not ideal, example. The Exemplar is thus not only a better example than the example, but also becomes an example for example. It is the example of examples, with respect to a particular case or issue. For instance, the examples that Derrida chooses to analyze from Kant's third *Critique* are not merely substitutable by other examples that he might equally well have chosen if it were merely a question that any example at all would serve his purpose. Rather the examples chosen, as chosen, become in that instance exemplary and hence Exemplars. They are not replaceable equally well by others, but rather entail some aspect of uniqueness which is itself precisely what is at issue. Ideally (if there was an ideality at stake here), if Derrida's reading of Kant was to substitute *other examples*, the *same results* would ensue. But this is not the case, as we will proceed to illustrate by example.

Derrida himself makes some reference to this status of examples as more than merely arbitrary and more than merely extrinsic, but only to Kant's text, and not to his own. His neutralization of the question of this status of examples is evident in the problematizing we mentioned earlier of the distinction between the margins and the center of Kant's text, in particular. By placing this distinction in question, suspending its relevance, he thereby opens up the possibility of reading the examples Kant chooses otherwise. Indeed, what is thereby made possible is that the examples are *perhaps* central and in no way marginal, extrinsic to the argument, or to the 'other logic' that organizes Kant's text. Derrida articulates this connection of the largest circle within the smallest circle as his definition of the abyssal structure which he 'finds' in Kant's text; namely, 'For it to be abyssal, the smallest circle should inscribe within itself the largest figure.'[19]

The example as a circle is, however, not a self-evident formulation unless one recognizes once again the rhetoric of reason that organizes Derrida's discourse on Kant, and deconstruction in general. This rhetorical stance situates the example as not only an example of something else, thereby indicating an intentionality within exemplarity, but also as an example of more than and less than what Kant intended or claimed it to be. In this more (and paradoxically less) we find the foundations for the inversions which Derrida's reading requires. The *example* then is always already, in Derrida's text (on Kant and others), an *Exemplar*. It is always already situated as chosen, as unique in its task and constitutive of a more and a less which dislocates it from any linear, univocal reading or interpretation. Thus do the levels of textuality open up within what is called the 'good' example, or the Exemplar. Now the question remains, however, as to what constitutes the 'good' example, what choices are made in order to choose it, or what preferences organize the deconstruction such that all margins are not equal, and the 'smallest circle' can itself be identified? This must now be our task.

Derrida's focus is not only explicitly on the examples Kant chooses and why he chooses them but also on what Derrida himself *designates as an example* (of something else; namely, that 'other' logic). For instance, the admission of a 'large difficulty' by Kant concerning the establishment of any a priori principle for aesthetic judgments prompts Derrida to claim:

> This here would have been able to constitute *an example*, as important as it would be, a great instance of the 'difficulty.' It is a question in truth of the *principal example*, of the *unique exemplar* which gives the meaning and orients the multiplicity. The examination of this example, concerning the aesthetic domain, forms *the* aspect of choice, *the* most important part . . . of the critique of the faculty of judgment.[20]

At this point, from a mere example turned *Exemplar*, the stakes could not be higher. The *inflation* has thus taken place such that this particular example has become '"in truth" the *principal example*, the *unique exemplar* which gives the meaning and orients the multiplicity.'[21] What could have greater value (or centrality)? This claim evidently relies on the rhetoric of truth and rationality, but at this point it is not clear that Derrida has any distance from the unique and exemplary claim being made here. The remainder of his interpretation confirms the commitment to these absolute stakes in that the examination, as he says, of this example (as an Exemplar) forms the most important aspect of the entire *Critique of Judgment*. Once again the transition from an example to the example par excellence is made here such that the smallest circle, Kant's guarded admission, becomes the largest in the instant that the example is transformed into an Exemplar. This process occurs throughout Derrida's reading and one could provide a long list of examples, mere examples, but let us leave the above to suffice as the Exemplar, in this case.

This *inflation* and its condition of possibility suggest a connection to Derrida's discourse which, as the discourse of Reason, in some respects, betrays, parodies, or satirizes what in the 'end' he will claim. The stakes here are Reason's stakes: *the* issue, *the* largest, *most central*, *most important*, *complete*, *total*, and *absolute*. Derrida's transition from one to all, or from the particular to the general, from a singular to a universal is evidenced in precisely his treatment of the example as an Exemplar. He seems thereby to be concerned to find the *rationale* for every step of Kant's text, each transition, each insertion of something particularly (in appearance) insignificant, extrinsic, external (marginal), or *parergonal*. It seems that the ornamentation, the marginal, parenthetical, and minimized claims of the footnotes are thus simply inverted to become their opposites; namely, central, essential, and intrinsic.

If this were the case, Derrida would certainly be performing, by deconstruction, an Hegelian move par excellence. All that is textual would be usurped within the orbit of Reason, all would be linked in a causal chain, that discourse could itself *articulate, thematize*, and thereby *rationalize* and potentially *communicate universally*, as Kant might call it. Is there, one might well ask, anything that 'saves' Derrida's reading from such a reading? Is there any other agenda or logic, indeed alogical logic, non-rational rationality at stake here such that the last word in deconstruction is not simply Reason (albeit inverted)? Certainly. It is the excess in the inflation itself, in the inflationary economy of mimesis, that organizes Derrida's choice which is itself outside the *logos* in its very mimetic relation to the same. Namely, the parergonality that organizes Derrida's text and Kant's text, a structure of exemplarity, which is not simply yet another circle that would entail an *Aufhebung* of the particular example within the general (example) or its law. We have not reached the level of the universal here, nor that of law, but of the *Exemplar*. The Exemplar is the good, ideal (perhaps) example, not the law of the example, we should recall. What this entails is a mirroring relation that has no third term; an instance of what Lacan called, the 'imaginary,' not the 'symbolic.' Thus the Exemplar relates not to the universality of the example, but to its *absolute specificity* and *particularity*. The Exemplar returns us to the time and space, the location and *topos* of the example, not its *logos*. Thus *topography* enters the deconstructive strategy as constitutive and orienting. *Topographical* reading of a text, namely, Kant's third *Critique* in this example, functions as an articulation of land-forms (styles), surface features (placings and locations of terms and issues; the order of presentation), and also depth charges (of archaeological importance). Thus, far from simply inverting the extrinsic to become intrinsic, as it might appear in Derrida's reading of Kant, the structure of exemplarity at work within this reading and within Kant's text as well withholds the *usurpation of reason*, stops it in its tracks by offering a layer of untameable, unframe-able plurality that Reason as such cannot totally control.

Thus *parergonality*, as the systematic, organized, and organizing framework of Derrida's deconstruction of Kant must itself be analyzed as it relates to and, in this case, organizes the structure of exemplarity. Parergonality is not simply the satirizing of the abyss, as Derrida puts it, nor is it simply the law of the relation between *parergon* and the *ergon*, but it opens out onto the lack that inhabits the *ergon* in order to make the *parergon* possible and makes its appearance as essential effaceable. That is, the lack in the *ergon* (the work) cannot as lack be recognized, cannot as such be named, Derrida claims. Rather, it is in evidence only by effect: the effect of the parergon which 'fills it,' albeit inadequately, incompletely and inappropriately, and this 'in' is of necessity. The *ergon* as *ergon* offers itself as complete, as not lacking, and hence the status of the *parergon* can be reduced to an extrinsic appendage, detachable and inessential. It is the hiddenness and the clandestine operation of filling the hidden lack which organizes the relation of *ergon* to *parergon* which will be analyzed here as the 'central' issue of parergonality and hence of exemplarity, in this case.

IV   Parergonality as exemplarity

The relations between the frame and the framed, or *parergon* and *ergon* entail a number of levels of textuality, from Derrida's standpoint. His relation to Kant as an example of this relation performs these processes which can be called parergonality. This is not to say, however, that Derrida's deconstruction forms a frame and Kant's third *Critique* a work of art, or the framed; despite appearances to this effect. The *parergon/ergon* distinction is one which floats, oscillates and ultimately can be shown to be a mirroring yet distancing relation of *différance*. It is a relation of doubling which belies the linear temporality of an origin/copy relation. The *ergon* is not simply prior (temporally or historically) to the *parergon*. Rather, they 'come into existence,' or are 'given' simultaneously. It is this simultaneity, however, that within the structure of parergonality presents itself as a temporal contingency of before and after which thus entails a certain attachability and in turn a detachability of *parergon* to an *ergon* already fully formed.

It is this false historicity that is revealed in the analysis of parergonality in Kant's third *Critique*, via the examples. The connection, however, between exemplarity and parergonality is not one of identity; nor is it simply the case that since the *parerga* chosen by Derrida are often (but not always) Kant's examples in this exemplary deconstruction, that the example is a *parergon*. This is also not to claim that the relation of example to Kant's text is simply one of parergonality. But exemplarity *as* parergonality is not a relation of identity, as we will now proceed to explain.

In order to explore the notion of exemplarity at issue here we must open up the space in which this process operates. The space is not in one place only, nor simply between terms, but it can be seen initially as precisely that. Namely, between the *exemplifier* and the *exemplified* there is a distance and a connection, and this relation is analogous to that of the frame and the framed. The exemplifier/exemplified relation inhabits what is termed an example or an Exemplar, since the latter is simply a type of example (the particularly good, proper, or ideal example). The relation of exemplifier to exemplified can be seen as arbitrary in the sense that the exemplifier makes its appearance as one possibility among others (which are not presented but could well have been; are not chosen but could equally well have been). The particularity of this exemplifier is thus effaced in order that it can be seen as directed towards (essentially in the service of) the exemplified. This arbitrariness, however, is not so arbitrary but rather is controlled by an internal relation (albeit hidden and effaced) between this particular choice of this particular exemplifier and what is to be exemplified by it. In other words, the exemplifier in fact relates necessarily to the exemplified, yet the independence of the exemplified from the exemplifier can only be sustained if this necessity is effaced and appears *as* arbitrary, accidental, extrinsic, and external. This entails an appearance of replaceability, substitutability as the status of the exemplifier in order to sustain the effacement. The question is why is this so, why is this necessary – the appearance of arbitrariness and substitutability – and what is at stake in the status of the exempli*fied* that it requires the appearance of independence from a particular exemplifier? Or, what is it about examples that disconnects them from their embeddedness in whatever context they are found and dislocates any indication of a necessary relation? Why must the example be seen merely as expendable?

We must turn towards the *ergon/parergon* relations in order to clarify this issue. Just as the exemplifier/exemplified relation is essentially double and characterized by the appearance of arbitrariness which in fact entails necessity, so too the relation between *ergon* and *parergon* is a double one in precisely the same respect. As Derrida has shown in Kant's text, the *ergon* is never fully complete, never fully finished, never fully indepen-dent, but rather entails an inner *lack* which *calls forth* (in an atemporal sense) the *parergon* to complete it. The painting is never without a frame, whether it is explicitly framed or not. In Hegelian terms, the immediate is never truly immediate but always mediated by some apparently external, detachable relation which can always be shown to entail necessity. Once again it would seem that this notion of parergonality *as* exem-plarity is locked within the universal of the law of reason, and thereby of a simple necessity. But this is not so for either parergonality or exemplarity. The relation of outside/inside, external/internal, extrinsic/intrinsic is never simple for Derrida, or Kant, via Derrida's analysis. The distinction is never pure, and can *never* (ontologically) be made pure, despite Kant's attempts. And this applies a fortiori to the transcendental-empirical distinction upon which Kant's entire project depends. We shall return to this.

This issue can be seen in terms of what Husserl called, 'inten-tionality.'[22] The example is always already an example *of* some-thing (else, or itself) as other. The structure of exemplarity (as perergonality) thus entails this reach, stretching or thrownness on the side of the exemplifier (as incomplete) to the exemplified (as incomplete). In Derrida's terms, this movement is from the parergon (as incomplete) to the ergon (as incomplete) and it is reversible. The reversibility makes the structure a logical relation rather than an historical one and thereby eludes the structure of mimesis as a temporal relation of an origin and its later arrival, the copy. This parergonal structure is thus in no respect one of origin and copy yet it entails an-other sort of *mimesis*.

Derrida calls it *economimesis*, or the economy of mimesis which entails *différance*, doubleness, and an internal opening in this 'same' (in the *ergon* and *parergon* alike) which is named by many as lack. This is also the internal abyss which opens up the condition of the possibility of the economy of the same as well as destroys its possibility of complete total closure (the conditions of truth, for Kant). The abyss can be encircled, effaced but never fundamentally filled in. In this sense the *parergon/ergon* relation itself lacks and calls forth (at least potentially) yet other frames, and so forth *ad infinitum*. The bad infinite lurks here within this unclosable opening, but this *relation* is *structured* and indeed it forms, via the repetition/alteration that does occur, a *logic*. The logic of supplementarity, *différance*, and in this particular case, that of parergonality, or what we will call exemplarity. The example of the example of the example etc., as a structure, can intrinsically never be completed. It is abyssal essentially, yet it is a structure that repeats. The question arises here as to whether there is thus an *ideality* lurking within this repetition which makes the repetition itself possible and hence, repeatable. The short answer is, no. What repeats is not the same, but something like (mimetic of) the same. It is the doubling itself that repeats, since the terms arise only as doubles and the relation of parergonality itself is always of necessity double; appearing as externality, in fact internally connecting. The other slippage of the logic of parergonality (and thus exemplarity here) from outside of the domain of *logos* as such, or the as such itself, is via the absolute irreplaceability or uniqueness of the examples or frames. The *choice* which locates this here and now is not repeatable, at this level. And this impossibility is ontological. Thus the structure of exemplarity here is an *as* structure not an *is* structure. It is a fictive foundation in the end, not on ontological one, an a fortiori not an epistemological one. But exemplarity, as perhaps the foundation of the as structure itself, does thereby ground (without itself being a ground) the possibility of epistemology and ontology alike.

To return to our example, of Derrida's relation to Kant, one might well ask whether Derrida's exemplary deconstruction as unique is in fact thereby an example of anything else? Namely, an example of deconstruction in general (if such a thing exists) or of his relation to Kant in general, or even philosophy in general. In other words, can his reading here be inflated to the status of an Exemplar in these respects, and if so on what grounds? These questions can all be answered in the affirmative in precisely the sense in which we have articulated the Exemplar, which is the good, ideal example but not the law. Derrida's relation to Kant as exemplified via the issue of parergonality and with that the structure of exemplarity here, can be justifiably seen within the framework he himself articulates. In other words, his reading of Kant is itself an example of itself, he performs what he is describing, declares what is being done at the same instant as doing what is being done. Again, the *parergon/ergon* relation as reversible can be offered as the relation between Kant and Derrida in so far as the lack, the abyss, the *sublime* in fact can, via Derrida's supplementary, apparently detachable frame of deconstruction (the *passepartout*) be shown to inhabit necessarily and with inevitability the Kantian project. This is not the sublime between the noumenal and phenomenal realms, nor between the transcendental and empirical, nor between the subjective and objective, but rather *within* each of these individual terms which thereby allows for, opens up, and even necessitates their relations to their respective others. In short, the relations between the empirical and transcendental, the pure a priori and impure a posteriori, as exemplars of the whole series of hierarchies in Kant's system have been shown in Derrida's analysis to be essentially, despite appearances, characterized by parergonality. That is, the distinctions and the attempted construction of the abyss between these terms by Kant have been encircled by Derrida's analysis, and, paradoxically, within each side or within each term of the distinction a lack (inner) has been revealed which is always already contaminated by the 'other' term of the opposition.

The results of such an analysis can only lead us towards what Kant intended in the first place and that entails a certain necessity and a certain desire, a certain need, and a certain uncertainty. In the search for the conditions of the possibility of metaphysics, Kant thought he had secured a firm foundation via critique, but via Derrida's deconstructive operations one can begin to see or hear that the critique itself rests on insecure or uncritical foundations, and, further, that another logic, that of parergonality or exemplarity, in this case, orients and organizes in a constitutive manner the demand for a transcendental logic which would ground all others. Let us turn finally to a notable admission by Kant which Derrida's analysis partially focuses on and partially analyzes concerning examples:

> Examples are thus the go-carts of judgment; and those who are lacking in the natural talent can never dispense with them.[23]

Despite Kant's condemnation of those who need to rely on examples due to a lack of natural talent or *Mutterwitz*, and despite his reduction of this reliance further to something akin to children's need (or those whose reason is not yet fully developed) his claim above tells us much more than his own rendition of its meaning says explicitly. Namely, that judgment *can* be supplemented with examples, that the *lack* of natural ability can be improved, and that child's play can be offered as a paradigm in which we (who understand better) can thus reduce examples, and with this exemplarity itself or parergonality, in the third *Critique*. Reliance on examples is admitted as a deficiency, but this deficiency (or lack) is imposed *ad hominem* on the one who learns by examples. What Kant did not discuss here is not the limits of examples but the very possibility of exemplarity itself, or what judgment might lack (and of necessity). By reducing the lack to a natural incapacity of some (persons) the issue is concealed at the instant that it is uncovered. One might also note the fact that 'examples as go-carts' are therein revealed as having no power of their own, no internal source of movement, but rather must rely on either a natural decline (or fall, the Fall?) in order to get moving (or be effective) or be an external force, an original mover that would set the wheels in motion. These issues do arise elsewhere, in Derrida's reading of Kant, and are not without some (perhaps eternal) significance.[24] For now, however, it is clear at least that the performance of parergonality itself exceeds the status of a mere example, replaceable, repeatable, imitable, or capable of identity, and thereby installs itself necessarily, albeit clandestinely, within Kant's text (via Derrida).

Chapter 5

HEGEL, DERRIDA, AND THE SIGN

Deborah Chaffin

The contours and strategic importance of Derrida's critique of idealism, and more specifically of the extent to which he 'takes Hegel seriously,' can be nowhere better viewed than in his treatment of Hegel's theory of representation and the sign. As he has many times stated: 'The problematic of the sign derives from a fundamental logocentrism, from a philosophy of consciousness or of the originary subject.'[1] In his protracted history of the notion of the sign in *Of Grammatology* as well as the shorter version presented in his interview with Julia Kristeva,[2] Derrida is concerned to show that the very concept of the sign has always depended upon, or been determined by, that fundamental metaphysical opposition: the sensible and the intelligible. His various treatments of the sign work to show that the metaphysical tradition has always treated the sign as a *transition* or bridge between these two moments of presence. Because the sign could only function as a provisional reference between presence in the form of the object (the sensible) and presence in the form of self-presence (the intelligible), Derrida views it as the *time of referral* which signifies self-presence: in the case of Hegel, it is the self-presence of the absolute as subject, or 'absolute subjectivity.'

But if we accept Derrida's argument that the history of the notion of the sign must be read as the history of the determination of Being as presence (as metaphysics), why would it have to follow that 'we cannot *do without* the concept of the sign' or abandon this 'metaphysical complicity'?[3] Derrida's argument is that we cannot give up this metaphysical complicity,

without also giving up the critique we are directing against

77

this complicity, or without the risk of erasing difference in the self-identity of a signified reducing its signifier into itself or, amounting to the same thing, simply expelling its signifier outside itself.[4]

In other words, Derrida holds that we *need* this problematic in order to put the *system* of metaphysics as a whole into question. And in the case of Hegel in particular, if Derrida can show that the signifier has been *reduced* to or *derived* from the signified, then he can argue that Hegel has *submitted* the sign to thought, and that the opposition of the sensible and the intelligible is systematic with the reduction of the sign to thought. In short, Derrida's focus on the problematic of the *sign* – on writing and language generally – allows him to develop an alternative to the traditional systematic relegation of the sign to the status of *transition*, as something merely provisional. On the basis of his critique of the history of the concept of the sign, Derrida can *lift* this site of the transition between two moments of full presence (the sensible and the intelligible) and effect a positively *displacing* and *transgressive* 'appropriation' of Hegelian logic.

Such an appropriation of Hegel cannot be achieved on the basis of the problematic of the sign, or writing and language, alone. In the section following I will show that *this* problematic is bound intimately to Derrida's understanding of Hegelian *Aufhebung*. Such a context will elicit the sense in which Derrida's own reading of Hegel may be viewed as *transformational*. I will then consider the import of this 'transformation' by focusing on Derrida's understanding of the role of *contradiction* in Hegelian *Aufhebung*. Finally, however, I will suggest that important aspects of the Hegelian arguments concerning the role and function of contradiction are still valid and should be rethought outside their Derridian affiliation.

I

In his 'Exergue,' or 'outwork,' to *Of Grammatology*, Derrida focuses attention on a triple movement of our 'logocentric' and 'ethnocentric' epoch. According to this analysis, the metaphysics of phonetic writing (= logocentrism) has controlled and ordered in one system:

1. *the concept of writing.* . . .
2. *the history of* (the only) *metaphysics,* which has . . . always assigned the origin of truth in general to the logos: the history of truth, of the truth of truth, [which] has always been . . . the debasement of writing, and its repression outside 'full' speech.
3. *the concept of science* or the scientificity of science – what has always been determined as *logic*.[5]

Because of the pervasive and continuing influence of this controlling order, even the science of writing – grammatology – may never be established as such. Indeed, both the idea of *science* and the idea of *writing* are themselves meaningful only 'in terms of an origin and within a world to which a certain concept of the sign . . . and a certain concept of the relationship between speech and writing, have *already been assigned*.'[6] Thus, modern semiology is itself constituted on concepts and presuppositions discernible in, among others, Plato, Aristotle, Rousseau, Hegel, and Husserl.[7]

Derrida's critique of Hegel's semiology can thus be understood as a moment in a general strategy of transformation, displacement, and reinscription at work in the Derridean project of grammatology. Viewed positively, the critique of Hegelian semiology allows Derrida to *avoid* a simple rejection of Hegel which would inevitably fix his own place within the Hegelian matrix. Such a strategy also allows Derrida to locate Hegel quite firmly within the history of the 'logocentric' tradition.

In 'The Pit and the Pyramid: Introduction to Hegel's Semiology,'[8] Derrida presents a detailed analysis of the Hegelian theory of speech and writing, and does so by focusing on two long Remarks from *The Encyclopedia of the Philosophical Sciences.* Both Remarks are found in the subchapter 'Imagination' in the chapter 'Psychology' within 'Subjective Spirit.'[9] As we shall see, Derrida's general critique is double-edged, for it aims to throw into question the *primacy* Hegel accords to psychology in his theory of speech and writing, and also to question the privilege Hegel accords the sonorous or phonetic expression.

But first, let us consider exactly why Hegel's theory of speech and writing – his semiology – falls within the sphere of subjective spirit, and more precisely within the area of psychology (and not, for instance, within anthropology or phenomenology – the two previous moments of subjective spirit). First of all, we should recall that Hegel's *Encyclopedia*, his most general presentation of the philosophic system, is divided into three parts:

    I. Logic: the science of the Idea in and for itself.
    II. The Philosophy of Nature: the science of the Idea in its otherness.
    III. The Philosophy of Spirit: the science of the Idea come back to itself out of that otherness. (Section 18)

The theory of signs, falling as it does within the third moment of the Idea or system of reason, is, then, a part of the philosophy of spirit. Since it follows the philosophy of nature, the philosophy of spirit is concerned to show *that* and *how* spirit 'frees itself' from nature, from its otherness. All three moments of this 'movement' – anthropology, phenomenology, and psychology – are concerned with this 'motion of freeing itself,'[10] but only the moment of psychology shows the *reality* of reason: the anthropological moment of subjective spirit shows reason to be the goal of nature, and the phenomenological shows reason to be the goal of consciousness. But the goal of the psychological investigation of spirit is to show that reason is the element of subjective spirit, that reason is the active power of spirit, and not just its 'goal.'

More precisely: the theory of signs is located within the first movement of spirit, in subjective spirit. Spirit in general is articulated in three parts:

1. Subjective spirit: the spirit's relation to itself, an only ideal totality of the Idea. This is Being-near-to-itself in the form of only internal freedom.
2. Objective spirit, as a world to produce and produced in the form of reality, not only ideality. Freedom here becomes an existing, present necessity.
3. Absolute spirit: the unity, that is *in itself and for itself*, of the objectivity of the spirit and of its ideality or its concept, the unity producing itself eternally, spirit in its absolute truth – *absolute spirit*. (Section 385)

And since Hegel's theory of the sign falls within subjective spirit and this determination of spirit is finite and transitory, Derrida argues that 'the sign indeed appears as a mode or determination of subjective and finite spirit as a mediation or transgression [*Ubersichhinausgehen*] of itself, a transition within the transition, a transition of the transition.'[11] In other words, far from actually providing a way *out of* itself, the theory of signs presents *a return to itself of spirit*, another version of the 'idealizing mastery' of the system as a whole.

Indeed, it would appear, as Derrida suggests, that the theory of signs is a form of 'idealizing mastery' in its very architecture: as a moment of intelligence (*Intelligenz*), representation makes the transition between intuition and thought explicit (Section 458, Addition). Representation (*Vorstellung*) distinguishes the activity of immediate intuition from the content intuited, transforming the sensible appearances which intuition has always already mediated. Throughout all the moments of representation – recollection, imagination, memory – such transformative activity is present. Indeed, in the production of signs, or language generally, intelligence *explicitly* posits its imaginative activities. Since signs are external, they escape the provisional character of the consciousness which produces them: as Hegel remarks,

> intelligence . . . *appears* in taking up sensuous content and forming representations for itself out of this material . . . it then gives its independent representations a definite determinate being (*ein bestimmtes Dasein*). (Section 458 Addition)

It is precisely at this point that Derrida locates the idealizing mastery at work in Hegelian semiology. I will now quote in full what Derrida claims in this regard, for it is the basis of his critique of Hegelian semiology.

> The sign unites an 'independent representation' and an 'intuition,' in other words, a concept (signified) and a sensory perception (signifier). But Hegel must immediately recognize a kind of separation, a disjointing which, by dislocating the 'intuition,' opens the space and play of signification. There is no longer in the signifying unity, in the welding of representation and intuition, an intuition like

any other. Doubtless, as in every intuition, a being is given, a thing is presented and is to be received in its simple presence. . . . It is there, immediately visible, indubitable. But insofar as it is united to *Vorstellung* (to a representation), this presence becomes representation, a representation (in the sense of representing) of a representation (in the general sense of conceptual ideality). Put in the place of something other, it becomes *etwas anderes vorstellend*: here *Vorstellen* and *represent* release and reassemble all their meanings at once.[12]

Derrida's point is that the strange 'intuition' present in the sign represents an *ideality*, the ideality of a *Bedeutung* or meaning. And as the unity of the signifying body and the signified ideality, the sign itself 'becomes a kind of incarnation.'[13] Thus, in general and most importantly for Derrida's project, 'the opposition of the intelligible and the sensory, condition the difference between the signified and the signifier, between the signifying intention (*bedeuten*), which is an animating activity, and the inert body of the signifier.'[14]

For Hegel, then, as Derrida notes, the proper and animated body of the signifier (the sign) is a *tomb*:

The body of the sign thus becomes the monument in which the soul will be enclosed, preserved, maintained, kept in maintenance, present, signified. At the heart of this monument the soul keeps itself alive, but it needs the monument only to the extent that it is exposed – to death – in its living relation to its own body. . . . The sign – the monument-of-life-in-death, the sepulcher of a soul . . . is the *pyramid*.[15]

Thus, in the final analysis for Derrida, *at its heart* Hegelian semiology remains within the seriousness of the negative, within the work of meaning and truth. The production of signs, the use of language, is an interiorization of spirit relating itself to itself with its sight set on truth. '*With its sight set*: conceived in its destination on the basis of the truth toward which it is oriented.'[16] Derrida's criticism is that Hegel's semiology remains within the chain of a dialectic tied to the *Aufhebung*. As his subsequent analysis in 'The Pit and the Pyramid' shows, all of Hegel's essential insights into language and representation are founded on dialectics, 'the resolution of the sign in the horizon of the nonsign, of the presence beyond the sign.'[17] And as he stated elsewhere, the submission to the hegemony of meaning present in his theory of language is 'the essence and element of philosophy, of Hegelian ontologics.'[18]

II

Since the sign works on the basis of contradiction, Derrida's understanding of Hegel's semiology as structured according to the movement of the *Aufhebung* is simply *one* instance of a much larger issue. Throughout all his major texts on Hegel, Derrida lays great stress on Hegel's reliance on negativity and contradiction, the essential characteristics of *Aufhebung*. In addition to the chief role this movement plays in Derrida's reconstruction of Hegelian semiology, it is also crucial for his sustained concern to distinguish *différance* from Hegelian difference; for difference, alleges Derrida, is determined in the *Science of Logic* 'as contradiction (*Widerspruch*) *only in order to resolve it, to interiorize it, to lift it up . . . into the self-presence of an onto-theological or onto-teleological synthesis.*'[19] Indeed, Derrida has argued that Hegelian idealism *is* a *relève* of all the binary oppositions of classical idealism, 'a resolution of contradiction into a third term that comes in order to *aufheben*, to deny while raising up, while idealizing, while sublimating into an anamnesic interiority (*Errinnerung*), while *interning* difference in a self-presence.'[20] In order to preserve meaning, then, *only* the *Aufhebung* will do; the very movement and structure of *Aufhebung* rests on the understanding of difference, or contradiction, as negativity.[21]

Now certainly it *is* true that Hegel's explicit treatment of contradiction in the *Science of Logic* begins with its identification as a *Wesenheit*, or essentiality. As a determination of reflection, contradiction (along with the categories of identity and difference) is treated thematically as a category of essence. But Derrida's focus on contradiction as *the* structure of *Aufhebung* also suggests that the Hegelian method itself *embodies* contradiction, that there is *no* important difference between the thematic and the methodological senses of contradiction. In the following, I will suggest that there are important reasons to acknowledge the difference between the thematic and the methodological uses of contradiction, and that this distinction underlies Hegel's position that in comprehensive thinking otherness is relevant only to the extent that it can be translated into the terms of thought (or the categories).[22] Moreover, any interpretation of Hegel's concept of contradiction according to which it would be dependent on *extralogical* subject matters will be shown to be much more ambitious than Hegel's theory itself.

In order to view the precise thematic determination of contradiction within Hegel's *Science of Logic*, I will first sketch its place in the *Logic* as a whole. The form of the categories in the *Logic* is a systemic one; it is only when viewed as a totality of *logical categories* related according to their own internal logic, that the structure of rationality Hegel presents can be explained to be true. It is only when the structure is so understood, that is, as an essentially self-related whole, that the being of rationality can be justified as the rationality of being. This characterization permits us to view an aspect of the perhaps unsuspected modesty of Hegel's project: ontology, for Hegel, does not claim to be exhaustive in the sense of including all entities (or extralogical subject matters) within its dialectical purview. Hegelian ontology rather claims to be able to explain being only in so far as being is rational.

The level of being in its immediacy, or that region investigated in the first book of the *Logic*, is only relatively rational. Yet the relativity of the rationality of immediate being is not judged on the basis of a criterion, as if imposed from 'outside being'. According to its *own* principles, those of being itself and negation, the sphere of immediate being is shown to be only relatively rational. The full significance of the other, in distinction from which alone being is determinate being, does not yet appear at the level of immediacy, for immediacy is 'indifferent' to its determining other.

The very indifference of immediacy pushes being to mediation: the determinateness of immediate being depends upon its being differentiated from its other. In order that such differentiation belong to being itself, immediate being's indifference to its other which determines it must be overcome. Because it is the *mediating other* of immediate being, reflection determines immediate being. However, this negativity of essence is also immediate and is, then, simply self-identical. But as self-identical, essence is self-related and so *posits* its own determinateness. Yet the determination of appearance – or reflective being – even though determined intrinsically, still has the ground of its appearance outside itself. The sense of appearance is thereby derivative, and cannot adequately be explained by reflection. As *immediate negativity*, essence cannot fully explain the sense it has as determinate being.

In the third, and final, sphere, the level of conceptuality, both sense and determinateness are fully integrated. Conceptual being is a negative unity which posits itself *in* its negative. Thus, in the being of the concept, otherness, or *real negativity*, is sublated. The sense of subjectivity is determined by the sense of objectivity; and objectivity possesses sense only through its negative. In the category of the absolute idea this mutual implication is posited. If being makes sense – if it is at all rational – it has the sense dialectical thought is able to explicate. Thus Hegel's philosophy attempts to resituate what is commonly understood to be given in experience into the form of thought. His account does not begin on the presupposition of the givenness of experience, but rather it justifies the theoretical acceptability of the given on the basis of theoretical principles alone. And Hegel's *Logic* provides an account of those principles which shows, finally, that thought itself is the principle of the account: 'not only the account of scientific method, but even the concept itself of the science as such belongs to its content, and in fact constitutes its final result.'[23]

Now, the *concept* (*Begriff*) of the account given in the final chapter of the *Logic* allows us to focus on the *methodological* meaning of the dialectic. For the concept of the account must show (i) that the categories elicited in the course of the *Logic* are normative with respect to that which they categorize, and (ii) that the individual categories have their normative status solely on the basis of their development *as* categories. In other words, there must be both a progressive and a regressive interpretation of the movement of the categories.[24] In the progressive reading, the account must build up an understanding of categorization without appeal to extracategorial items. While the regressive reading must provide a justification for the status of each of the categories as moments in the progressive understanding of thought's normativity.

As my account of the overall structure of the *Logic* has indicated, the first phase of the account of the categories does begin with categories which are *immediate* or *indifferent* to each other *and* to the account thought gives of them. However, this progressive understanding of the movement of the categories must result, finally, in a *categorial* expression of what it means to be a category. Thus, in the final sphere of the *Logic*, the level of the concept, we view categories which are neither indifferent to each other nor to what thought makes of them. In order that the categories of the first phase will be justified, there must therefore be access to them from the third phase. The logic of essence, the second phase of the *Logic*, provides this intermediate sphere by showing that the determinations present in the categories are relational (*not* indifferent to one another), but are nevertheless still indifferent to the sense thought makes of them as explanatory or normative.

Development between the spheres or phases of the *Logic* cannot be explained only on the basis of the phases themselves. Each phase must be internally complex so that its development from beginning to final determination can be viewed. The categories themselves provide this complexity and each can be understood as a term of the development of one phase of the *Logic*. Each category is thus a *logical function*,[25] and can be explained in terms of its systemic meaning within the *Logic* as a whole. This leads to the *thematic* understanding of individual categories.

However, the *Logic* also requires a principle of development which will elicit the logical function of *each* category: the dialectic is this principle. More precisely: determinate negation, or the precise way the dialectic is applied to each category is the principle of development of the *Logic* as a whole. This, then, is the *methodological* understanding of the dialectic.

In Hegel's presentation of the category of contradiction, we can differentiate both the methodological and the thematic senses of the dialectic. Moreover, such a differentiation is crucial in order to view, finally, the extent to which Hegel, in Derrida's words, 'determines difference as contradiction.'[26]

In the logic of essence, Hegel gives a first development of the necessity inherent in thought's own activity. Reflection is not the mere distinguishing of moments in an intellectual process, but rather an act of distinguishing which takes place *only* because in being aware of itself as distinguishing, thought is aware of itself as process. Both this intellectual process, and that which is able to be distinguished within the process, are next used self-reflexively: reflection turns on itself and dissolves and cancels its own negative essence. 'Being, in its determining (*das resultierende, unendliche Zusammengehen mit sich*), has thus determined itself to essence, a being which, through the sublating of being, is a simple *being-with-itself* (*ein einfaches Sein mit sich*).'[27]

In the logic of essence, being is dissolved as immediacy; this act of dissolution is what comes under analysis. In the logic of essence, thought internalizes or 'recollects' (*erinnert*) itself from out of immediate being. Through such mediation, knowing 'finds' essence:

> Cognition certainly cannot stop short at manifold *determinate being*, nor yet at being, *pure being*; the reflection that immediately forces itself on one is that this *pure being*, the *negation* of everything finite, presupposes an *internalization*, a *recollection* (*Erinnerung*) and movement which has purified immediate, determinate being to pure being.[28]

Even though being is still *a* being in essence, it is still a being within which everything determinate and finite is negated. The 'internalization' or 'recollection' that takes place in essence is an intellectual act which arises from relating; because of its movement into itself through the *self*-sublating of determinateness and otherness, essence constitutes the transition from the sphere of being *per se* to that of conceptuality, or concept as being in *and* for itself.

Hence, the most general determination of essence is that it *came forth* from being; consequently, essence is the first negation of being for it posits *within* itself negation or determination. By thus giving itself a determinate being which is equal to its being-in-itself (or that which it has posited within itself), essence becomes concept. At first, however, essence is not yet for itself: the determinate being essence gives itself is not determinate being as it is in and for itself, but determinate being as *determined* by essence, as *posited* by essence. Accordingly, as simple, essence remains within itself with the moments of illusory being, determinations of reflection (identity, difference, and contradiction), and ground.[29]

Thus, at first, the category of contradiction is construed as simple negativity: since it is one of the categories of reflection it is merely *formal*, it simply belongs to the structure of reflection. More precisely, contradiction is *derived* specifically from the category of difference because that category alone is unable to provide an account of the relatedness of the relata under consideration in essence (the positive and the negative). The attempt to elucidate the co-ordination of the relata and their relatedness motivates the move from difference to diversity and opposition and then to contradiction and ground.

The category of contradiction emerges, finally, as the structure of relatedness in which each relata is determined to be what it is by denying its own self-identity as excluded from the other relatum, and yet each relata identifies itself with that other.[30] But if the relata *are* equivalent, then relatedness itself is contradictory, and, as Hegel points out, 'the initial unity which results from contradiction is the Null.'[31] Thus both relata 'destroy themselves,'[32] and to the extent that something is self-contradictory, it is indeterminate, and the merely formal category of contradiction issues in a 'ceaseless vanishing of the opposites into themselves.'[33]

However, as Hegel immediately points out, 'contradiction contains not merely the negative, but also the positive . . . the result of contradiction is not merely a nullity.'[34] The movement present in contradiction, 'the self-excluding reflection,' is a *positing* reflection which has withdrawn into its ground:

> The resolved contradiction is therefore ground, essence as unity of the positive and negative. In opposition, the determination has attained to self-subsistence; but ground is this completed self-subsistence; in it, the negative is self-subsistent essence, but as a negative; as self-identical in this negativity, ground is just as much the positive. Opposition and its contradiction is, therefore, in ground as much abolished as preserved.[35]

Hence, the category of contradiction simply elicits the motivation for the transition to ground, and is *not* a 'stage' in the movement in the way that the categories of identity, difference, and ground are stages in the dialectical movement of essence.[36] In other words, the *category* of contradiction does *not* determine the *dialectic* as self-contradictory. It is rather the case that the category of contradiction (the thematic sense of contradiction) *indicates* the logical defect of regarding the relata (the positive and the negative) as related symmetrically; it shows that the structure of essence *cannot* be expressed in terms of the symmetries of simple self-identity and mere difference. As the category of ground shows, the proper relation between the relata is the asymmetrical, or structured, unity of ground.

What has emerged from this discussion of the thematic sense of contradiction, then, is that, as an initial category of essence, contradiction simply shows what must be avoided in a categorial account of thought's comprehension of being. Contradiction shows that there is a *logical defect* in regarding the positive and the negative as symmetrically related. In other words, the *category* of contradiction shows the failure of identity and difference to account for the structure of reflection. Thus, reflection, construed as symmetrical relatedness, cannot account for the differences which the otherness of being and a categorial account of being make to each other.

More generally, the logic of essence may be viewed as simply the *first* step of the dialectic of the *Logic* as a whole: within essence, the dialectic (as *method*) posits the negation to the logic of being. In essence, the initial otherness of being, *as indifference*, is progressively categorized as identity, difference, and ground. The logic of essence is the way *thought* categorizes its own limitation: it renders the otherness of being in its own categories so that otherness can itself be categorized. In the logic of the concept this second stage of the dialectic is accomplished: the categories of the final stage negate the limitations of the logic of essence by comprehending them in new categorial determinations which articulate being by incorporating all previous otherness.

Further, since this dialectical method is merely the explanation of the *logical functions* of the categories, the *Logic* does not have to impose an *external* principle of method on the categories:

> *Method* may appear at first as the mere *manner* peculiar to the process of cognition, and as a matter of fact it has the

nature of such. But the peculiar manner, as method, is not merely a modality of *being determined in and for itself*; it is a modality of cognition, and as such is posited as determined by the *concept* and as form, in so far as the form is the soul of all objectivity and all otherwise determined content has its truth in the form alone. . . . the method has emerged as the *self-knowing concept* that has itself . . . for its subject matter.[37]

The method is the same as the content of the *Logic*; to be a category is to be a moment in the development of the *Logic*. And since the *Logic*, on this interpretation, makes no claims regarding extracategorial reality, the adequacy of the dialectic isn't to be measured by comparison to that extracategorial reality. One advantage of this reading is that we can understand the difference otherness *does* make to thought, and such otherness can be shown to determine thought, or comprehensive thinking, itself. Secondly, this reading can *justify* the distinction between the thematic sense of contradiction and the contradiction proper to the method; a reading of the *Logic* according to which the *Logic* would make claims regarding extracategorial reality would be unable to distinguish between the two senses of contradiction.[38]

This issue of the distinction between the two senses of contradiction is of crucial significance for Derrida's project. As he has described *différance* (the process of differentiation), 'it can no longer simply be subsumed by the generality of *logical* contradiction . . . [it] permits a differentiated accounting for heterogeneous modes of conflictuality, or, if you will, of contradictions. . . . To reduce *différance* to difference is to stay far behind in this debate.'[39] In the terms of our discussion, if thought in the *Logic* had to comprehend reality outside its categorial determination, then thought and reality would *both* be contradictory, and determinate negation (the second step of the dialectic) would simply preserve these contradictions at the expense of sense. But surely this is *not* the result of the *Logic*, nor is it the result of Derridean *différance*. Indeed, *Derrida's* own distinction between a merely '*logical* contradiction' and 'a differentiated accounting of contradictions' does not appear to be so far removed from what I have spoken of as the 'thematic' and 'methodological' senses of contradiction.[40]

III

In spite of Derrida's polemics against the Hegelian *Aufhebung* as being merely at the service of an onto-theological or onto-teleological synthesis, I hope to have shown that such a reading of Hegelian logic is ultimately unsatisfactory. Just as Hegel's theory of speech and writing, his semiology, cannot be *reduced to* the logic of representation,[41] so too the Hegelian *Aufhebung* cannot be reduced to being the symbol of an idealizing mastery. As my interpretation has argued, Hegelian logic does *not* rest on self-consciousness or the absolute subject as the foundation of meaning. Rather, Hegel's philosophy attempts to *resituate* what is ordinarily taken as given in our experience into the form of thought, and he attempts, in his *Logic*, to provide a self-justificatory account of the theoretical principles which justify our acceptance of such reformulations.

In the final analysis, the Hegelian *Aufhebung* turns out to be modest in a way I don't think Derrida would reject: for Hegel, thought does not occupy a spurious elevation above the world of experience, but rather begins and progresses within the limits of meaning and explanation. Hegel, like Derrida, does not question the irrationalities and sheer otherness of the world; but Hegel's philosophy presents us with a means for rendering that otherness intelligible in the only way it can be for us. If the world makes sense, then the Hegelian *Aufhebung* is not the force of the negative in the service of totality, but rather the force of the negative in the service of human understanding.

Chapter 6

DRAWING: (AN) AFFECTING NIETZSCHE: WITH DERRIDA

Ruben Berezdivin

RÜCKBLICK (Retrospect) – Seldom do we become conscious of the genuine pathos of any period of our lives as long as we are taking part in it, but always rather think that it is the only possible real state for us, thoroughly *ethos* and not pathos – to speak and distinguish with the Greeks. Today, a few musical tones recalled for me a winter and a house, and an extremely solitary life, along with the feeling I lived in at that time: I thought that I would forever go on living like that [*ewig so fortleben*]. Now though I understand that it was wholly pathos and passion [*Leidenschaft*], comparable to some moodily-painful and soothing music, the like of which for years one mustn't hear, much less for eternities – otherwise one would become too over-earthly [*zu überirdisch*] for this planet.[1]
[Friedrich Nietzsche, *Fröhliche Wissenschaft*, section 317]

In assessing Derrida's relation to Nietzsche, we may start with something simple: there is no privileged position from which to judge it, it must be reinterpreted along a certain vantage point. With deliberate melodrama, I choose the way of the affective, of tonality (Hölderlin's famous *Wechsel der Töne*),[2] 'musical' pathos, attempting to set into relief what cuts across Nietzsche's and Derrida's corpuses (alive dead one the other), what about the body affects them, beginning with a certain problematic concept (whose recent history goes back to Kant's first *Critique*):[3] self-affection.

While affecting a certain set of guidelines for its trajectory, the present text aims to evaluate a certain destination or issuance, a dispatch or *Schickung*. The issue affecting the text, folding it upon itself and granting it its proper dimension, bears on the thought of a specific mission, missive, or message, emitted such that in the desire to communicate it affectively the thought's

92

own possibility is essentially (tautologically) affected with its eternally recurrent impossibility or impotence, now become condition of (im)possibility, 'deconstructing' along a certain angle Christian metaphysics. (The or 'this' text aims at a *symploke*, an interweaving, of the thought of eternal recurrence, self-affection, and textuality.)

The primary referent of Derrida's encounter with Nietzsche in his most recent texts is Nietzsche's (telling of his) life[4] which constitutes a peculiar object, on the one hand dealt with by Nietzsche in his autobiographical and infamous *Ecce Homo* and on the other in Derrida's *Otobiographies* (whose plural is already worrisome). Since the referent is someone's life, the issue of life accompanies these texts as well, in a singular specific emission, and specifically life in its non-oppositionality to death.

I shall here write as if Nietzsche's 'truth' were dictated to me and shall derive from that angle the interpretative affect subsuming the present reading, a mood of (hopefully) *gay distress*. That affect programming the forthcoming reading in the intertexture of two powerful texts will take itself, in the light of Nietzsche's own doctrine of the affects, as an interpretative will to power, seeking to overpower in interrelating to the other two texts the plural dissemination of binary textuality.

The focus will be on life, specific and general, as retold by Nietzsche and reinterpreted by Derrida, with Nietzsche's metaphysics, as countersigned by Heidegger[5] as a sort of conventional code to direct us and interfere with the pregiven wavelengths crossing each other constituting this present text as a communication across distances.

I Affecting a self

What is the tonality we can detect in Derrida facing Nietzsche? What change of tone or affection, what 'retrospective pathos' (following our exergue's distinctions)? Nietzsche's pathos surnamed 'distance' over many texts[6] may be described preliminarily as an inconspicuous, apparently submerged, but dynamically powerfully explosive will to destroy traditional morality while discovering within itself the gaiety of a Dionysian affirmation that essentially resists direct assertion (requiring instead constant and stylistic obliquity). Following the exergue from the *Gay Wissenschaft*, a pathos necessarily presents itself during its happening as an ethos, as a relatively fixed and stable disposition, allowing cognitive and affective perspective, proving retrospectively to have been a mirage designed by the will of memory. It is the affects that control 'life,' the pathos of things inscribed and emergent as a will to *command*:

> *To will – that is commanding*. Commanding however is a definite *affect* (this affect is a *sudden explosion* – eager, clear, exclusively one thing in the eye, an innermost conviction of superiority, a certainty that the will shall be obeyed). (*KSA*, vol. 11, 25, 436)[7]

This 'commanding' affect happens indeed as a 'sudden' release of energy, in an instant of decision, asserting the will as a commanding presence in order to command the very present in becoming stamped upon it. Remarkably this affective will becomes aware of its presence only retroactively, while commanding it is 'spontaneously' at work in achieving its work. The affect taken over the command post constrains other wills, affecting them with its desires, and which it (as it were) ranges on its side as means to its end, mustering their force together through differential integration, dividingly conquering, and thus regimenting them similarly to how a general ranges over his troops, commandingly, with his very stride (the example of presenting arms being an early instance used by Nietzsche to think through the question of the will and of cause–effect).

Always at war with each other and only affecting themselves reciprocally, the affects command the inside Nietzschean scene, its pathology, his organic–theoretic scene. Behind, the still more 'physiological' drives, which are represented by the affects, while above, sublimely and intelligently, calculatively self-conscious, stands reason as a central agency responding to the politics of the affects and bringing about the governance of the will as a pseudo-singular entity.[8]

The affects, however, are not psychological 'entities,' for they do not belong to the realm of being at all:

> Affects as counterparts to physiological groups having a sort of unity of becoming, a periodic process. (*KSA*, vol. 11, 25, 185)

It should not be asked 'Who interprets, then?' but interpreting itself as a form of the will to power has existence only as an affect (but not 'being,' rather as a *process*, a becoming). (*KSA*, vol. 12, 2, 151)[9]

Affects belong neither to being nor to becoming. The dominant pathos of a stage of existence conceals itself as ethos, an affected morality or code of conduct whose temperamental origin or tonality, dominant as mood ('*Stimmungen*' in *KSA*, vol. 10, 7, 136), leads thinking to the belief that these affects lie behind and control our will as metaphysical motives or motors, a presumed ontology, a psychological theory Nietzsche indefatigably exposes as illusory, for psychologically, there is no will. The dominant affect, while affecting the self with its tonal attunement, disaffects its thought, rendering it effective, and provoking a disposition that sublimates its process of becoming into a stable duration oblivious, for all practical purposes, of its pathological origin. The recovery of that dominantly latent pathos concealed by the ethos can only take place retrospectively, by means of a special mnemic signal or trace awaking a hermeneutically suspicious memory, an affective memory whose very dwelling upon being would consist in a retroactively natural self-affection, a passive–passionate pathos whose past is evoked only when a certain staging of its history is recalled in order to be dwelt on again and again, for and as itself.

Hence it may be said that a sort of self-recall constitutes being's dwelling and leads what persists being, during the relative stability of a self-oblivious life stage, by means of the passionate and pathologic, to maintain the illusions of ontology, whereas self-identity is previously constituted by the trace of self-relation in self-affected *différance*:

There is no law; every power at every instant draws the ultimate consequences. . . . A quantum of power is designated by the effect it brings about and it resists. . . . Adiaphory is lacking (in itself it would be highly conceivable). Essentially, it is a will to subjugate and to protect from subjugation, not one towards self-preservation. . . . We require unities in order to reckon. . . . Let us eliminate these additions. . . . Nothing remains but dynamic quanta in a relation of tension with other dynamic quanta, whose essence indeed consists in their relation to all other quanta, in their producing effects upon them – will to power not as a being, not as a becoming, but as *pathos*, that is the most elemental fact, from which later there emerges a becoming and producing of an effect. (*KSA*, vol. 13, *14*, 79; *WM*, sections 634–5)

Affects would thus be 'power relations' and their consistence, their insistence, not a matter either of being or becoming, neither 'Parmenides' nor 'Heraclitus,' but an interpretative differential force that defers or postpones permanence while affecting an illusory hold, differentially bringing presence about as a determinate specific effect, affectively commanding within a chain of obedience or hierarchy of affects struggling with each other and *always already* in a process of establishing themselves and becoming confused, retroactively, with the status quo, set to function as the real.

The affective 'punctuation,' the textual staging of a certain period – state or juncture – in one's life, recalled to itself to dwell in a passionate, self-affected and affecting, thought as a mnemic trace of a pathological memory committed to re-collecting and remembering its own pathos *as* passage and passing away of a portion of life, as life's impassioned self-survival, in this way lends itself, as affective dispositionality, to the performance of a telling story in which that very portion of life is autobiographically recounted and thus repeated as eternally recurrent, whence the auto-bio-graphic re-trait or retreat in *Ecce Homo* affecting the passages we have been quoting, always more or less out of context.[10]

II The return of the passage

How is this autobiographical drive contracted, drawn, acquired? Why should it be written down? Why, in any case, should memory have to contract with itself in order to be affected with its own passion, its past and passage, by (auto)-inscription or signature?

Derrida affects Nietzsche ('s signature), at once *draws* and *with-draws* Nietzsche's signature (for and) from *itself*. Such, if it had any, would be the hypo-thesis underlying the present text.

The recalling of myself as past passion and passage has to be relayed to my 'present' self and conveyed to my 'future' self, it must contrive – in order to take place – to unify the temporal 'biograph' by tracing itself *across* time, plotting its own graph and drawing it *along* by drawing it *forth* in drawing it *in*, inscribing or imprinting it. This self-draughting machine affects biography as auto-graphy, draws (its) life from itself in drawing it *upon* itself, drawing *out* its life signed *as itself*. Thus is a biography self-contracted, drawn, affectively signed and confirmed.

Here the interface or border (*bordure*, Derrida calls it)[11] between the life and work of an author must be 'crossed.' On this border-line we must persevere, allowing for the effect of a certain *dynamis*, a virtual differential force[12] to play upon and affect our text in interaction with Derrida's (on) Nietzsche, affecting the biographic inscription with the patho-logy or patho-graphy of a specific biological factor. The border-structure[13] and problematics of the biographic text draws its limits and derives its power from this locomotion. It is in this (derived and derivative) place that we shall find that abyss where the signature stamps upon its counter an affirmative jubilation (as eternally recurrent) *without* confirming the statute of a protective self-consciousness.[14] It is not the recall of conscience but the memory of a passion erasing its past in passing to a self-affirming demise, exposing the self to the elemental, that will be our destination – which does not preclude the restitution of the *effects* of consciousness in a structural *après-coup*.

In the border, along the line of this interface, approaching our destiny, the question resurfaces: why should a biography be necessary for life; why must a pathos auto-affect its inscription with life through a supplementary de-scription narrating its own history? As a self-contracted 'oath' to tell the truth about my past, plotting its passage by means of narrative, auto-biography can always fail to arrive at its destination; and if this autotelic stricture is necessarily affected with a possible flaw in the emission of its message, how does the original code get affected? How is (possible) failure inscribed and transmitted in relaying a message? Indeed, since the Derrida–Lacan–Poe debate,[15] we 'know' that a missive involves the fatality of possible catastrophe as condition of its own emission. In the limiting case of biography – when emitter, emitted and emissory are all the self-same in various instances of itself – what are the results of this inscribed flaw in the destined mission of recounting and retelling 'my' life to 'my' 'self'?

Turning now (finally?) to Derrida's text on Nietzsche's biography, *Otobiographies*, the focus would seem altogether different than ours. There, it is a matter of determining how, in order for the utterances of *Ecce Homo* to be legible, Nietzsche must be granted a certain credit (credibility) that at the time of writing he did not have, whence the structural necessity of that sort of writing (but it will affect retroactively all writing) to make sense of itself by drawing credit from a (possible) future whose arrival cannot be guaranteed. That is, *Ecce Homo* depends upon a speech 'act' that performs its deed only by drawing sustenance from a future code of the language, a most peculiar turn of events. Then again, Derrida fixes on a passage in which the intention to recount *to himself* Nietzsche's own life story is 'dated' by the anniversary of his birth,[16] by means of which an abyssal self-reflexive gesture is highlighted in the text linking it to the thought of the 'eternal return,' while at the same time, in a later gesture, the writing is shown to be intertwined with a certain 'fascist' strand which complicates the 'politics' of auto-biography immeasurably. And all of this is treated along prefatory and preliminary remarks whose liminal space Derrida guards jealously, opening up his preliminaries to deferred continuation.[17]

It is thus that we will follow Derrida's reference along the liminal surface of certain selected passages and study the criss-crossing current of Nietzsche's text along Derrida's angle.

With autobiography the issue of 'life death' in Derrida's sense (from *The Post Card*)[18] is naturally co-implicated along with the divested self. Brought along into the present text, since Nietzsche's life is at issue, issued and transmitted across texts, narrated, dissected, discussed, and drawn along, the motif must be followed here. The 'simple' opposition of life versus death can no longer be tenably presupposed in reading either Nietzsche or Derrida if the complications of a self-affected and self-affecting message are to be taken into 'account.' As Derrida briefly observes in Nietzsche's case:

What is called life – thing or object of bio-logy or bio-graphy – does not face anything opposite itself, death, the thanatological or thanatographic, therein lies the first complication. Whenever life becomes the object of a science, it suffers grief [*a du mal*]. . . . All that, the grief, the delays it entails, directly concern the fact that a philosophy of life is always accommodated by a science of life. . . . Which would lead us to assert that all sciences acquiring their scientificity without delay or residue are sciences of death, and that between death and the statute of a scientific object there is a co-implication that *interests* us and our desire to know. (*Otobiographies*, p. 42; *E*, 6)

'To know is to dissect,' whence the problematic of a science of the living. (The point here is not that ethically we cannot study the living, as K.O. Apel contends, but that the co-implicatures of investigator and investigated invaginate the experiment.)[19] The 'so-called living subject' of a 'biological discourse' 'is party to or part of the investigated region' (ibid.), wherefore the living is always already inscribed within bio-*logy* as a part that participates, *takes* part. That convoluted or invaginated structure affects all biography: whenever someone treats in his own name his life, the involution can but grow.

But then, whoever speaks of his life is or will ultimately be dead, and his auto-inscription must perforce remark upon this elementary *Tatsache*, and doubly: on the one hand, in so far as the normal interests of speaking on one's behalf, capitalizing on one's self-investment (with whatever economic and temporal delays and detours) will no longer strictly hold for the instant of the inscribing utterance; on the other, since the very structure of life as lacking opposition to its other(s) must bear issue within the autobiography as such:

To be dead means at least this, that no benefit or ill, calculated or not, can *return* to the bearer of the name. Only the name can inherit, hence the name, and not the bearer, is always and a priori the name of someone dead. What returns to the name never returns to the living. (*Otobiographies*, p. 44; *E*, 7)

The interest of what returns resounds to the name of the author as dead, naming, for instance, Friedrich Nietzsche in so far as he was always already (going to be, necessarily, biologically) dead. A priori death affects the name of the auto-scription, of the signatory, and of his/her signature. The sign in signing affects itself with its own *différance*, its fatal difference from the living author whose fate it decisively survives, thus allowing the author to 'speak from beyond the grave.'[20]

The legacy of a retroactively self-bequeathing 'will' inscribes on its affective command – uttered, emitted, issued – death's gravity. A certain economy or law of 'returns'-home is at work in autobiography, affecting its style and scriptural code, just as life must be affected by its presumed opposite to be at issue. Indeed, for Nietzsche death and life are not 'genuine' opposites:

> We cannot for ourselves think becoming except as the passage [*Übergang*] from a persistent 'dead' state to another persistent 'dead' state. Bah, we call the 'dead' motionless! As if something motionless existed! The living not as the opposite to the dead but merely as a special case. (*KSA*, vol. 9, *11*, 150)

> Fundamentally false *value*-estimation of the sensitive world against the *dead*. For we are the dead! We belong to it. And yet with sensitivity [*Empfindung*] superficiality and deception are set loose. What do pain and pleasure have to do with *real* processes! – they are something secondary that does not penetrate the depths. But *we* call it the *inner* and regard the dead world as *exterior* – basic falsehood! The 'dead' world, eternally in motion and without error, force against force! And in the sensitive world, everything false, darksome! It is a *feast* to pass from this world into the 'dead' world – and the greatest desire of knowledge is directed at holding up for this false world eternal laws, where no pleasure or pain or deception exists. (*KSA*, vol. 9, *11*, 70)[21]

Life would be a *Spezialfall*, a special case of death in which deception and falsehood lie installed along with perspective (which, unlike Leibniz, Nietzsche excludes from the inorganic). Life for Nietzsche requires perspectival projection, and that projection posits opposition in order to be able to think and calculate:

> Only after an imaginary counter-world [*gegen-Welt*] originated, in contradiction to the absolute flow, could *upon that basis* something be recognised. . . .
> I only recognise something true in opposition to something livingly untrue. . . .
> Without the assumption of a kind of being opposed to the truly real, we would have nothing against which to measure compare and imitate; error is the presupposition of all knowledge. (*KSA*, vol. 9, 11, 162 (my emphasis), 171, 325)

Gegensätzlichkeit, opposition and setting into opposition, pertains to the organic intellect which construes becoming by comparison with the scheme of opposition of self-identical being. But how does that affect the issue of autobiography? To recall its issuance, recalling it upon my self, when it is a matter of life as my subject, opens up a breach in my life, suspending and deferring its immediate urgencies, making room for time wasted from practicalities, time thus self-granted, in which I allow myself to retell who I have been and what I have become.[22] Punctuated by the conversion of pathos into ethos, a life-stage will have passed on forever, but I bring it back, I affect myself to recollect it, passionately. How was that past life mine at all?

> The movement of *différance* does not supervene upon a transcendental subject, it produces it. The auto-affection is not a modality of experience characterising a being that would already be itself (*autos*). The *différance* produces the same as the link to itself within difference from itself. It produces both the self-same and the non-identical.[23]

To identify the 'same' required things to be folded up at the very instant when uniquely happening they pass away in a passive rapture (*Entrückung*) of time.[24] The constant (*beständig*) return of the same is required for (re)cognition, and this recurrence marks the self with its affection or affectation, so that time gets pseudo-transcendentally unfolded, drawn apart, and drawn forth. This eternally recurrent 'now' as the instant imprinting being upon becoming[25] mimics the eternal recurrence of the same redoubling the identity of beings and super-imprinting a supplementary remark on the presence of beings, invaginating its constant becoming.

There is in Nietzsche's thought of eternal recurrence a structure of 'probity' (*Redlichkeit*) that unmakes what logic constitutes, namely sameness and consequentiality, a probing honesty that can dominantly affect life with the 'heaviest thought,' the impossible, gravest thought, into interminably dying[26] that at once ties and unbinds the bonds between life and death affecting the two with each other's measures and limits:

> Beyond all their oppositions, without possible synthesis or identification, it is indeed a matter of economy as law of the proper (*oikos, oikonomia*), an economy of death controlling [Freud's] whole detour [in *Beyond the Pleasure Principle*] and unremittingly seeking its own propriation, the proper happening (*Ereignis*) rather than life *and* death or life *or* death. The drawing-out or curtailing of the detour would be at the service of this properly economical or ecological law of itself as proper, of the auto-mobile auto-affection of the *Fort–Da*.[27]

Self-affection *produces* the subject at least since Kant's revolution in thinking, but now in addition it issues into an economy of life death where the thus produced self seeks at bottom its own manner of self-extinction, its own self-styled vanishing. This thanatotropism inherent in economy leads the self to seek derivative autonomy, to stamp its own identity only by means of a differential play of forces within the perspective of a given temporal and mortally wounded projection.[28] This *reckoning* to the end, confirming and affirming the interminably open deathless dying which inspires the eternal recurrence constitutes a double signature, signature countersignature, where the chance or hazard of the reckoning, deriving differentially self-identity, integrates its own fatality into the fortune of its own implacable detour by way of itself.

III Nietzsche('s) self drawn

We have just spoken of probity in passing. I read it following Jean-Luc Nancy's recent work,[29] from which I extract two notes:

> *Redlichkeit* names perhaps in Nietzsche *at once* the ultimate moral truth of metaphysics and something which removes that truth from itself.

> *Redlichkeit* must perhaps confront what at once confers on truth and retires from it its own truth, to wit, also what in every thought confers and takes away thought; not some 'unthought' that could be surrounded and reappropriated, but (if I dare say) an 'unthoughtfulness' (*impensement*) or let us say the straying (*égarement*) of thought away from itself; briefly, that *madness* that in spite of everything Nietzsche does confront. (*IC*, pp. 70–1)

Stressing the self-affection inherent in such probity, loyalty, or sincerity, its 'necessity of contra-dicting itself resolutely and incessantly' (ibid.), let's seek confirmation from Nietzsche's *Nachlaß*:

> Probity against ourselves is older than against others. (*KSA*, vol. 9, 6, 236)

> Drives we have in common with animals; the growth of probity makes us more independent from the inspiration of those drives. That very probity is the result of intellectual work, namely whenever two opposed drives set the intellect in motion. (*KSA*, vol. 9, 6, 234)[30]

Self-probity, precondition of honesty toward others, requires self-affection by means of which the 'intellect' represents the drives, called 'affects' upon self-affection, which ever fight for partial or substantial recognition and dominance in the willing center, vying for representation of their desires. Indeed, the will may be seen as a commandingly dominant self-affected drive,[31] a suddenly exploding affect arousing respect by its commanding presence. Such an auto-inscribing will releases of itself its own legacy as a non-representable 'thought' generating a self-probity that ultimately transcends even the pursuit of truth, leading to a tragic catastrophe that affirms Dionysian-style the abyss of truthlessness and the need of error and deception for the perseverance of life and desire.

The will as such, in its self-bequeathing auto-legation, seeks to affirm 'life death' in striving for power as over-power-ing,[32] and when conveyed in an explicit auto-legation it prescribes an auto-description that is consigned to the future 'wills' or inheritors of the divided and divisive message, upon whose decisive confirmation the eventual fulfillment of the 'truth' of its 'self'-confirming utterance depends, in so far as it transmits truth *as well* as the means to organize and enjoy power, a truth of *sorts*.

The self-affection of the will affects eventually, in the event, identity and temporizing (producing temporal span, *Spannung*), exposing the timely and untimely, inscribing the mark of passion on itself as passivity, pastness, passing on, perspectivally projecting its own domain, drawing itself along to a future that arrives as return, a self-turning as already being dead, in which the return cancels and uplifts its own economic gain, a homeless unnostalgic return home, recurringly:

> F.N., this identity that he vindicates, is not possessed by means of a contract with his contemporaries. He received it from the unheard-of-contract he drew with himself. He is indebted to himself, and by means of what remains of his text due to his signature has implied us therein.
> (*Otobiographies*, p. 47; E, 8)

'I live upon my own credit,' 'my life is merely a prejudice': these twin statements from *Ecce Homo* are thus interpreted by Derrida in so far as he reads in them an involuted iterative structure that affects the normal strictures of autobiography by means of the 'Yes, Yes' of the hymeneal signature (which cutting another dimension overflows the text along a border neither inside nor outside the text, or both),[33] a signature by whose means Nietzsche releases a text-remnant, itself generated by the supplementary dynamics of the signature affecting its own deferred double affirmation which draws the autobiographic diachronic past along and overboard. The credit self-drawn in telling himself, celebrating his life death, his phantom life, entails that the text be legible only via future readers and by way of their multiple disseminated code of reading(s), whence the explosion and exposure of the text, complicated by the self-imposed-imposture that Nietzsche's undecidable sincerity adds on to the utterances, rendering them indefinitely suspect (as sincere) and hence *in truth* at once legible and illegible, from the perspective of his code or of ours.

To read such an 'overboard', 'transgressive' textual remnant would then require an interpretation which, fulfilling hermeneutic constraints in advance, through the imposition of a violence non-recuperable by sincere truth-seeking, crosses styles or stylets with Nietzsche 'himself',[34] differentially and confirmingly countersigning the text for him, in his name (as living dead), while of necessity taking account of the economy of the reading's own life death and the *différance* of its 'own' destination, thus crossing purposes with hermeneutical practice in a self-prescribed transgression.

The derivative, non-foundational, identity that would be claimed by and for Nietzsche as subject of biography can thus only signify itself, and herein lies Derrida's overwhelming insistence and the strength of his reading, by affecting its generation by an open-ended double signature, stylistically retracing the weave of the regenerate text and refolding it on its self-utterability (*Redlichkeit!*), exposing its will to verification and desire for self-presence in truth while 'at once' drawing truth across as instance of legitimation. At the same time, the attempt cannot be avoided (of desiring, self-presently) to help Nietzsche speak for himself through his others, his would-be readers, on behalf of a Nietzsche always returning and coming forth from the incredible future while only having been in an immemorial past (Levinas!)[35] or in a nondescript unexperienceable present.

This self-affecting inscription, auto-scripture both self-identical and iterative, repeatable and unique, produces the 'life' of the subject of a biography self-written, an abyssally reflected life in its own recounting, *drawing* (upon) *itself*. The 'self' is thus linked to the life death *différance*, a proper derivative linked differentially, through a calculus of chance, with other affirmative stylish wills-to-power divested by a singular fatality of their own inheritance, wills whose reading reaffirms this generative auto-scription drawing open the dimension of the heteroscriptual, prescribing a general text, like de Man's 'Social Contract',[36] drawing open a law of the auto-bio-graphic text pursuing 'truth' as the writing of life's fatality destined to life death without beginning or end, interminably.

Whence follows the need to affect retroactively (if that hadn't already happened by singularly and unpredictably other means) all Nietzsche's *corpus* with a generalized auto-inscription, a self-drawn contract in which meaning is filtered to utterances by the projective (future-directed, creditable) perspective of a self seeking to outlive itself in the future passing of its life, exposed to the powers of the others who come along the way by chance and surmount the impossibility of reading (double-edged, stretched, stitched) without either paraphrasing or meta-phrasing Nietzsche's 'himself.' A reading that would be a reaffirmation of the Yes! Yes! along the edge of a perpetually recurring life death in *différance* crossing the borders miraculously to the 'other' shore and returning, like Orpheus.

But then, the self-contractual credibility remarked on in the text may be assigned to all (Dionysian) writing beyond and aside of the genre of autobiography.[37] That script is also a secret message from the labyrinth of the unconscious requiring an affective release of the conserving present while all the time prescriptively commemorating the dead in a literally endless feast.

IV Case suspended: the survival of the signature

The drawn self-contract, between the living and the eternally recurring, alive dead, Nietzsche, the posthumously famous one, has always already sealed and con-sealed a countersigned signature retelling Nietzsche's life to his selves, affecting to narrate it *for* him in his name, in an undecidable imposture, which as his readers we must assume upon ourselves in order to enter into the play of the text and its (im)possible legibility, its draughtsman's contract. That countersignature affecting the act of signing uniquely and singularly, stamping one's unique seal, affects the signature with the affirmation of the eternal return of the 'same' and its conditions, such that, as the clause would have it, its legal prescription, only when and if others read it passionately and self-affectedly, between affect and affectation, can they affect the text and be affected by it in its impressive signature, defying time's passing and passage in a drawn out, drawn along, and drawn forth life death.

Life death self drawn: such would be the (ph)otography, the positive or negative, basal or acidic, por-trait of a self-surviving Nietzsche, drawn along by a gallery of his co-authors and co-readers, especially a certain late-comer derivately behind all the rest, drawing upon a special case of death, one which in falling due remains suspended in time's abyss, phantomatically returning as the name of what comes again, self-affecting his presence otherwise, his own pure vestige.

Derrida's encounter with Nietzsche: as an affirmative co-signer, affected by Nietzsche's self drawing – but the issue or sending of that drawing draws lots and resources, upon a certain economy of luck.

And that for Nietzsche's fate, his luck, was not all good. But that is another story.[38]

Chapter 7

'ÇA CLOCHE'[1]

Sarah Kofman

Translated by Caren Kaplan

I Man: *anthropos* or *aner*?

We know that the title of the colloquy is a quotation, referring to the title of a paper that Derrida delivered at an international conference in New York in October 1968 – 'Philosophy and Anthropology.'[2] At the start, Derrida underlined the political significance of all philosophy conferences, a significance reinforced by the international character of such a meeting. Writing in April 1968, in an historically and politically determined horizon, just before the events of May, at the moment when the Vietnam peace negotiations began, at the moment of the assassination of Martin Luther King, Derrida questioned the political implications of a conference which put an accent in its own title on the 'universality of the *anthropos*,' an action which tended to erase singular ethnic differences in the name of a 'humanism' which, whatever its form – atheist or not – is fundamentally metaphysical (as Derrida recalled, citing Heidegger: ' "every humanism remains metaphysical," ' metaphysics being the other name of ontotheology').[3] Perhaps the final end of a conference on the universal *anthropos* referred to a need to *master* differences; erasing differences, that is to say – *mastering* them.

New York 1968 – Cerisy 1980: the philosophical scene, historically and politically, has changed little. If this colloquy has kept a title so strongly marked by metaphysical humanism, does it not run the risk of implying that a need to master differences has once again crept in? Because the scene *has* changed in twelve years we must ask if the need to master *sexual* difference,

108

in particular, has not crept in (even if this is obviously not the *will* of the colloquy's organizers). When we think of the 'ends of man' today how do we escape this tendency? Is this colloquy designed to rescue, assist, or erect (in every sense) man – man no longer understood as *anthropos*, the sexually neuter, universal man, but as *aner* or *vir*? It would seem that the subtitle of this colloquy – 'Concerning Derrida's Work' – at once lifts any such suspicion. It is true that the text published in *Margins* does not underline the danger of mastering sexual difference. Derrida's other texts since *Of Grammatology*, however, continue to denounce metaphysics (and therefore humanism and all discourses of the 'ends of man') as phallogocentric. *Glas*, in particular, rings a death knell not only for phallogocentrism but also for a colloquy on the 'ends of man' (understood as the sexually neuter, universal *anthropós*).[4] A warning resounds throughout Derrida's texts – the ends of man are always in the final analysis those of 'masculine man.' The benefits that man reaps from his speculations on the ends of man or on the 'ends of nature' (another way of further concealing the true ends of such speculations) are always masculine. From behind one of those peepholes where he surveys, among other things, the eagle and its sublime flights, Derrida observes that sexual difference sets the foundation (through scientific givens, and above all in the notion of *Aufhebung* – the central concept of sexual relations which permits Hegel to articulate an entire discourse of ontotheoteleology) for phallocratism and most traditional hierarchies (that is, the opposition of passivity and activity, of form and matter). Derrida brings up (*relever*)[5] the equivalent of a 'slip' as symptomatic of this goal of mastery: the 'we' (*wir*) used by Hegel at the moment when he exposes the constitution of the system of virility: 'With man, to the contrary, we (*wir*) have the faculty of feeling active, the swelling of the heart, etc.'[6] Behind his peephole Derrida exclaims: 'Who are we? Are we the masters? Are we the id? Are we men? And has it always been this way? And who brought us here?'[7]

Similarly, Derrida reminds us that Kant's anthropological discourse has as a central object, not man in general, but woman. This anthropological and humanist discourse pursues phallogocentric ends under the cover of a natural finality (although the phallogocentric system is very complex and contains within it what undermines and neutralizes it; although it is also, as always, a kind of feminism). Appealing to this hidden teleology justifies all developmental inequalities, all the dissymmetries which Kant ascribes to sexual difference. It is the corollary to a denial. The characteristic of the feminine sex to appropriate the masculine does not stem from categories, goals, or forms of human consciousness; it is not modeled on the principle of our own finality, on the 'end we give ourselves' (again a 'we'), but only on a profound instinct which would direct women to create reserves of masculinity as compensation for an eventual widowhood since man is, by nature, finished. This characteristic is ruled by nature's only goal: the preservation of the species and the refinement of society by the feminine. It does not model itself on human finality, nor, a fortiori, on any masculine finality – for example, Immanuel Kant, who remained single to protect his sex from feminine appropriation. Writing on the fundamental principles of dietetics in *The Conflict of Faculties*, he recommended bachelorhood to whomever wanted to be certain of a long and happy life, for:

It would be difficult to prove that most people who reach an advanced age had been married. And it is not such a bad political principle to multiply marriages, extolling matrimonial life as a long life, although, proportionately, experience furnished only a few examples of people who became extremely old side by side.

II The ends of Freud

I would like to show that when Freud speculates on women one can always find the pursuit of phallogocentric ends in operation, concealed behind a pseudo-scientific discourse which denies all 'speculation' and bases itself only on observation. This discourse wants to be positivist. This sterile and foolish opposition of observation and speculation in Freud's text is only radical precisely when 'speculating' on women, since Freud does not hesitate to acknowledge in *Beyond the Pleasure Principle* that the death instinct is a purely speculative hypothesis – necessarily speculative – limited by a kind of halting, limping progression.[8] In such a discourse one finds evidence of a phallogocentric finality, the most intelligible sign being (beyond the denial of any speculation) the appeal to 'demonstration,' to a natural teleology, to a benevolent Mother Nature. This Mother Nature, as *deus ex machina*, always arrives in time to help man (*vir*) justify that he, and he alone, is the final end of nature; that *he is the favorite* of a mother who is completely fulfilled only through bringing a male child into the world (one of the results obtained by Freudian speculation). By appealing to nature as a grandiose sublimation of the mother, Freud makes her, and women in general (little favored by this Nature who only gave them an incomplete sex and an incurable penis envy – from here stems all their misfortunes), complicit in a discourse which represents them as nature's cast-offs (a complicity necessary to cleanse Freud of any suspicion of anti-feminism). 'Analysis Terminable and Interminable,' literally Freud's last word on women, concludes with a *rejection of femininity by both sexes*. Constituting the rock of indisputable biological fact which all analysis smashes against are the symptoms of this rejection: castration anxiety in men and penis envy in women. This is the final word at the end of analysis, the word at the end of Freud. Since 'Analaysis Terminable and Interminable' is one of his last texts, it seems that the attempt to have the last word (on women) only led Freud to his final word (like Spinoza, who died as he arrived at the point of withdrawing all political rights from women, leaving his *Political Treatise* unfinished). This is what Freud had always dreaded. A terror of death accompanies his writings on female sexuality. It is only towards 1921–3 that he properly addresses women, publishing in haste, afraid of death, without waiting for his results to be confirmed or disproved by observation. The same anxiety about death is evident when the *Traumdeutung* was published, since in this text he exposed for the first time this thing so horrible to see, this thing that could not be directly looked at, the sex of the mother – horrible in its desirability. Freud is constrained by the dread of having to blind himself, to cover this sex with a thick veil; in other words, to speculate, to elaborate pseudo-solutions, the fictions which screen the unobservable and which transform woman into a never-solvable enigma.

This 'ideological' recourse to nature (or another variant – biological science) justifies an obsession – woman's infamous penis envy. In a general sense this speculation justifies Freud's phallogocentrism. For example, it is only in 1923, in *Infantile Genital Organization*, that the primacy of the phallus is affirmed. Here Freud introduces the idea of a third stage – the phallic stage – a phase which recognizes only one type of genital organ, the masculine organ. In this phase (which already 'merits' being named 'genital') one finds a sexual object and a certain convergence of sexual tendencies around that object. Freud only introduces this supplemental stage when he discovers the radical difference of the young girl's pre-oedipal sexuality (the obverse of Mycenaean civilization). One can read this finding as an apotropaic defense designed to conceal the surprising character and disquieting implications of this discovery. Nothing else in the text explains why Freud needed to wait until this date to discover or invent the existence of a third stage. Nothing else explains the contradictions between the text of 1923 and *Three Essays on the Theory of Sexuality* (1905), contradictions that Freud did not hesitate to address in supplementary notes added later, where he devotes himself (edition after edition) to a profound revision of infantile sexuality. This marks, at the very least, a vague affirmation of a 'progression in knowledge,' induced by a changing intention, over the course of time. As a last resort he appeals to a biological prototype (*Vorbild*) that cannot be totally accounted for: 'According to Abraham, it (phallic organization) has a biological prototype in the embryo's undifferentiated genital disposition, which is the same for both sexes.'[9] Another example can be found in 'Female Sexuality' where Freud critiques traditional psychology and its biologically based determinations that correlate masculine to active and feminine to passive. This biological model is only capable, he says, 'of inferring erroneous analogic reasoning.' Since speculation is inappropriate, this appeal to Abraham and his biological prototype is an attempt to try to justify the simple theory of infantile sexuality (the belief in the non-differentiation of the sexes based on the child's inability to recognize the existence of the vagina) that is more or less fantastic in spite of the nugget of truth it is always supposed to contain. The preference shown for the male sex *in utero* must be transformed into a fact reflecting nature's wisdom.

Freud appeals to Abraham's prototype of the embryo (elsewhere it appears as an appeal to Ferenczi's 'paleobiology') to establish the primacy of the phallus. Yet, he also declared this very prototype fantastic and speculative in order to 'establish' penis envy, to dislodge it from an archaic origin and attach it to the stage of sexual differentiation. In this way, Freud constructs an *unsurpassable primary phenomenon* – a rock that cannot be moved. Recourse to this speculative paleobiology is given as supplemental 'proof' to add to those offered by clinical observation, that is to say, the dream during one of his illnesses (at least how he interpreted it, since the manifest dream content is never given), as well as those offered by literature – *Judith and Holoferne* (*Judith und Holoferne*) by Hebbel and *Virgin's Venom* (*Das Jungferngift*) by Anzengruber. Once analyzed, these 'proofs' only confirm that Freudian 'theory' always proceeds in a circular fashion. In 'The Taboo of Virginity' Freud states:

> In the paleobiological speculation Ferenczi has traced back this hostility of women – I do not know if he is the first to do so – to the period in time when the sexes became differentiated. At first, in his opinion, copulation took place between two similar individuals, one of which, however, developed into the stronger and forced the weaker one to submit to sexual union. The feelings of bitterness arising from this subjection still persist in the present day disposition of women. I do not think there is any harm in employing such speculations as long as one avoids setting too much value on them.[10]

Since his dream about Irma, such a 'kettle rationale' is customary with Freud: (i) I do not speculate, I observe – it is Ferenczi who speculates; (ii) at any rate, it is not always harmful to speculate; (iii) these speculations only have value to the extent that they corroborate my own observations, my ideas – Ferenczi should not 'overestimate' them.[11]

Freud's obsession with penis envy – introduced as the foundation of the virginity taboo – is a panicked reaction to the disquieting and strange female. It is the dreaded woman that Freud accuses of castrating men at the same time that he, not nature, is in the process of castrating her by definitively endowing her with an incomplete sexuality, with basic penis envy. He attributes this castration after the fact to Mother

Nature, once again making her an accomplice to her son. In 'Femininity' penis envy is made a primary phenomenon that does not result from the vantage-point of observation but stems from Freud's inclination (*Wir sind geneigt* – *Wir*, making us masterful? *Wir/Vir?*). Freud recognizes that other psychoanalysts, especially female analysts, are more inclined to make penis envy a secondary phenomenon, admitting other tendencies (*Neigungen*), thereby diminishing the primary importance of penis envy and increasing the emphasis on other factors. Who makes the distinctions between these diverse tendencies – between these opposing theses and texts which defend all anticipated theses according to their particular dispositions? Who will decide among all these speculations? In the case of penis envy, it is Freud's masculine conviction which tips the balance in favor of the innate. It is nothing more than his conviction in favor of a natural, biological foundation – a nature which tips the balance in favor of man – which consigns women to an incomplete sexuality; an immediate, irresistible, and definitive penis envy.

A last example of this appeal to a natural teleology that camouflages phallocratic finality concerns the correlation of masculinity and activity. This example is even more interesting because Freud's move is complicated – a double move. In one sense, against every metaphysical tradition, Freud strives to differentiate between active and masculine, passive and feminine, emphasizing that, for example, the opposition active/passive arises earlier than the opposition masculine/feminine (the first appearing at the sado-anal stage and the second at the genital stage). Furthermore, in neatly distinguishing between the biological and psychoanalytic sense of the terms 'masculine' and 'feminine,' he leaves women (in the biological sense) the potential to be masculine in the psychoanalytic sense – that is to say, active, as well as the opposite. Therefore, active and passive are no longer the essential property of either sex. The libidinous instincts of individuals of both sexes show an equal preference for activity. Freud emphasizes that a correlation of activity to masculinity and passivity to femininity is too simplistic. And when he makes the same correspondence himself he claims that it is only in accordance with convention (this is the case when he qualifies the libido as masculine).

Strictly speaking (not according to convention), the libido does not appear to belong to any one gender (*Wir können ihr selbst kein Geschlecht geben*):

> There is only one libido which serves both the masculine and the feminine sexual functions. To it itself we cannot assign any sex; if, following the conventional equation of activity and masculinity, we are inclined to describe it as masculine, we must not forget that it also covers trends with a passive aim.[12]

As in any metaphysics, Freud makes another move (sometimes in the same text) beyond the terms of convention which tend to associate masculinity with activity and femininity with passivity. Thus, biological and psychoanalytic meanings perfectly support each other: the masculine becomes the assemblage of subject, activity, and penis, while the feminine is the locus of the passive object. Since the sado-anal opposition passive/active welds itself at puberty to sexual opposition it becomes possible to affirm that there are some differences between girl and boy from the beginning (that the former is always already more passive). For example, if the two sexes demonstrate a preference for the active role they do not reverse roles with the same energy. This difference in their behavior permits a withdrawal of any conclusions as to the relative strength of masculinity and femininity as demonstrated in their sexuality.

This explains why conventional labeling of the libido as 'masculine' ultimately seems neither conventional nor arbitrary. Freud rejects the idea that there can be a convention that would authoritatively qualify the libido as feminine. Nothing, he says, can justify the joining of the words *feminine* and *libido*. Ultimately, both nature and its teleology provide a rationale for 'convention':

> More constraint has been applied to the libido when it is pressed into the service of the feminine function, and that – to speak teleologically – nature takes less careful account of its (that function's) demands than in the case of masculinity. And the reason for this may lie – thinking once again teleologically – in the fact that the accomplishment

of the aim of biology has been entrusted to the aggressiveness of men and has been made to some extent independent of woman's consent. . . . The sexual frigidity of women, the frequency of which appears to confirm this disregard, is a phenomenon that is still insufficiently understood.[13]

In this manner, nature itself requires the weakness of women's sexual desire to ensure male sexual aggression, thereby ensuring the reproduction of the species without women's consent. Woman's frigidity would then be seen as part of and essential to a plan no longer attributable to nature alone. Under the cover of fulfilling the biological destiny of the human species – its reproduction – the final ends of man are attained by subordinating woman's sexual desires to man's desire, holding them in a rigid dependency. Under these conditions, when a woman has strong sexual demands she is an absolute anomaly in nature and she will not accomplish her biologically destined task. In short, she is not truly a woman. Such a 'woman,' if she is not homosexual, will have at the very least a strong 'masculinity complex.' According to Freud, she will possess 'a large quantity of activity' like that ordinarily characterizing men, thereby assimilating biological and psychological meanings: 'The essence of this process is that at this point in development the wave of passivity is avoided which opens the way to the turn towards femininity.'[14] If such a woman does not envy man's penis it can only be that she is herself, by nature, a man – the only reason Freud can imagine for a woman's lack of penis envy, for her failure to recognize the 'fact of her castration,' for her refusal to subordinate her sexual desires to those of man as a natural finality, or a cultural finality (to preserve the traditional opposition of nature/culture acknowledged by Freud).

In effect, 'The Taboo of Virginity' appeals to a natural teleology, to an unjust nature (or mother) who, in one way or another, marks her preference for men. 'The Taboo of Virginity' recognizes that these are cultural rules which have the sexual subjugation of women as an aim. Freud attempts to demonstrate that a certain degree of sexual subjugation is necessary if the threat of polygamous tendencies is to be contained and the civil institution of marriage maintained. But he does not really explain the necessity of the subjugation of the female sex. Freud argues that woman's subjugation (which can go so far as the total loss of her independence and the absolute sacrifice of her interests) is necessary because she remains obsessed with the one who first conquered her initial resistance and alleviated her sexual desire. Thus, woman's first sexual experience guarantees her compliant and permanent possession.

Beyond all these speculations which appeal to a natural teleology, these are the ends of man: to fix the instability of feminine oscillation, to make her capable of resisting new impressions, to incite her to sacrifice her sexual interests . . . to man's advantage. The ruse of masculine culture is the presentation of the repression of female sexuality as psychic phenomena; to sacrifice the sexual interests of woman, to subject them (without her consent) to man's aggression. In his 'Lectures' Freud wrote that he still considered woman's frigidity to be insufficiently understood, but we can view it none the less as one of the consequences of this subjugated state – not as its precondition. Freud never says this. 'The Taboo of Virginity' explains frigidity as a reaction to the narcissistic wound which occurred at defloration: 'that a woman's *immature sexuality* is discharged on to the man who first makes her acquainted with the sexual act.'[15] The virginity taboo of aboriginal peoples permits man to economize such dangers as castration or female frigidity. At a more developed level of civilization the assessment of danger gives way to the undertaking of subjugation:

> It must strike the observer in how uncommonly large a number of cases the woman remains frigid and feels unhappy in a first marriage, whereas after it has been dissolved she becomes a tender wife, able to make her second husband happy. The archaic reaction has, so to speak, exhausted itself on the first object.[16]

Thus, man's end is the subjection of women, assuring their placid and permanent possession. This subjection alone allows man to surmount his castration anxiety, the anxiety he experiences in the face of women's bitter hostility – their penis envy, their need to revenge their having been so unjustly provided for or deprived by 'nature.' What Freud never states is that this infamous penis envy, this obsession which haunts all of his texts, is also a way to fix woman in a stable position, to permanently end the oscillation between masculine and feminine – the origin of the enigma of woman's sexuality (as Freud defined it). It is a way of mastering their bisexuality to the advantage of either their femininity or their masculinity. It is a way of subjugating women while making them accomplices to man's desire since women's penis envy, even as it arouses castration anxiety, reassures men that they do possess a penis. The 'theory' of penis envy is a speculation, a fiction, a reaction to the panic provoked by the female sex, by the mother. This panic is analogous to that which causes the collapse of the throne and the altar.[17] In the face of the dread of castration, this apotropaic solution, therefore, permits the creation of the homosexual economy.[18] It alone permits, by combining horror and pleasure, the colossal erection of man. If the debasement of the sexual object is necessary for man's sexual well-being then one can say that the fiction of 'penis envy,' in spite of Freud's denials, functions to permit the debasement of woman, man's love of the whore. To create the economy of the whore, the woman who cannot evoke the mother (as if the figure of the whore comes from a split with the maternal figure), necessitates the costly solution of the brothel and all the dangers that it implies for man's health:

> The man almost always feels his respect for the woman
> acting as a restriction on his sexual activity, and only
> develops full potency when he is with a debased sexual
> object; and this in turn is partly caused by the entrance of
> perverse components into his sexual aims, which he does
> not venture to satisfy with a woman he respects . . . to be
> really free and happy in love [he] must have surmounted
> his respect for women and have come to terms with the
> idea of incest with his mother or sister.[19]

III 'My excitement is the oscillation' – for a generalized fetishism: Derrida

The Freudian solution still permits the creation of an economy of fetishism. Fetishism makes love-relationships easier. According to Freud, most fetishists are perfectly happy with it.

When they start analysis it is not because of the fetish, since it is not, in general, experienced as an unpleasant symptom. Thus, one can ask why Freud considered this solution to be pathological (and, therefore, why penis envy is a 'better' solution, allowing heterosexual relations to be evaluated as 'normal'). In short, why is it so bad to be a fetishist? With fetishism there remains a certain oscillation, an 'indecidability.' To 'speculate on this indecidability' is to lose before one begins. On the conscious level, the fetishist is content with his fetish. Entering analysis, what comes to light as the adopted solution is merely a compromise – such a thing is never perfectly satisfying.

It is the question of fetishism, linked to indecidable oscillation (and, thus, to the gamble of speculation), which resounds throughout Derrida's *Glas*. Beginning with a reading of Freud's text, he proposes a generalization of fetishism as a first stage in the deconstruction of phallogocentrism (following a completely Nietzschean methodology), a stage which includes indecidability and oscillation: 'My excitement is the oscillation.'[20] Following a discussion of Hegelian speculation *à propos* the fetish, where he concludes that a certain indecidability of the fetish oscillates between a dialectic (of the indecidable and the dialectic) or an indecidability (between the dialectic and the indecidable), Derrida begins his reading of Freud: 'As far as the fetish is concerned, what use is speculation? For such a question, one loses one's head (*le cap sans cap*), it is indecidable.' On the one hand, grafting a reading of Freud on to a reading of Hegel allows one to question whether the benefits Hegel derives from his speculations on the fetish are perhaps in the same order as the benefits accrued by the fetishist himself. This permits, on the other hand, the reinscription of Freudian notions of castration, of fetishism, in the circle of speculative dialectics, putting them in relation to the process of *Aufhebung* and to truth. In the most general fashion, such a reading grafts Freud's text on to a metaphysics which has always tried to master the indecidable and the intolerable – oscillation. Thus, to be a fetishist is always bad. The founders and destroyers of religion are always against fetishism. To be against religion does not disturb the economy of metaphysics and religion. The criticism of fetishism is a critique common to the detractors and founders of religions, symptomatic of a *common will*: the unveiling of the column, the erection of the thing itself, the rejection of the substitute; a will doomed to failure since the indecidable never lets itself be mastered. On the contrary, fetishist oscillation disturbs metaphysical categories, creates an oscillation between the dialectic and a totally other logic, that of the indecidable. It necessarily entails speculation which oscillates between a move to master the oscillation and a move which both unsettles and solicits oppositions, a speculation which drifts to, among others, the opposition of fetish/non-fetish, substitute/thing-itself, and masculine/feminine. What is gained is a generalization of the terms most devalued by the metaphysical hierarchy: fetishism, the substitute, the *Ersatz*, supplementarity. Because the feminine is characterized by oscillation, it, too, gains in this operation. It is this double move that Derrida deciphers; particularly in Freud's text on fetishism, a text which oscillates, which doesn't quite ring true – a particularly speculative text. Derrida goes as far as to say (this time against a literal reading of the text) that when Freud addresses the question of fetishism he himself states that he is taking a speculative route, although at the same time Freud attempts to shore up his speculative hypothesis with some weighty arguments (the famous argument based on the athletic supporter is one).[21] On the contrary, Freud departed from this speculative approach when he devised his description of fetishism, admitting that it was a risky train of thought and that he had been wrong to commit himself to it. He wrote elsewhere, and this time not concerning fetishist splitting, but the distinction between neurosis and psychosis: 'soon after this I had reason to regret that I had ventured so far.' 'Returning to my description of fetishism, I may say that there are many and weighty additional proofs of the divided attitude of fetishists to the question of the castration of women.'[22]

Just because Freud, like the fetishist, did not openly admit it, does not mean that he did not speculate. The strongest denial is always most significant. In a discussion of Rousseau, Derrida distinguishes between that which a text openly declares and that which is smuggled in (*fait en contrebande*). We don't need Freud's confession – on the contrary. What is the end of such a reading (since a bad reading is not possible . . .)? What strategy does Derrida pursue here and to what ends? What, and for whom, are the benefits of this operation?

First, Derrida shows that this text on fetishism is, like every text, heterogeneous: concerning the fetish there are at the same time both decidable and indecidable statements which dismantle the system of oppositions on which the definition of fetish as penis substitute (the mother's) rests, and reconstruct, beginning with its generalization, a 'concept' of the fetish which would no longer let itself be contained in the traditional opposition *Ersatz*/non-*Ersatz*, or in any opposition. For example, 'the argument of the athletic support belt [*gaine*]' (and those systematically like it) is cited by Freud as a consequence of his definition in spite of the fact that the indecidability which its 'subtle' character introduces would contradict his definition. The singularity and subtlety of the case of the 'athletic support belt,' like any fetish, contains opposing interests within it, making it particularly resistant. Derrida concludes (in disagreement with Freud) that the instability of the fetish already supposes some kind of relationship with opposing interests, inscribing itself in a general economy of the indecidable. Thus the fetish, in general, due to its indecidability, would constitute an excess of power in relation to all oppositions, destabilizing the opposition *Ersatz*/non-*Ersatz*, denial/affirmation. This operation is what Freud, who elsewhere retains the definition of the fetish as penis substitute, could not openly recognize as the thing itself. Freud will thereby oscillate as fetishist between two positions and will be compelled by this to *speculate*.

> The fetish – in general – only comes to exist in as much as it begins to ally itself to opposites. This double link, this double ligament, then defines its most subtle structure. The consequences must be brought out. The fetish economy is more powerful than that of truth – the decidable – of the thing itself or of a discourse deciding castration (*pro aut contra*). The fetish cannot be opposed. It oscillates like the clapper of truth which rings out in the hollow of a bell.

However, here Derrida's reading does not ring true since he simultaneously attributes too much and too little to Freud; too little, when he suggests that the definition of the fetish implies a simple distinction between the thing itself and its *Ersatz* (as in the metaphysical tradition). The text ends, in effect, by stating that the normal prototype of the fetish is man's penis; thus Freud begins by saying that the definition of the fetish as penis substitute could be deceiving if he did not emphasize that:

> it is not a substitute for any chance penis, but for a particular and quite special penis that had been extremely important in early childhood but had later been lost. That is to say, it should normally have been given up, but the fetish is precisely designed to preserve it from extinction. To put it more plainly: the fetish is a substitute for the woman's (the mother's) penis that the little boy once believed in and – for reasons familiar to us – does not want to give up.[23]

Is such a description less deceptive than the preceding one (which was not raised by Derrida, who locates the deception in the second definition)? It is not only that it breaks with traditional metaphysics, that is to say with the idea of the penis as 'thing itself,' since this implies a fetish imagined by the infant, a *belief* that implies both the denial and the affirmation of castration. There had never been a 'thing itself,' only an *Ersatz*, a prosthesis, an originary supplement to the panicked reaction of infantile narcissism. Adult fetishism repeats this spontaneous infantile fetishism. This fetishism is not the substitution of the 'thing itself' or of the truth, since substituting the imaginary penis of the mother always suggests the play of supplementary difference in the 'thing itself.'

If the *Ersatz* is originary there would no longer be an opposition *Ersatz*/non-*Ersatz*. Freud dismantles the traditional logic of fetishism in his new definition (surely less deceptive than the first) because it alone permits the concept of a generalized fetishism. So understood, this definition no longer implies an actual rupture with the argument of the athletic support belt. Derrida is correct in stating that 'the slightest instability of the fetish already supposes some kind of link between opposing interests.' But Freud did not say otherwise since there cannot be fetishism *without compromise*; compromise between the affirmation and denial of castration, the *split* itself implying the possibility of two incompatible currents, in contradiction to a logic of consciousness. If one decided in favor of one of the two currents there would be no need to construct a fetish. Either one would have to completely deny reality or recognize what Freud called the reality of castration. The argument of the athletic support belt, as refined and subtle as it is, is therefore a consequence of this definition of fetishism. From the beginning, Freud argued that all cases of fetishism have the same general solution. The argument of the athletic support belt only has paradigmatic value, while the fetish in general is, for Freud, by nature 'indecidable.' Freud says that as far as he is concerned it has the qualities of a *compromise*. Perhaps it attributes too much to him to purely and simply associate compromise with indecidability here. In any case, the conduct of the fetishist, who both venerates and despises his fetish, shows that the fetishist is not completely for either of the two aspects (that is, neither for or against castration), nor is he for both aspects simultaneously. The fetishist oscillates between two contrary hypotheses without being able to decide between them, not being able to decide between the 'thing itself' and its supplement, nor between the sexes. This oscillation could only stop if there was an absolute split between the two aspects and the complete disappearance of one of them. But the benefit of fetishism consists in playing in two scenes at the same time, in speculating on the equivocacy and the ambivalence of the fetish according to the more or less complex needs of its economy, in being more or less lost to this play (because the castration or non-castration of woman is always in doubt and therefore 'his' own castration is not certain).

Derrida's reading strategy assimilates compromise (only possible if there is a split between two aspects) and indecidability (which does not necessarily imply a logic of the unconscious). Such a strategy emphasizes the indecidable element in this economic speculation, and reminds us that to speculate in this way is always to lose. If one keeps to a literal reading of Freud's text, one could say that Freud, like the fetishist, plays all the scenes; that of decidability as well as indecidability. Perhaps the heterogeneity of Freud's text can be brought to light only by an entire strategy of reading the operation of 'subtle and refined' displacements.

Such a reading strategy ensures that Derrida can introduce the concept of a generalized fetishism (that of the *Ersatz*, the fake, the original prosthesis) which opens the space of play, of oscillation, of indecidability – the space where literature originates. *Glas*, in its very form, puts this fetishism into play, this generalized indecidability which overturns phallogocentrism and all metaphysical oppositions. What is gained and what is lost in this play? And *who* wins and loses (if one can still ask such a question)? What 'ends' does Derrida pursue? ('Derrida' – is he really the 'author' who signs his name to *Glas* . . . *Glas*, which sounds the death knell of the 'author,' the 'proper name,' the 'signature'?)

IV   The double erection[24]

First, in *Glas* there is never a single end, but, like fetishism, a play between at least two sites at the same time: 'designs which can never be reduced to one alone' since the happiness or unhappiness of the one that oscillates between the two resides in the 'between.' This structures *Glas*'s division; its *Colpos*, its double knolls, its two hills, its double columns, its double supporter – each being itself double (creating the possibility of a double reading – instigated by indecidability and 'textuality'), divided into two by an antagonism, a *double bind*. Thus, the argument of the athletic support belt is erected as a general law (the law that, elsewhere, concerning *La Foie du jour* or *L'Arret de mort*, Derrida calls double invagination?): it envelops all this which 'like a glove or like a flower' (see *The Maids* by Genet) 'overturns everything without losing a certain form.'

Double designs, a double posture or postulation, exacting a double discourse, a double writing, two texts written at the same time; and a double gaze, profound, stereoscopic: a cross-eyed reading, a squinting imposed on the reader, which, in dividing, makes one nauseous, dizzy, losing all sense of where the head and body of the discourse is located. 'When his mind is present, it reminds him that the law of the text is within the other, and so on.' Suppressing the margins, the frames, annulling and blurring the lines which separate one text from another, preventing all fixing of boundaries, slicing, domination, hierarchy. 'In writing two texts simultaneously, which scene is being played here? Who plays it? Who wants what or fears what? Of whom?' These questions are inscribed in the columns of *Glas*. A preliminary response can be found there and refuted in advance: that to write two texts at the same time, in behaving like a hysteric in a crisis or like a fetishist, erecting a double partition, having a double erection (*à bander double*), this operation is to make oneself impregnable, to make writing impregnable. This is the absurd limit of a mastery that erects two columns, claiming to keep constant guard on a double discourse, letting one eye cross the other to let nothing escape, like the Stranger in the *Sophist*, who, to better trap the beast that he pursues, tries to chase it with both hands, abandoning neither term of the dichotomy. But it is true that to write two texts simultaneously can be read as a powerful and paralyzing apotropaism, like the erection of a supplementary column to guard against castration – 'If I write two texts at the same time, you could not castrate me, if I delineate, I erect' – thus, to write doubly is also and always at the same time to castrate oneself, to split one's desires while doubling them – certainly to try to make oneself impregnable but always to lose in the end. Desiring to play in two scenes simultaneously, like the fetishist, means to lose from both sides. One never actually plays, one only oscillates from one posture, from one postulation to another; one 'plays only at pleasure,' one writes.

I separate my act and my desire. I mark the division and always escaping you, I stimulate ceaselessly and come nowhere. I castrate myself – I thus remain myself – and I play at pleasure. Because if my text (was) impregnable, it will (would) be neither taken up or retained. Then who would be punished in this economy of the indecidable? But if I linearize myself, if I put myself in line and believe – foolishness – that to write only one text at a time would amount to the same thing and must still be figured as the cost of the margin. I win and lose at every jab of my spear. Double posture – double postulation. Contradiction within oneself of two incompatible desires. I give it the title of the *double erection*, practically giving it shape, and putting it into play: a text bound in two senses. Two times bound. *Bande contre bande.*

One always loses to this strange, *unheimlich* play, this doubling, because the duality of the columns or orifices necessitates passing from one breast – *sein(g)*[25] – to the other. There is the material impossibility of putting the hand or the tongue on both at the same time – the impossibility of mastery, of manipulating everything like a pen. There is no death knell (*glas*) without the intervention of an entire machinery in which any so-called absolute knowledge would itself be just one of the pieces: 'At the very moment when you believe yourself to be engaged, released, manipulated, orchestrated, believing that you make the liquid music ascend and descend while playing the pedals, you have nothing to do with it.' And if you persist in this desire to manipulate, peeking through the peepholes behind which you hid to spy on this primal scene, you run the risk of seeing this doubling, these two columns, all this disquieting machinery getting into gear to crush you, to toy with you, threatening to collapse on top of each other, leaving you no way out. You probably already dreaded this, to see the columns of the synagogue collapse on you, when the Jewish child looked at you from afar and probably from the bottom up, the stripped Torah unsheathed, its two columns (legs spread) extended to the ends, then rolled up again, bound, before you, yourself, had to lend a hand to this ceremony much later. This vision, a forbidden manipulation which you say you dreamed about for so long, influenced the arrangement of all the pieces of your life – no doubt the origin of your generalized fetishism, of your indecidable oscillation, of your necessary double liaisons. But which you? Derrida? The one who signs his name to *Glas* (*Glas* which plays with the proper name, the signature, as the identifying mark of a specific author)? If the signature is 'a network as well as a name' then *Glas* sounds the death knell of autobiography and the psychoanalysis of the author: it would not be possible to analyze the clapper of a bell. Does 'Derrida's' childhood memory find itself grafted onto a recollection of the Torah made by Genet, a non-Jew, in *Our Lady of the Flowers* (which, along with the Torah, shapes *Glas*): 'When the rabbi slowly unrolls the Torah, a chilling mystery grips me, like when a column is unveiled.'

'Derrida's' childhood memory is not the explanatory principle of the writing of *Glas* and the Torah is not the paradigmatic text. In *Glas* there are more series than paradigms. The Torah is part of a series that includes Genet's *Our Lady of the Flowers*, *The Miracle of the Rose*, along with '*Ce qui est resté d'un Rembrandt*, with *L'Arrêt de mort* by Blanchot, an arrested title, suspended between two meanings. The series continues with Kafka's *The Country Doctor*, grafting itself on to *Madame Bovary*, etc. All these texts are in a series with texts signed by Derrida, among others: 'The Double Session,' *La Vérité en peinture* (and the question of the double colossus, of Van Gogh's pair of shoes which are not truly a pair), with 'Living On: Border Lines' (on Blanchot's double narrative, the question of double theory and double triumph), etc.[26] *Glas* is a ringing bell, an oscillating pendulum between texts, which, according to Blanchot's title, accompanies without accompanying, escorts texts. 'The text does not write itself on either side. It strikes between the two. The place that would have pre-occupied the clapper, namely the *Colpos*.' 'I write myself on the beam (*la hune*) between them.'

The relationship between these texts is not one of example and copy but a relationship of quotation, plagiarism, infatuation, translation, transference, re-editing, 'apocalyptic superimposition,' 'cryptic obsession' (all terms you can read in 'Living On') – all possible in the absence of a paradigmatic text, of a complete *corpus*, and of a fetish. Each text, says *Glas*, is a machine which multiplies the communication between readings, observing and answering each other. Divided and bound at the same time they become, as far as their code and their sex is concerned, indecidable. They speak each other's language without knowing it (like the two women of *L'Arrêt de mort*, according to the crazy hypothesis of 'Living On'): the procession of one text, of one language, into another, the full flood of this procession over the banks of another language, washing away all sharp limits. No more frame, no more border, no more certain boundaries between a text and its outside, the end and the beginning of a text, the unity of a *corpus*, the title, the margins, etc. – more than a differential network, a web of traces indefinitely referring to each other. Each text transforms the other, and, a fortiori, what writes itself between them, resembles no other form, no other genre, no other mode of literature or philosophy. Ring the death knell of code and genre!

Everything that can be said of the text can be said of sex: there is in *Glas* a *sexualization of text* and a *textualization of sex*. The question of sexuality as indecidable oscillation repeats textuality – it is the same thing – like the pealing of bells between texts. The written double column is like a diabolical double sex which in its duplicity breaks with all oppositions and hierarchies. Each sex, like each text, binds the one to the other, becoming indecidable, speaking the language and in the tongue of the other, penetrating the other; neither feminine nor masculine, neither castrated nor non-castrated, not bisexual, but striking between the sexes, because sex is always already double; doubly sheathed and erect, it's a double bind. A sex with double ligaments, doubly connected, double spurs, double styles, which binds and counter-binds, which binds only to get an erection, which gets a bigger erection only through a previous 'castration' (since if castration has never taken place one still cannot say that there is no castration), in any case – sliced, incised, slashed by the other. Even more powerful when cut, divided, the erection has an oblique aspect, what Derrida calls the *antherection*, which makes it spill out, fall, reverse itself.

This powerful, erect sex, doubly bound, can only, however, 'play at pleasure.' Genet cites Tiresias, cited in *Glas*; Tiresias – patron of actors: 'Seven years in men's clothing, seven in women's, because of his dual nature his femininity hounded his virility, both in play in such a way that he never had any rest, that is to say, a fixed point on which to settle.' Tiresias–Dionysus: the power of sexual pleasure and its play are not antinomies, and one can perhaps only 'truly' be pleased while playing for pleasure.

V From 'The Question of Style' to Stilitano's style: m'ec writing[27]

The power of *Glas*, its potency, comes from the play of the double erection, the double bind of text and sex. It presents a generalized fetishism, a writing which erases all oppositions, those of sex, of castration and non-castration, in favor of affirmation, double affirmation. This writing, as it mixes sexes and genres, enacts a necessary lapse of taste. Within the confines of this reading, we replay the ceremony of *Glas* – the inverse of a purification. We begin with what is left of the other, the little bits, the stumps – the quotations play with these remains. *Glas*'s two columns are always mangled at top and bottom and slashed at the sides; wounded, colossal columns mark the entry into double play. Stilitanesque columns (*Glas* can be directly grafted onto 'Nietzsche and the Question of Style') – they hold themselves straight up like flower stems or like bandaged heads which only lift themselves up to be bound, like heads wrapped up after decapitation, crowned, glorified, and restored by this very decapitation (like the beheaded martyrs in the paintings of Fra Angelico that are in the Louvre; bloody heads, glorious): the glorification of what expires, falling like a turd.

Our Lady of the Flowers opens with an archive of all the heads which fall, condemned to death. But in falling, the head is already raised again. In this case, it surges, it erects itself precisely, decidedly. To be decapitated is to appear – erect: like the swathed head and like the phallus, the erect stem, the style of a flower.

Following the logic of the *antherection* the Stilitanesque columns are oblique; what remains is stronger after being cut:

The more that remains, the harder it gets. The logic of the *antherection* should not be simplified. It does not become erect in opposition to, or in spite of, castration; in spite of the wound or the disability, emasculating the castrated. The disability itself bandages while binding. It is this which . . . produces the erection.

Hegel–Derrida reads this as the entire history of the Jewish people beginning with Abraham. It is Stilitano who draws his strength, glory, and magnificence from his stump, from his mutilation – one could say from his castration if this 'term' did not hold up the text. It is Stilitano who rises and falls, more alive than dead, thanks to these cuts.

A Stilitanesque column is not erected afterwards to disguise a deficiency, a castration; it is a prosthesis that is not preceded by castration.Nothing remains upright without it. It stands erect. It is a machine, a postiche and a pastiche, an ornamentation, a parade (an umbrella, a screen, a parachute, etc.), an originary supplement. Indecidable as far as sex is concerned, Stilitano affirms himself as male as well as female, or as self-loathing queer, as transvestite.

Everyone becomes erect and is incorporated in the

transvestite, opposites in every genre. The incorporation of each sex supposes both the incision and the supplement in the interior of the double erection. But as soon as a supplementary incision creates the double erection, the question of this undecidable double sex arises, which encompasses father and mother at the same time.

Thus, Stilitano's postiche, the bunch of grapes, cannot be read as a big and strong fetishized penis substitute but as a fake wound. This feminine tendency is the *antherection*. A Stilitanesque column is also a marked column, covered with scars, inscriptions, and tattoos: 'The ceremony of *gl* takes its shape, then, from the "Order of Tattoos" whose institution is recounted in *The Miracle of the Rose:'* words and designs inscribed on each column, incisions, mingling of black ink and red blood to transfer a contract to the skin, to handle the text. And *à propos Glas*: 'kinds of incrusted peepholes in each stone column, slits, venetian blinds, murderers look out so as not to be imprisoned in the colossus, tattoos in the body's wrinkled skin.'

The making of tattoos – a fine needle's thousands and thousands of little blows, beating just to the point of drawing blood, the most extravagant figures displaying themselves in the most unexpected places. . . . All that blue grimacing on white skin covers the child with an obscure but powerful prestige, as an indifferent and pure column becomes sacred under the inscribed hieroglyphs, like a totem pole.

Columns notched on the side, etched, tattooed, incrusted to supplement strength, for power and sexual pleasure . . . for *'jouissance féminine'* – if one could say that such a thing still exists in a generalized fetishism which makes the opposition of feminine and masculine oscillate. Because: 'tattoos are also like the carving of precious stones, cut like the ones the Dayaks of Borneo put in after an incision on the surface of the penis to increase female sexual pleasure.' And if this is the final end of all this machinery, this ceremony, it would be the very inversion of Freud's ends – the inversion of phallogocentrism's aim to subordinate women's sexuality to men and their desires. At first, in *Glas*, the columns are not smooth and intact, they are not ornamented afterwards, they are not broken into like the phallic columns from India which open and close the Hegelian procession in *Glas*, where notches, excavations, openings, hollowings, holes, deep lateral marks unexpectedly appear on columns which originally could not be cut into. *Glas* also tolls for the end of the limit between a column and its ornamentation, its *parerga*, its balconies, its fluted edges. There are such columns on the brothel in Genet's *Balcony* – each column is a fake, concealing peepholes, corridors, balconies.

What relationships are maintained between these two columns which can appear – here a metaphysical vision – opposed; setting up one against the other, not communicating; like the antagonism between feminine and masculine, literature and philosophy? But they are not in opposition; they are heterogeneous. Generalized fetishism does not lead to either sexual or textual non-differentiation: a column does not speak the language of the other, obeys neither the same rhythm nor the same law; they differ from one another as the galactic from the dialectic; they are like two colossal towers erected in double solitude, without any apparent connection. They are not opposed but heterogeneous, they communicate between themselves. Because these columns are not yet cut into, because they are double, oblique, because there are peepholes, they establish between them a series of exchanges, winks of an eye – they bind together and unbind in passing. They penetrate each other: every penetration suspends opposition (because no substantial opposition can be found). Particularly, sexual opposition finds itself compromised in this agglutination, infatuation, coupling of sexes, texts, and terms. 'Each term divided in two adheres to the other, coupling in a passionate manner, drunk as a bell-ringer at his hanging rope': it is the effect of the *Gl* (paste, glue, spit, sperm, chrism, unguent forms the unidentifiable conglomeration of this ceremonial), moreover, the *general law of the equivalence of terms*, of opposites which continuously change places where:

each sentence, each word, each stump of writing finds itself related to each other, in each column and from one column to the other: each envelope or girdle incalculably reverses, returns, replaces, recoups the other: infinite exchanges of two columns which gaze at the inverse; what gives shape to this general equivalence is always the flower and the glove.

in order that the supposed opposites maintain an equivalence and reflect each other, the flower must turn itself back like a glove and its style like a sheath . . . these gloves are not only artificial and reversible signifiers, these gloves are almost fakes . . . and *The Maids*, like the Jews of the other column, are both castrated and castraters, spiders or umbrella sheaths, filled and emptied by the phallus that Madame doesn't have.

the law of oscillation and indecision which marks the flower's incessantly instantaneous return: penis/vagina, castration/virginity, erection/flaccid, natural organism/ disarticulated artifact, one's whole body/fetishized piece, etc. There is no choice here, of disjunction or accumulation. My excitement is the oscillation.

Each column raises itself in impossible self-importance (it is a metaphysical ideology, if you will) but finds itself more or less interlaced, intertwined, wrapped around the other like a vine – flowing into the body of the other. This is the writing of *m'ec*, the inverse of Man, of the general equivalence of subjects and opposites, of mixed genres. Due to a complex depurifying machinery, *m'ec* writing tolls the death knell for phallogo-centrism, the end of all oppositions, that of man as well as that of woman, in favor of *jouissance féminine* – if feminine means indecidable oscillation.

The generalization of fetishism reverses hierarchy in favor of the most devalued term and permits a general equivalence, the flowing of one into the other, the communication of what appeared to be incommunicable. It is a 'stage' which leads to affirmation (already present in the generalized fetishism that it alone makes possible), or rather, to double affirmation since this is linked to 'the one who engages in the language of the other.' It leads to a 'Yes, yes,' to a request to the other to 'Come,' to the sign of the hymen, to an alliance where one body flows into another, transforming both, leaving neither complementary poles intact, 'infatuated' with each other. The passage from generalized fetishism to double affirmation, which is a step beyond, from Genet towards Blanchot, a step beyond indecidable oscillation towards the neutral which takes neither form . . . 'neither' is fundamentally affirmative. Perhaps it is in this step beyond that we discern not only the death knell of phallogocentrism, but even new ends – not only the end/s of man, or of woman, but the end of 'I/we.'

What does this means to me: this 'we' which holds us together and where we are neither one nor the other? Perhaps it is none other than myself, forever me without me, the relationship that I do not want to open, that I reject and which rejects me.

I could distinguish myself from it, only to hear it all while hearing myself in it, immense *parole* which always said 'We.'

The happiness of saying yes, of affirmation without end.[28]

Debate[29]

Participants: Sylviane Agacinski, Françoise Clévenot, Jacques Derrida, Sarah Kofman, Phillipe Lacoue-Labarthe, Jean-Luc Nancy, François Raux-Filio, Jaqueline Rousseau-Dujardin, Jacques Trilling.

Clévenot: Does *Glas*'s generalized fetishism permit a female fetishism? And wouldn't Derrida's childhood memory of the synagogue be impossible for a girl who would be relegated to the side, without a frontal view of the Torah?
Kofman: Generalized fetishism, defined as generalized oscillation, does not exclude a female fetishism, since it implies the generalization of the feminine and the end of the privileged phallus which ceases to be a fetish. Regarding the childhood remembrance – I was the one who added that Derrida looked in a fetishist manner at the Torah from the bottom up. And the specific topology of the synagogue did not prevent me, a little Jewish girl, from looking at the Torah, open, closed, from the bottom, from the top, and my father – the rabbi – showed it to me, moreover, in hiding. . . .

Derrida: Does the passage in *Glas* on Freud and fetishism play the role of a central lever into the text and is the generalization of fetishism the key? On the one hand, in *Glas* there is not one but *two* analyses of the text on fetishism in the two columns, an important duplicity. On the other hand, I tried not to privilege any particular passage. Therefore, I resist a move to create a key to the text. Because one could do the same thing, for example, with the Hegelian theory of fetishism, etc. Likewise, there is no one memory of childhood, there is childhood memory, supposing that it is authentic: all this is put into play at each moment.

Kofman: For me, generalized fetishism is not a transcendental key either. But in rereading *Glas*, starting at that point, many things became clearer. And it does not seem to me that one can do the same reading of Hegelian fetishism unless you read Hegel beginning with Freud – as you do.

Derrida: It's a fact and, empirically, I could not write this without knowing a little Freud. . . . I will add that 'key' is a theme in the text, the syllable '*clé*' (key) is submissive to a certain reading. As a text on keys, it presents itself as a ring of keys – each reader can select the one they like best. In your case, the key was Freudian fetishism, but that was not in itself the key to the text. And this conforms to what you have said about generalized fetishism. Perhaps I was inattentive to a certain rhetorical movement on the question of Freud's rhetoric in his text. But it is very complicated and secondary here. The essential point in what you have said concerns the fact that I give *too much* or *too little* to Freud. When it comes to gifts there is no measure, and with the gift of a reading, it is always too much or too little. Not being concerned with *one* Freud or *one* of Freud's texts, I tried to locate the 'weakest' passage which reproduces classical thought, showing an inconsistency. Perhaps you would say that I give too much in reversing what I extract from Freud's text to make another Freud who would be capable of receiving it. In order to save Freud from the too little that I would give him, you say that what functions in his text on the *thing itself* is – and you are right – the mother's penis. It is not at all the metaphysical thing itself to which the substitute would be opposed, it is already a construction that is called fantasy: I completely agree. But for this fantasy to keep the status of a prop in relation to which other fetishisms would be substitutes, is nevertheless to remain dependent on a formal logic of one or many metaphysics of fetishism. Because in the classical metaphysics of fetishism in Hegel, Marx, etc., no one could believe that the thing itself existed: each time there was always also a construction, something which came to occupy the place of the thing itself. In Freud's case what I called the thing itself was the signified or signifying prop which leads to the same kind of logic that prompted my questions. In the passage from the oscillation of generalized fetishism to double affirmation, to completely follow your meaning, the emphasis on double affirmation is perhaps greater in subsequent texts. But there is no historical continuity. Already in *Glas*, and before *Glas*, double affirmation is the condition of a discourse on fetishism and of a generalized fetishism.

Kofman: However, Freud says that it is less deceiving to speak of the mother's penis substitute than the man's. Why is it less deceptive? Isn't it because only this new definition makes the passage to a generalized fetishism possible?

Derrida: Yes, it is a great advance. . . .

Kofman: In addition, what relationship is there between the compromise Freud spoke of and the indecidable as you define it?

Derrida: There is always an irreducible link between the logic of the indecidable and compromise. The idea of compromise implies an attempt to master a contradiction which in fact does not yield a solution, a stop. It is because there is indecidability that everything is put into gear – fetishism, compromise, etc. But I do not think that the indecidable is understandable in any other way than as compromise. I call this the economy of death in the same passage.

Nancy: If there was *one* Derrida in your talk, it seems that there are two Freuds; one begins at the point where Derrida, in giving him too much and too little, puts the operation of his generalized fetishism into effect, and another Freud whose ends would be the subordination of the feminine and who would no longer have any connection with the Derridean operation.

Kofman: In the first part of my presentation I drew upon Freud's texts which bear upon femininity and which result in a radical rejection of femininity, in as much as this is defined as a permanent *oscillation* between the virile position and the feminine position, an oscillation unbearable for man because he never knows to which sex he belongs. Finally, Freud stopped this mobility, cadaverized the woman, fixed in an immutable position, at the age of thirty. . . . This time, in 'Fetishism,' the oscillation of the fetishist, and no longer the oscillation of woman, is in play. Fetishist compromise, its oscillation, is only understandable through the logic of the indecidable. But Freud does not so much valorize oscillation because it is never an ideal for him: it always remains a *pathological* compromise even if the fetishist is happy with his fetish before going on the couch. In Freud's 'theory' he substitutes the fiction of woman's penis envy for the fetishist solution, which would be the *normal* solution. However, due to a complete reading strategy, the text on fetishism permits Derrida to introduce a new 'concept' of fetishism, oscillation, the feminine.

Derrida: I do not pose generalized fetishism as an ideal either, nor valorize it as such. . . .

Clévenot: Could one say that sometimes you suggest that generalized fetishism is a benefit to women?

Kofman: No. I only wanted to emphasize that in relation to metaphysics and Freud, in relation to the rejection of fetishism and of the feminine, the generalization of fetishism is a first positive stage which, moreover, already implies double affirmation.

Trilling: Two points: (1) Freud did not say exactly that fetishists are happy. He designated fetishism as a failure in the face of, one could say, the indecidable; (2) We have said 'the mother's penis' too much. I would say, rather, the impossibility of the representation of the absence of the mother's penis. Thus, it is not on the order of a substitution so much as it refers to the notion of 'thing.'

Kofman: The fetishist's contentment is clearly affirmed in Freud's text; in any case, the fetish is never experienced as something painful, which is why Freud admitted having few fetishists among his clientele. The 'compromise' is a result of the analysis. It goes back to a split rather than a repression as with the hysteric. The hysteric also plays every scene but, as opposed to the fetishist, suffers and is unhappy.

Trilling: There is no evidence that hysterics are always unhappy and one must question the notions of unhappiness, suffering, pleasure, displeasure. In fact, the impossibility of compromise in the representation of the penis's absence does not function economically in the same manner for the fetishist as for the hysteric.

(After agreeing that penis envy is the goal of analysis and that one cannot leave it at that, *Rousseau-Dujardin* indicates that she would not proceed in the same manner as Kofman in reading the Freudian text, that she would put more of an accent on the cultural context, and on the indecidable nature of all this, that Freud would not have had the mastery of the consciousness of this indecidability. Taking 'The Taboo of Virginity' as an example, she points out the strangeness and the indecidability of a text which puts the emphasis on the virginity taboo while Freud's cultural context valorizes virginity. *Kofman* responds that this is exactly the problem posed by the text. Freud resolves it by showing that there is only an apparent contradiction, that the taboo among primitive peoples is based on man's castration anxiety in the face of woman's penis envy, whereas among civilized peoples this same anxiety finds itself compensated for by the permanence of woman's subordination, conquered by the first one who deflowered her. *Rousseau-Dujardin* and *Trilling* point out that the one who deflowers a woman ensures both her affection and her permanent hostility; this is why Freud considered second marriages happier than first ones. *Rousseau-Dujardin* then returns to the problematic of self and other which would never be dealt with, as such, by Freud. The woman would never have been seen as other, but as the same – yet inferior. However, Freud would have at least destabilized the notion of the same. *Kofman* emphasizes that there is, however, in certain texts a recognition of woman's radical alterity, in particular beginning in 1923, but there is a correlative detour which consists in the demonstration of the primacy of the phallus and the girl's penis envy; a triumph of the same because, as *Rousseau-Dujardin* says, the truth is unbearable.)

Agacinski: You interpret penis envy in terms of masculine benefits. This fiction, according to you, would construct an economy of castration anxiety. Now it happens that this is already the result of the interpretation of sexual difference as much as castration; castration is also a fiction. The fiction of penis envy protects the fiction of castration. In as much as castration is a fiction – from what is it protected? Would this not be sexual difference? But then are the benefits only masculine?

Kofman: Do not confuse castration with castration anxiety. The latter, which stems from the menace of castration in so far as it is an anxiety, is real. This is where the fiction begins; it is when the little boy, under the effect of his anxiety, perceives the little girl's sex for the first time. In a panicked reaction, he transforms the situation like magic, that is to say, he denies what he perceives: spontaneous fetishism, corollary to a fiction of castration; the clitoris is 'seen,' then, as a little penis. In his 'theory,' Freud resumes, in man's favor, the 'theory' of the little boy's sexuality which protects him from narcissistic anxiety. For the protection to be effective, the boy's construction must be shared by the girl; in other words, it must be given as fact and not as fiction. In Freud this is where 'penis envy' is situated, as a sign of the girl's own recognition of the *fact* of her *castration*: the fiction of penis envy and that of castration are *stricto sensu* identical and they protect man from castration *anxiety*.

Agacinski: Yes, but you take castration anxiety with all its content, its representations, as a given. . . .

Kofman: A given in an analytic context.

Raux-Filio: It is never only a question of imaginary castration.

Kofman: That is not in Freud but in Lacan.

Agacinski: At least there is a real castration in Freud's text, that of the little girl since she must establish the fact of her castration.

Kofman: This 'fact' is the boy's fiction that she finally realizes is to her benefit – to the greater benefit of Freudian fiction.

Trilling: The threat of castration can have a protective value, it can protect the narcissism of the child.

Kofman: You asked: is it only to protect man? Freud managed to show that this operation affects girls as well.

Agacinski: Yes, that I have not been persuaded of.

Rousseau-Dujardin: She must resign herself anyway?

Kofman: Yes, according to Freud, if she wants to become a woman; but to become a woman she does not have to accept this fate.

Chapter 8

ON DERRIDA'S 'INTRODUCTION' TO HUSSERL'S *ORIGIN OF GEOMETRY*

Rudolf Bernet

The reader of Derrida's 'Introduction' to Husserl's *Origin of Geometry*[1] is confronted by a complex text which in the course of reading soon expands into a bewildering labyrinth of the most diverse inter-textual references. Despite its apparently quite academic subject matter and the classical style in which it is written, Derrida's first published work already introduces the reader to one of the fundamental themes in Derrida's own thought, namely the textuality of philosophy. On the one hand, this is due to the fact that the textual basis of Derrida's own text is rather intricate. Derrida's 'Introduction' was conceived for the French translation of a Husserlian text which originated in connection with Husserl's *Crisis of European Sciences and Transcendental Phenomenology*. This text by Husserl was only published after his death under a title supplied by E. Fink as *The Question concerning the Origin of Geometry as an Intentional–historical Problem*. On the other hand, Derrida's efforts to situate this posthumously published text within Husserl's work as a whole as well as within the history of philosophy in general, makes it a test case for philosophical con-textuality. In addition to this, the legitimate desire of the contemporary reader to discover intimations of Derrida's own later work in his interpretation of Husserl contributes much to the reader's almost despairing sense of feeling at a loss before this text.

It is hardly surprising, then, that this first work of Derrida has been more or less equally ignored by the standard interpreters of Husserl's work and by the supporters of Derrida's thought. As far as the Husserlians are concerned,

Derrida's text may have seemed too abrupt, far too immersed in details and altogether too eclectic in its reliance on quite disparate schools of Husserl interpretation. For their part, Derrida's own disciples usually show little interest in Husserl and any attempt to pursue the traces of Derrida's thought here, where it conceals itself beneath the cloak of a self-denying and almost subservient display of Husserl scholarship, may have struck many of them as an unnecessary detour.

One should expect the author of an introduction to Derrida's text to act as a sort of fore-reader for other readers. As a good reader he must have lost his way in the multivarious byways of this text, but as a fore-reader he is supposed to lead other readers to their goal as rapidly as possible, that is, to hold back from such a good reading. But any acquaintance with Derrida's subtle and varied reflections upon the problematic status of all such introductions, forewords, and prefaces can only strengthen the fore-reader's impression that he confronts an impossible task. In addition, the nature of the text for which the present text is supposed to be an introduction is particularly complex, since quite apart from the fact that we are dealing with a translation, Derrida's own text presents itself as an 'Introduction' to a fragmentary Husserlian text which originated in a much broader context of its own. Thus even the question concerning precisely which text this introduction is really concerned with is far from evident.

In what follows I shall restrict myself to the text of Derrida's 'Introduction' and present some of the paths which I have explored in my experience as a reader. In this connection I am particularly concerned with Derrida's contribution to a better understanding of the limits of Husserl's transcendental phenomenology and with the question concerning the extent to which Husserl's text on the origin of geometry has exercised a decisive influence upon Derrida's own thought.

In a subsequent attempt at self-interpretation, Derrida identifies the question concerning the 'historicity of ideal objects' and their expression in language and especially in writing, as the central concerns of this introduction to the *Origin of Geometry*, and of his work as a whole.[2] Husserl's analysis of the constitution of geometrical objects such as the theorem of Pythagoras offers Derrida, as it already offered Husserl himself, the opportunity to raise the more general questions concerning the constitution of the various kinds of ideal objects. Not only science works with ideal objects, but the possibility of human life as a whole rests on the presence of non-natural, that is, cultural–ideal objects such as texts, works of art, social and political institutions, ritual forms of behavior, etc. Derrida's attention goes mainly to the linguistic embodiment and transmission of ideal objects, as well as the historicity of science in general. In doing this, Derrida takes his bearings entirely from the conceptual framework provided by this text and Husserl's work as a whole, in particular from the separation between real (factual) objects and ideal (essential) objects, as well as the separation between external (empirical) history and internal (a priori) historicity. Anyone who simply dissolves these differences, like Merleau-Ponty, is charged by Derrida with abandoning transcendental phenomenology, or simply with empiricism (cf. *I*, pp. 111ff., 77ff., as well as, implicitly, p. 120).

In general terms, *ideal objects* for Husserl are spiritual formations which have their origin in human activity and especially in human thought, and not in nature. Thus, already constituted spiritual objects cannot be sensibly perceived either. They are understood in their sense-content and are optimally re-thought in their original meaning. Compared with natural objects which are located in objective space and time and can only be perceived perspectivally, ideal objects have the decisive advantage of being universally available and consequently strictly objective. Such ideal objects are secure from the chances and changes of nature and cannot be claimed as a private possession by any individual subject. This immutability or 'omnitemporality' (*I*, p. 71, note 69), this universality and objectivity make the ideal object into the 'absolute model for any object whatever' (*I*, p. 66).

Derrida's original contribution in his commentary on Husserl's text lies above all in his detailed examination of the question of why Husserl should have chosen geometry in particular as the point of departure in his consideration of the historicity and linguistic embodiment of ideal objects. The examination of this question not only leads Derrida to some interesting conclusions about the various kinds of ideal objects and the way in which they are bound to real objects, but also allows him to make the extremely important distinction between ideal objects in the sense of essences and in the sense of 'Ideas in the Kantian sense.' These distinctions then permit Derrida to investigate in an exemplary phenomenological manner the peculiar linguistic nature of ideal objects as well as the intentional–teleological transmission of their original truth-content. In turn, this determination of the way in which an ideal truth is linguistically fixed and transmitted gives rise to a new understanding of the infinite idea which guides scientific progress. Finally, this phenomenological investigation of the rational historicity of science issues in a 'phenomenology of phenomenology,' that is, in the question concerning the language of phenomenological science itself as well as its guiding idea of infinite progress and its foundation in the responsibility of the phenomenologist. Thus the phenomenological investigation of the *Origin of Geometry* leads us to the very limits of phenomenology and especially to the conclusion that a purely phenomenological understanding of phenomenology itself is an impossibility. In what follows I should like to dwell a little longer upon certain stages in Derrida's explorations of these limits.

Derrida's interest in a phenomenology of history or a 'critique of historical reason' (*I*, p. 29) is characteristic of the period in which his text was written and contrasts with the later Derrida who distances himself from the philosophy of history as a typically metaphysical enterprise. A closer reading, however, shows that Derrida's almost unqualified defence of Husserl's understanding of history repeatedly forces him into a polemical confrontation with the relevant literature, particularly that of the 1940s and 1950s. Husserl's phenomenology of history is emphatically distanced from the kind of hermeneutic philosophy which invokes the name of Dilthey, as well as from the ontology of facticity inspired by Heidegger. Unlike Dilthey, Husserl is not concerned with the appropriation of a pre-constituted and historically transmitted realm of objective spirit but rather with the original constitution of this realm. Transcendental phenomenology investigates the essential conditions of the possibility of the constitutive origin of objective spirit and not its origin as a peculiar fact. This latter escapes the phenomenological approach in principle and requires a transition from

Husserlian phenomenology to ontology in the Heideggerian sense (*I*, pp. 150–1).

Nevertheless, the constitutive origin of ideal objects is a historical origin. Derrida repeatedly emphasizes that, in the realm of ideal objects, notions such as constitutive origin and historical transmission, origin and telos, cannot be separated from one another. That is why the phenomenology of the historical constitution of ideal objects also issues naturally in a phenomenology of the constitution of history or a phenomenology of historicity. In opposition to most other interpreters of Husserl's later work, Derrida also emphatically insists that this phenomenology of history is to be strictly separated from Husserl's so-called 'genetic phenomenology.' In the phenomenology of history we are not concerned with asking how the established validity of an ideal object is built up in its logical sense from the various levels of experience. Rather we are concerned with asking how the original sense of an ideal object is subsequently constituted for the first time in the process of historical reproduction, communalization, sedimentation, and transmission. In Husserl, the question concerns an archaeology which is not interested in some original fact but one which asks how this originally insignificant fact can subsequently come to acquire such a significant meaning and one which is never definitively closed.

Derrida understands Husserl's historical 'return inquiry' (*Rückfrage*) as a form of communication in which we subsequently ask at a certain distance how, why, and with what intention something has been sent to us (*I*, p. 50). In this way the process of historical transmission is likened to the 'telecommunication' systems which never function completely smoothly. And it is well known how much Derrida is inspired by the system of postal communication in his later work as well.[3] Just like the recipient of a letter, Husserl in his 'return inquiry' also struggles with the problem of an inevitable 'delay' (*I*, p. 152). The original sense can only be grasped subsequently (*I*, p. 49), and its significance and historical potency depends upon its dispatch, that is, on the manifold forms of communication through which it is torn from its place of origin (*I*, pp. 63ff.). We could express this in the language of geometry and say that there is no vector which proceeds from sender to recipient. Rather, the historical origin, its transmission, and the teologically anticipated goal constitute a 'circle', as Husserl says, an 'interplay' which we can only follow in a 'zigzag' fashion (*I*, pp. 50ff).

What is true with respect to this relation between historical origin and transmission, is also true for the connection between empirical history and a priori history: we can only investigate the a priori of history phenomenologically by taking the historical *facts* as our point of departure. For their part, however, they can only be recognized as *historical* facts by virtue of an understanding, implicit at the very least, of the essence of history. Whenever we deal with history we soon discover that we are continually moving in a circle. It is not surprising therefore that we protest most violently against a linear understanding of time precisely when we are orientated towards historical time in particular. It is a further service of Derrida's text to have shown that Husserl's later philosophy of historicity necessitates a revision of his earlier phenomenology of time.

In defining the nature of this circularity in the process of historical transmission Derrida advances beyond Husserl in so far as he considers negligence (*I*, p. 36, note), forgetfulness, and concealment (*I*, p. 105), misunderstandings (*I*, p. 82), in short betrayal, as necessary ingredients in genuine transmission. However, this infidelity does not arise from some empirically grounded incapacity of our intellectual powers. It determines the essence of historical transmission and it could thus be described as ontological finitude. Thus transmission is at once preservation and loss, and the return inquiry is at once an exposure and a concealment of the origin. Derrida analyzes this paradoxical finitude or 'indecidability' in the historical transmission of an event preeminently with reference to writing, the phenomenological determination of which greatly occupied Husserl in the *Origin of Geometry*. Writing is at once the condition of the fecundity of an origin and the cause of its loss. Writing makes possible the development of an original sense and also produces the loss of sense which takes place in this development or in every (scientific) advance. This indecidability in (written) communication and transmission remains a central philosophical theme in Derrida's later work as well. Thus it is no surprise that Derrida soon began to treat historical

events and experiences as particular forms of the universal
structure of the written sign or of the 'trace.'[4]

The interplay within the historical constitution of ideal objects
and the circle of origin and transmission which constitutes the
historicity of ideal objects also reveals that ideal objects are
exposed to a double danger: they threaten either to lose their
spirit in the form of bloodless abstractions, or to lose it in the
letter. These two dangers arise from the fact that on the one
hand such spiritual objects become detached from the natural
'life-world' through the process of 'idealization' (*I*, pp. 117ff.)
and, on the other hand, they require a process of 'embodiment'
(*Verleiblichung*), especially embodiment in the form of written
language (*I*, pp. 87ff.). The historicity of ideal objects is essentially linked with these two kinds of danger. I should like to go
into this problem more closely in what follows.

The constitution of ideal objects, that is to say, the process
of objectivation of an originally subjective and transitory
evidence, is accomplished in *language*, and particularly in
writing. As prior steps in this process Husserl mentions retention, reproductive repetition, and the communicative communalization of original evidence. Derrida investigates each of
these steps individually, yet if we read the text and particularly
the notes very closely, we see that the result which emerges
everywhere is the same as that which emerges with the analysis
of writing: not only does the progressive objectivation of original evidence proceed with a progressive loss of substance but
we find once more that the balance of gain and loss is shared
equally at each individual step of the way.[5]

On the other hand, writing is radically different from the
previous steps in the constitution of the ideal object in so far
as it liberates the original insight from any possession by any
existing subjectivity or intersubjective community. Thus writing
generates an anonymous and 'autonomous transcendental field'
(*I*, p. 88) which is comparable to the ego-less 'field of consciousness' described by A. Gurwitsch on the basis of his phenomenology of perception. Writing promotes intellectual flexibility in
the cultural world which always already embraces us and upon
which we can only impress a personal stamp by exerting
considerable creative force. But the anonymity and the independence of writing also make possible a radical loss of sense, the

burying of the intentions and the cultural world of an author, or the indecipherability of a stone inscription (*I*, p. 88). Because of this possibility of radical loss, writing confronts us with 'the transcendental sense of death' (*I*, p. 88),[6] as no other phenomenon does. Perhaps we must even say that transmission and the loss of sense do not simply hold the balance in writing but rather that the very possibility of loss contributes to the significance of the text in a quite essential way.

The insertion of the analysis of language into the context of the constitution of ideal objects means that Husserl is concerned with 'constitutive language' rather than with constituted language (*I*, p. 78). What interests Husserl is the service that language performs for thought, the preservation of sense, its accessibility and the possibility of its progressive articulation. In fact, however, this determination of the constitutive function of language already presupposes a decision about the way in which it is itself constituted. In Husserl's view, language is constituted by thought procuring for itself a 'spiritual corporeality' (*geistige Leiblichkeit*), particularly in writing. As a *proper body* (*Leib*) writing is not simply a sensible body (*Körper*) or thing. On the contrary, it is an expression which directly belongs to the sense or the meaning-intention. As a *spiritual* proper body, writing is divested of all facticity and materiality and is reduced to the intention of self-expression, to the 'intention of writing (or reading)' (*I*, p. 97). Husserl considers writing as the pure, that is, transcendental possibility of the embodiment (*Verleiblichung*) of an intellectual truth rather than as a kind of empirical–contingent inscription upon a stone, a piece of paper or a video-screen. The 'book' is the exemplary model of such an ideal form of writing, that is, of an 'archetypal unity' whose spiritual and 'indestructible' corporeality must not be confused with all those exemplars through which the book materially presents itself (*I*, pp. 90ff.).[7]

While it is true that Derrida does not present an explicit critique of this separation between constituting and constituted or between ideal and factual language, he does present the phenomenological argument that both these moments are always simultaneously present in the phenomenon of language. Language and, in particular, writing are always simultaneously and indecidably the 'movement of the essential and constitutive possibility of embodiment' (*Verleiblichung*) as well as 'the place of factual and contingent sensible embodiment' (*Verkörperung*) (*I*, p. 92; cf. also p. 97). If we ascribe a moment of essential and thus irreducible facticity and materiality to writing in this way, then the danger of 'the annihilation of the world' or even merely a burning of books affects writing not simply as sensible body but as spiritual corporeality as well (*I*, pp. 94, 97). The spiritual essence of a universally valid sense which is deposited in writing is always endangered by factual events and defence-lessly exposed to acts of individual caprice or the brutal violence of natural catastrophe.

Derrida thus draws the conclusion that along with the appearance of ideal truth in writing, we must always simultaneously investigate its potential disappearance (*I*, pp. 93ff.). If the possibility of the gradual exhaustion of sense through the facticity of writing and the possibility of the burying over and loss of sense belongs to the (spiritual) essence of writing and of language in general, then we must also ask ourselves whether there can be such a thing as a purely spiritual, that is, purely expressive, language at all. Can our thought in fact rely upon finding an adequate and definitive presentation in the spiritual corporeality of ideal linguistic expression? Derrida also asks himself this further question even if only in the form of a (very important) note (*I*, pp. 69ff., note 66). He speaks here of the vulnerability of sense on account of the irreducible facticity of linguistic expression and of thought's own vocation for silence which springs from this.[8]

As I have already mentioned, in addition to linguistic embodiment the process of *idealization* also plays an essential role in the historical constitution of ideal objects, as well as in the dangers to which they are exposed. In the case of geometry, according to Husserl, we throw a 'garb of ideas' over the things encountered within the world of sense-perception (*I*, p. 118). Just as the linguistic garb of expression both reveals and potentially also conceals an ideal truth, so too the geometrical garb of ideas promotes the precise investigation of the life-world and simultaneously runs the danger of completely sacrificing the concrete foundation of sense in the life-world to scientific abstraction. In Husserl's view the crisis of the objective sciences is also a consequence of the fact that the linguistic garb of expression and the mathematical garb of ideas have a tendency to detach themselves from their sense-foundation or even to substitute themselves for this foundation. Of course, here too, the solution for this crisis cannot possibly lie in removing this garb and returning to the naked pre-scientific truth.[9] Derrida quite rightly insists that the 'life-world' is a concept derived from the theory of science and one which can only be grasped from the perspective of the objective sciences as they have been handed down to us. Furthermore, to clarify the meaning of the 'life-world,' natural experience is not enough. Rather, what is needed is a phenomenological form of scientific investigation.

Alongside this scientific investigation of the pre-scientific culture out of which geometry, for example, emerged (*I*, pp. 122ff.), we require above all a much better understanding of the process of idealization with which every science begins. In the case of the 'mathematization of nature' which goes back to Galileo in particular, one 'substructs' geometrically and exactly defined concepts like those of 'straight line,' 'circle,' 'surface,' etc., for a description of the factually infinite variety of individual bodies in space. This transition is based in particular upon a sensible typicalization of the perceptual field, that is, on a still inexact morphology of sensible ideal-types (*I*, pp. 122ff.). Thus the sensible 'morphological-type' 'round' or the pure sensible idea of 'roundness' mediates between a round empirical thing and the ideal geometrical spatial form of the 'circle.' In Husserl's view the imagination plays an absolutely essential role in this process of substruction. In a footnote, Derrida observes that the imagination is characterized by an 'ambiguity' similar to that involved in the whole process of idealization or substruction which imagination makes possible (*I*, p. 125, note 141). On the one hand, the imagination liberates the spirit from the fetters of empirical actuality, while, on the other hand, understood as a purely reproductive capacity, it remains exposed to all the confusions of the factual world.

However, Derrida's most important remark about the process of idealization concerns the fact that the formation of a morphological ideality by means of the imagination in particular, while preparing for the grasping of an exact geometrical essence, does not really ground it (*I*, pp. 133ff.). The transition from the sensible to the geometrical ideality thus remains a 'leap,' an act of radical theoretical 'freedom' and 'decision.' The geometrical ideality ultimately has its origin in the 'project' which aims at an infinite progress of knowledge (*I*, pp. 127ff.). The exact ideality of the geometrical object is thus a virtual limit which can only be understood as the pole of an infinite process of approximation. As a correlate of an infinite progress of knowledge, we can find no better way to describe the geometrical object than as an *'Idea in the Kantian sense'* (*I*, p. 134, note 159).

According to Husserl, 'Ideas in the Kantian sense' represent essences of a quite particular kind which are only fully and rationally intelligible as the *telos* or as rules for an uncompletable process of knowledge. However, they cannot be understood as completely constituted ideal objects. For this reason, the idealization through which the ideality of the geometrical object is constituted is not simply an 'intuition of an essence' either (*I*, p. 135). Thus, Ideas in the Kantian sense are ideal objects which constitute or are still to be constituted, while the other essences are constituted ideal objects. A particular mode of intuitive givenness belongs to both these kinds of ideal object. In particular the question of outstanding importance is whether, and if so precisely how, Ideas in the Kantian sense can be grasped in an adequate intuition. When we look more closely we can see that this question does not merely concern the epistemological status of geometrical idealities alone, but also the phenomenological givenness of the perceptual 'thing in itself,' of the unity of the infinite world-horizon, of the total unity of the inner flux of consciousness (*I*, p. 106). Thus the question concerning the intuitive givenness of geometrical idealities leads directly to the question concerning the role of adequate intuition within phenomenology in general, and thus to an investigation of what Derrida later calls Husserl's 'metaphysics of presence.'

In Husserl's phenomenology these Ideas in the Kantian sense enjoy a quite particular mode of presence which is moreover never satisfactorily clarified (*I*, pp. 136ff.). On the one hand, they are objects of an intuitive and even adequate insight. In an exercise of phenomenological seeing we can grasp the necessity of an infinite progress of knowledge with complete evidence. Thus phenomenology not only discloses the ever more comprehensive and ever more richly articulated visibility of an object but it also discloses the visibility of the rules, that is, the conditions of the possibility, of this infinite progress of knowledge. And phenomenological intuitionism celebrates its greatest triumph in this vision of the idea of the infinite. On the other hand, the insight into the nature of the infinite goal of knowledge is also an insight into its unattainability. The insight into the infinite nature of both the goal and the task of human knowledge cannot be separated from the insight into the finitude of human knowledge. Insight into the possibility of an infinite progress in visibility simultaneously allows us to experience the impossibility of unlimited visibility. The Idea in the Kantian sense is an intention without an object (*I*, pp. 139ff.) or an anticipation of the *invisible ground of visibility* (*I*, pp. 138ff.).

Derrida's analysis of the 'Ideas in the Kantian sense' and the consequent impossibility of encompassing the ground of phenomenology itself within the phenomenological purview, owes much to Husserl's idea of grounding theory in *ethical responsibility* (*I*, p. 141). The phenomenologist encounters the idea of infinity not as the visible ground of visibility but as a challenge to serve a reason which is constantly endangered: the absolute of phenomenology is 'the absolute of a danger' (*I*, p. 149). The real motivation behind Husserl's thought is thus revealed as the danger which threatens the presence of ideal objects in writing and transmission and the impossibility of a phenomenology of a phenomenology, rather than the conquest and administration of a realm of unlimited presence and visibility. The authentic idea of infinity in Husserl's phenomenology represents a resolute decision in favour of a task which can never be finally mastered, an orientation towards an unattainable goal. The inauthentic idea of infinity is the Idea in the Kantian sense which has been rendered visible in an overview and intuitively mastered, that is, the mere knowledge of the conditions of the possibility of the infinite task. It has frequently been overlooked that in *Speech and Phenomena*, too, Derrida's critique of Husserl is still determined by the tension within Husserl's thought which is already noted here.

The 'ethico-teleological' motivation behind Husserl's thought (*I*, p. 136) and an understanding of how this motivation ultimately undermines rather than founds the possibility of phenomenalizing the infinite, emerges also from the analysis of the *temporality* and *historicity* which are proper to the Ideas in the Kantian sense. Derrida's analysis of the temporality within which the infinite task of phenomenology unfolds leads him to the conclusion that even the Idea in the Kantian sense is incapable of encompassing the total unity of this infinite process of knowledge or containing it within the visibility of a 'living present' (*I*, pp. 136ff.). The living present is irremediably ruptured by the interconnection between the now and retention after the fact and protentional infinity. From this Derrida draws the conclusion that an original presentation of the temporality of the infinite process of knowledge is only possible at the cost of denying our facticity or 'death' (*I*, p. 137). The temporality of phenomenology itself cannot be appropriately determined within the framework of any analysis of the essential structures of time-consciousness which remains purely formal. In reality the temporality of the idea which determines phenomenological practice is historical in nature (*I*, pp. 141ff.).

Phenomenology follows in the wake of reason which reveals itself in history step by step and contributes to the unfolding of a teleologically determined rationality. Consequently phenomenology remains bound to a prior event and pursues an absolute which it cannot precede. Phenomenology cannot assume a position at the end of history (from which it might sit in judgment) by the miraculous means of an infinitude which it has rendered completely intelligible as a Kantian Idea. The historical absolute from which phenomenology draws its justification is thus a 'passage' (*I*, p. 149), 'a presence which is deferred without respite' (*I*, p. 153), or a 'difference' (*I*, p. 153). The task of phenomenology lies in progressively disclosing this absolute (*I*, p. 142) with 'delay' (*I*, p. 152).

As is well known, 'difference,' 'postponement,' 'delay,' and 'deferred action' also play an absolutely central role in Derrida's later work. However, it is very striking that in the present work Derrida still deals with these themes in the context of a transcendental philosophy – albeit one of a new kind – of a phenomenological reduction which reveals deferred self-consciousness and the delay involved in philosophical thought (*I*, pp. 152ff.). What then were the reasons which prompted Derrida to break with this conception so soon after the appearance of the 'Introduction' to Husserl's *Origin of Geometry* and to equate his repudiation of a phenomenology of visibility with the *repudiation of transcendental a priorism* or 'logocentrism'?

I believe that it is possible to trace some of the reasons for this break back to the 'Introduction.' Undoubtedly the most important element in Derrida's attempt to 'problematize' the transcendental–philosophical separation between the a priori ground of possibility and empirical facticity is his increasingly profound reflection upon the nature of the written sign. Thus Derrida's later critique of the 'transcendental signified' (*'signifié transcendantal'*) (cf. for example, *De la grammatologie*) is still clearly based upon the analysis of the ambiguity of writing which he had already developed in the 'Introduction.' If, that is to say, the 'spiritual corporeality' and the 'material body' of the signifier are indeed inseparably entwined with one another, then we can no longer maintain the spiritual independence of the signified either. Sense is not the ground of the possibility of language since as 'trace' or 'primal writing,' it remains stamped by the materiality and facticity of the structure of the sign.

In *De la grammatologie* the critique of the 'logocentric' philosophy of language is directly connected with the charge of 'ethnocentrism.' This recalls the passages in the 'Introduction' where the idea of the teleological rationality of history as well as the consciousness of historicity in general are grounded in the spiritual essence of 'Europe' (*I*, pp. 114ff.). Here, once again, we must ask ourselves whether or not Europe is not simultaneously and indecidably a spiritual essence and a historical fact, and with what right the European idea of rationality can still count as a criterion for understanding alien cultures in their difference (*I*, pp. 113ff.). In his later work, Derrida's emphasis upon the facticity of reason as it manifests itself in various forms of 'indecidability' finally leads him to a critical engagement with the philosophical idea of foundation as well.[10] It is already possible to find approaches to this radical interrogation of philosophical reason in the 'Introduction,' especially in Derrida's reflections upon the 'transcendental earth' understood as the universal soil or ground of human experience (*I*, pp. 83ff.).

As is well known, Derrida's thought revolves constantly around the questions concerning the facticity of language and writing, the exclusions which never fail to leave a trace and the presuppositions which can never be recuperated. Of all the 'indecidables' which Derrida discovers in the 'Introduction' to Husserl's *Origin of Geometry*,[11] the most influential is the one which concerns phenomenology itself. It is hardly surprising that Derrida affirms his distance from Husserl most emphatically when the question concerns the language in which the insights of transcendental phenomenology are formulated (*I*, pp. 69ff., note 66). The radical incapacity of transcendental phenomenology to tear itself free from its natural empirico-factual basis reveals itself in the impossibility of a transcendentally pure and thus purely expressive ideal language. The facticity of the linguistic sign and its manifestations as a linguistic body in social documentation, constitutions, testaments, libraries, and archives or in written records and prescriptions, remain paradigmatic phenomena in Derrida's later work as well. But this extension of Husserl's phenomenology of ideal objects simultaneously undermines with increasing confidence any possibility of philosophizing in a transcendental manner. In his deconstructive analysis, Derrida is less and less concerned with exposing the indecidability in the relationship between the transcendentally constituting and the transcendentally constituted, than he is with affirming this indecidability as the fate of philosophical thought and setting it uncompromisingly to work as a matter of philosophical responsibility.

Chapter 9

DERRIDA, HEIDEGGER, AND THE TIME OF THE LINE

Hugh J. Silverman

Die Zeit der Linie
Le Temps de la ligne
The Time of the Line

What time is it in New York? What time is it in Paris? What time is it in Vienna? A line links three cities – perhaps not a straight line, but surely a straighter line than New York–Paris–Rome. But even if the line is straight, there is difference in time. New York is not the same time as Paris, but Paris is the same time as Vienna. Noon in New York; six o'clock in Paris and Vienna. But the more or less straight line that New York–Paris–Vienna makes does not make the same difference in time. And even though Paris and Vienna are the same time, it still takes another two hours (by plane) to get there. Yet again, one might say that New York, Paris, and Vienna – in the 1980s – are of the *same* time. But what time? *Welche Zeit? Eine Neue-Zeit* – no longer simply modern but distinctly post-modern. What sort of time is this new time that calls itself post-modern? The Renaissance of the fifteenth and sixteenth centuries had to wait for Burkhardt in the nineteenth century to receive its full self-understanding as the 'Renaissance.' There must be something peculiar about a time which can name itself while also giving sense to an antecedent time. To name itself *post*-anything (post-impressionist, post-industrial, post-capitalist, post-structuralist, post-phenomenological, post-analytic, post-partum, post-critical, post-modern, etc.) announces that the previous time is at an end, that a new time is on the rise, and that it is self-consciously *avant garde*. This new historical time is rather the time of periods and moments, epochs and centuries, then and now. It does not occur by traversing different time lines, different time zones, different countries and cities. As a post-historical time, it partitions itself off as different from what is past, establishing a threshold, a gap, or an end which has become a beginning. But my purpose here is to speak of another difference and another time – the time of the line. But what line? If it is not the line between past and present, not the line from New York to Paris to Vienna, not the line of the tramway or underground, not the line *behind which* one stands for an eye test or when waiting for passport control, not the line *on* which one must walk for an alchohol test, not a police line-up, nor a line (that is a *queue*) *in* which (or, if one is from New York, *on* which) one stands with devoted seriality waiting for the bus, not an artist's line or the line on which one signs one's name, the line of an argument, a line of reasoning, or a line of thought, then what sort of line could it be?

The line in question – not the line of questioning – is the line about which Heidegger discourses with Ernst Jünger (in *The Question of Being*)[1] and which Derrida inscribes in his memorial to Jacques Ehrmann (that is, his celebration of Shelley's *Triumph of Life* in 'Living On: Border Lines').[2] But here, too, the line is not the same. Both Heidegger and Derrida mark out a line of difference while also differing in their respective accounts (and at the same time approximating each other). This inscription of difference at the juncture between Heidegger and Derrida is a *philosophical* line of difference – and not a historical, artistic, geographical, chronological, or linguistic line. But what is the meaning of the inscription of a philosophical line of difference? Such a difference is marked out by two philosophical enterprises that are brought into conjunction – particularly when both formulations are established by another text in which the line itself is in question.

Here the time of the line is a reading of two philosophical texts: one by Heidegger, the other by Derrida. They each delimit themselves in terms of a rather unique philosophical position, a set of strategies, and a specific complex of queries. Yet there are some common themes, not held in common, only like common land in which both the Heideggerian text and the Derridean text participate, in which both operate at the limits of their own proper territory. This ground – which is hardly foundational – is a differential space, a domain without identity, a line of difference where the line as *topos* is placed on the line in a reading of the line.

I Heidegger

In *Zur Seinsfrage* (1955), Heidegger writes to Ernst Jünger concerning his essay *'Uber die Linie.'* *Uber die Linie* could be understood as either *de linea* or *trans lineam*. The division itself between these two understandings of *über die Linie* is crucial for an account of Heidegger's concern when examining this title.

De linea – concerning the line – is the investigation or inquiry about the line. The line itself is *in question*. Here the line is in question in the same way that 'experience' is in question for Montaigne in the last of his essays,[3] or 'studies' are under consideration in Francis Bacon's *Essays*,[4] or 'grammatology' is at issue for Derrida in the book of that title.[5] Archaic in form, discursive and essayistic in practice, the proposition *de* or *peri* designates a discourse on a topic that is to follow. Aristotle uses this form when speaking *about* interpretation (*peri hermeneia*).

Trans lineam is the 'going across,' passing from one side to the other, or the transport across. 'Crossing over' the line is getting safely to the other side. The line then separates two sides: it is a kind of obstacle or division between the here and the there. Like the 'Trans-Europe-Express' (TEE, for short) or a Trans-Atlantic flight, it gets the traveler from one place to another. Such transports are not simply a crossing over from one side to the other as in border disputes or in choosing up teams or determining one's affiliation. But then *trans lineam* is of another order when understood as a transportation line (viz. the London 'Circle Line,' the Paris RER, or the Vienna U-Bahn).

Uber die Linie can also be understood as 'above' the line: *meta-linea*. When Aristotle – in the book *after* the *Physics* – wanted to speak *about physics* – not purely as nature – but as the study of first principles ('metaphysics'), he found it necessary to go *above* nature, to discuss nature *from above*, from a *higher* point of view, from a perspective that takes into account the *causes* and *conditions* of nature. But to be *above* nature and to be *above* the line are not the same. To be above the line is to *hover over it*, to *examine* (or *think about*) it, but also to be *superior* to it, to take a position of greater authority, greater power, greater strength in relation to it. Machiavelli's counsel to the Prince was to manipulate one's circumstances so as to always retain the upper hand. To be above the line then – and *above all* (*überhaupt*: in general) – above the line is to have an overview of it, to see its perfections and imperfections, its advantages and disadvantages. Merleau-Ponty characterized this sort of 'overview thinking' as *la pensée de survol* and correspondingly expressed his dismay at its employment as a philosophical strategy.[6]

When Nietzsche's Zarathustra[7] comes down from the mountain, he finds – in many instances – that he has come too early. He thereby goes *over* (*über*), *above, back up* the mountain – from the heights he can see afar. However, from above, Zarathustra cannot communicate. He must go under (*untergehen*) in order to speak, in order to address the people. If they do not wish to hear of the *over*man (the *Übermensch*), they will not hear and Zarathustra will – once again – be obliged to return, to again *go over, above* – back up the mountain – over the line, even above the tree line.

Hence *Über die Linie* is (i) to discourse *on* the line, (ii) to *go across* the line, and (iii) to *stand above* or oversee the line. Heidegger is less certain of this third sense – and yet only by 'standing above' (making itself different from) can the relation to itself be made thoroughly clear. Heidegger also wants to say that these different senses of *Über die Linie* belong together. They are all understood in the response to Jünger.

But what Heidegger is after is not just a reflection on the different senses of *über die Linie*. There is a special line that concerns him – a line in which all three senses are raised. This line is the one that differentiates Being from beings. The Being of beings (*Sein des Seienden*) – the is-ness of that which is – establishes a line of difference between what is and its Being. This line of difference is not anything – Heidegger reaffirms that it is nothing of content or even of substance – and yet there is a difference between Being and beings, a difference in the relation beings have to Being. This line of difference is marked by a genitive, the 'of' – what Heidegger elsewhere calls the ontological genitive (the Being of beings). Like the 'time of the line' the difference between 'time' and 'the line' is that the genitive designates the non-sameness of the two.

Heidegger claims that the Being of beings, the line of difference, designates the 'essence of man.' The 'essence of man' (*Das Wesen des Menschen*) is the nothingness designated by the line of difference. In the 1920s Heidegger called the affirmation of this difference *Dasein*. By now announcing it as the *Menschenwesen*, he reaffirms the place of difference without reifying it. But what is the Being of beings? Why does the 'essence of man' (*Menschenwesen*) constitute this place? And how does Heidegger propose to designate it?

The Being of beings marks a line. Heidegger proposes to inscribe this line by writing the relation of a being to Being as B̶e̶i̶n̶g̶. In effect, then, Being is a double line – a crossing (*trans, über*) and a crossing over (and out) of two lines. Not only is the line traversed once but it is also crossed a second time. This double crossing is the *trans* rendered twice. To speak about this double line is to speak about (*de, peri, über*) the line – but in this case in its doubleness. And further the crossing of the line designates the respect in which Being stands *above* (*über*) beings in their particularity. Being, Heidegger says, is always at the horizon of beings, just above or beyond beings (or any particular being). Being then designates the *über* as 'concerning' Being (*de Sein*), as 'across' Being (*trans Sein*), and as 'above' or 'over' (*Sein als über*). Being as *übersicht* cannot be understood as *pensée de survol* – hence it is crossed out, marked off as what cannot have a transcendental position, as what cannot stand apart, cannot be – on its own – without the Being of beings. Being, then, is a crossed word, a puzzle of sorts, whose enigmatic character is designated by B̶e̶i̶n̶g̶. The question of Being (the *Seinsfrage*) then marks the 'of' as the line between Being and beings, as difference – not overview, as crossing out, not separating off – as a matter of concern (*Sache des Denkens*), not some auxiliary interest. But what sort of line is it that becomes polysemous, that has the many senses of *über*, proliferated in the space of difference, and marked out by a cross, a sign, a *chi* . . .? As essence of man, the difference as line, as polysemous, as multiple otherness, as not the same, and as crossed out, constitutes a space that is not a space, not a concrete line, not a mark of what is – but rather a mark of what *is not*. Between Being and beings, the ontico-ontological difference cannot be, it cannot constitute a positive entity. Hence Heidegger calls this line of difference – nothingness. Nothingness here is not a vacuum, not a chaotic emptiness. Rather it is what *is* not – for both Being and beings *are* and Being is *between* yet neither one nor the other.

The Being of beings is also – particularly in the later Heidegger – an event, but not an event in time. The event of the relating of beings and Being is an event of significance. This event is not some everyday occurrence, some ontic occasion that will pass into another happening perhaps without even notice or remark. This event, or advent, is of major importance, for it marks the very call of Being, the accounting for any being's relation to Being, the appropriation of the ontico-ontological difference, the mark of temporality itself. In the Heideggerian formulation, this happening is ecstatico-ontological. This means that the ontico-ontological difference is not simply a difference constituted for all eternity. Rather this difference is precisely the event or happening of a being that is already outside itself. The event of the relating of beings to Being occurs in time, but it is ecstatic in that it goes outside itself, outside time. *Ex-stasis* departs from the static, the stable, the solid, the everyday. In so doing, it brings about an occurrence of otherness, an alterity with respect to a being's identity. But again, this alterity is not simply otherness; it is also the happening of the otherness, the coming to pass and marking of otherness, the passage from identity to difference. Heidegger calls this event of difference: *Ereignis*.[8] *Ereignis* is the ecstastic, happening of a being's difference from itself, namely, the time of its relation to Being – which is another 'time' than the time of everyday being.

Just as *Eigentlichkeit* is the condition of being most one's own, namely, 'authenticity,' so *Ereignis* is the happening of what is most one's own. The *Eigen* is what is one's own, the *Eigentlich* is the description of a being – a human being, for instance – which is most its own; and *Eigentlichkeit* is the condition of being most one's own. Albert Hofstadter would translate it as 'ownliness.' Similarly *Er-eignis* is the appropriation of what is one's own.[9] And what is most one's own for a being is its relation to Being. Hence what is most one's own is its difference from itself, its marking of a line between what is itself, its

159

own, and what is other – not just distinct from it (a mere *Unterscheidung*) but a difference (*Differenz*) of the highest order, namely the ontico-ontological difference, the difference that traces its relation to Being. For the relation to Being is no everyday relation.[10] It is also not a relation to just any otherness. Rather it is a relation to *its own* otherness, a relation to that otherness that is most its own, most authentic, most the particular relation to itself. Hence, the appropriation and appropriateness of otherness in the ontico-ontological difference is the event of crossing over the line that a being sets for itself, not necessarily actively but simply by defining itself as what it is, that is, by *being* what it is. The line between what it is and what it is not, between its being and its relation to Being is the very line of difference, the line whose event of occurrence is *Ereignis* itself.

What does it mean for difference to happen? And how is it marked? In 'The Origin of the Work of Art,' Heidegger demonstrates that the difference marked in the happening of the artwork is a difference that is best called (by) 'poetizing.'[11] 'Poetizing' is not only the naming of the relation to Being in terms of the artwork, whether it be a poem, painting, or building, but it is also the 'calling' of Being. For Heidegger, Being is not simply in relation to beings. Rather it is also called *to* Being and called *by* Being. The *Ruf des Seins* is the 'call of Being' in that beings are drawn to Being. Beings are marked by their very alterity – and this alterity is the 'call of Being.' This is to say that the identity of a being includes its relation to the is-ness that all beings have in common. This is the 'call of Being.' Being is even 'heard' by beings. That is, there is a 'belonging-togetherness' of beings and Being. This *Zusammengehörigkeit* of Being and beings is the hearing (*hören*) of the relation of beings to Being. All these marks of the relation of beings to Being: 'naming,' 'calling,' 'hearing,' and 'belonging' are the very features of the line between beings and Being, the traces of the difference that is already inscribed in beings themselves. 'Poetizing' is the saying of the ontico-ontological difference in the event of the truth of an artwork, in the disclosure of a painting, in the bringing out of concealedness of a poem, in the making open of a temple. 'Poetizing,' then, for Heidegger, is the saying of the time of the line.

The saying of the time of the line can also occur from one poem to another, from the time of one poet to another. This is Heidegger's point in 'Wozu Dichter?' (1946).[12] Hölderlin writes of 'the destitute time' of the nineteenth-century age in which he lives. He remarks in his poem – and with characteristic romantic despair – that there seems to be no way out of this unfortunate time and therefore asks: 'What are poets for in a destitute time?' He is speaking of the age in general. For Hölderlin, it is an age in which the gods 'have fled' leaving only their 'traces' (Spuren). In this time, Hölderlin remarks c.. the abyss (Ab-grund) in which he finds himself. The time of the abyss is a falling away from the ground (Grund). It is a sense of being cast off, broken away from the ground, the foundation, the solid mooring. By contrast, Heidegger notes, Rilke detected that in *his* time – a number of decades later – the possibility of falling back to the ground is in evidence. Poets may be able to fill the gap, the line of difference between ground and abyss, between definitive assurance and hopelessness. Poets may be able to offer some solace, some disclosure, some opening up of what seemed closed off. The truth of poetry, according to Heidegger, is this disclosure, this opening of a clearing (Lichtung) in the space of difference, in the event of the Being of beings, in the appropriation (Ereignis) of the line – not only in Rilke's time, but also in the time that is distinguished, marked off, separated from the destitute time that Hölderlin identifies.

II   Derrida

And what of the line between Derrida and Heidegger? Has its time come? Has its time come into its own? What time is it that marks the line of difference between Derrida and Heidegger? In some respects, the reading of Heidegger offered here is already a Derridean reading, already a thinking that situates itself in the line between Heidegger and Derrida. And yet where Heidegger's text inscribes the *crossing* of Being, the *crossing out* of Being, the naming and thinking of Being, Derrida's text – and particularly 'Living On: Borderlines' (recently published in French as 'Survivre')[13] – formulates another line of difference. The thematization of the line of difference itself will make it possible for an inquiry into the line between Heidegger and Derrida.

However, without understanding how the line operates in Derrida, it will not be possible to formulate the place between the Derridean 'line' and the Heideggerian double-crossing of Being (that is, ~~Being~~), what Derrida will call Being *sous rature*.

Derrida's line of difference – also multiple – designates not a relation to Being, not a generality for a particularity, not the *essence of man*, but rather the relation between Shelley's 'Triumph of Life' and a memorial to Jacques Ehrmann. Just as Heidegger is addressing Ernst Jünger and his *Uber die Linie*, Derrida is also addressing a person (now and then passed away) – a professor of French at Yale (in the context of other colleagues all at the time still at Yale, including Geoffrey Hartman, Harold Bloom, and J. Hillis Miller). The topic is not the 'question of Being' but rather the 'triumph of life' – or one might simply say: *'living itself.'* With Derrida, *living* is not a *topos* which is given centrality in his text. 'Living' permeates Derrida's text while 'living on' moves to the edge of his text. Indeed, as the text is constructed, there are in fact two texts: the main text (the *Haupttext*) and a second long running footnote that *under-lies* the main text. The second text – not really a *secondary* text – goes *unter* (not *über*). This second *Unter-text* serves as a memorial with dates and other chronological marks referring to Jacques Ehrmann, whose initials would name the self or subject – *le 'je'* – which is not other. What then is the relation between sub-text – or under-text – and the over-text (*Ubertext*)?

The over-text is concerned with Shelley's poem – written in Italy, during a journey – in fact, his *last* journey. Shelley's poem remains unfinished: life is triumphant in the poem but not in the author. The poem's unfinished character gives it the quality of a cliff whose edge marks off a limit. At its limit, the poem calls for an abyss. In fact, Shelley drowned. For Derrida, the abyss is not as it is for Heidegger an *Ab-grund* – a falling away from the Ground (*Grund* or *Sein*), a marking of the ontico-ontological difference as event. For Derrida, the abyss is the margin, the edge, or end of Shelley's poem – incomplete and unfinished.

At the edge of Shelley's poem, Derrida juxtaposes another text – this time Blanchot's *L'Arrêt de mort* (translated as *Death Sentence*).[14] More than half a century separates these two texts. Yet, by juxtaposing the two, Derrida inserts a new line. The

Blanchot narrative (short story or *récit*) comes after the Shelley poem. Derrida places them side by side – just as Heidegger's *Zur Seinsfrage* and Derrida's 'Survivre' are juxtaposed here. Shelley's text (in English) announces the prevalence and achievement of life. In its placement, the poem is also Shelley's very death knell (his *glas*). Hence the 'Triumph of Life' is a triumphing *over* life – namely, *death*. Correspondingly, Blanchot's *L'Arrêt de mort* is a proclamation of death – to come – to be executed by an edict of the judicial system. But literally an *arrêt de mort* is a stopping or interruption of death – hence: life. So Blanchot's text is formulated as at once the stopping of death and the proclamation of death – a kind of annunciation: birth and crucifixion, death and resurrection. Shelley's poem pronounces at once the affirmation of life and the success of death over life. At the juncture of the two texts there arise the very basic questions of life and death, living and dying, survival in life and the coming of death. The line 'between' marks the achievement of life and/or death as a question. On the line – here the line between *The Triumph of Life* and *L'Arrêt de mort*, there the borderline between the main text 'Living On' (on these matters) and the sub-text 'Borderlines'; under the line – the inscription of living itself is turned into a *speech act*, an inscribed performance of the ontico-ontological difference. The borderline marks the place of living – not towards death (*zum Tod*) as in the early Heidegger – but as marked out in the text, as indicating – between the *Übertext* and the *Untertext* – the vitality of living itself. Living itself can only be a theme in a text – but between the texts, as in Heidegger's ontico-ontological difference, the disclosure of living itself comes alive.

To keep in mind all that Derrida says about Heidegger would be an enormous, if not an infinite, task. Yet there are some key moments such as 'Ousia and Grammé' (1972) and the recent *De l'Esprit* (1987)[15] where Derrida comments directly upon Heidegger texts. Often there is the concern for what Heidegger has omitted or left out. In *De l'Esprit*, for instance, Derrida remarks that Heidegger continually sought to avoid (*éviter* or *vermeiden*) anything that has to do with 'mind' or 'spirit' (*Geist* or *geistige*). He seemed to want to keep the matter of mind or spirit apart from the rest, beyond the pale, outside the corpus of his work. Hence for Heidegger, the mind would be, it seems, another matter, other even than the very matter of the Being of beings. In this sense, the mind – a concern that preoccupied the whole generational lineage from Descartes to Hegel to Freud – has been absented from Heidegger's inquiry into the meaning of the Being of beings. Hence, just as Sartre rejects the Husserlian transcendental ego, so too Heidegger rejects the preoccupation with mind (*Geist*). In this way, he leaves aside the matter of a mind–body distinction, the concern with a self–world relation, the fear of the psychosomatic, the obsession with the empirico-transcendental doublet. Derrida's reading of Heidegger as placing to one side the dimensions of mind or spirit marks a line along the edge of the Heideggerian enterprise.

If there is no place for mind in Heidegger, then can Heidegger himself, or at least his writings, be kept in mind? As Derrida shows in his reading of Plato's pharmacy, such an action would require '*memory*.' For Heidegger, memory is not a mental event. Rather its opposite (forgetting, oblivion, concealedness) is invoked in order to give an account of truth, for truth is the disclosure, revealing, bringing out of concealedness, the denial of what has been forgotten. The task of thinking, then, is a kind of memorial activity, remembering what has been forgotten, disclosing what has been hidden or buried within the western philosophical tradition itself.

But even as a mental activity, memory is itself limited. One cannot keep so much in memory. Hence the need to 'write it down.' Writing an account of Heidegger (or of anything for that matter) obviates the necessity to hold it all in memory. However, just as memory is limited, writing is also limited. The limits of writing show that there is always more to be written down. Yet to note down all the memory traces would not only produce a massive result but would also leave an uninterpreted mess. At the border between memory and writing is the line that separates the two. An epitaph is a writing down of what is to be remembered – most notably, the person. How is Heidegger to be remembered? For his philosophical writings, for his teaching of students, for his political (or non-political) activities, for his party affiliations, for his familial relations, etc.? Biographies will tell. Subsequent disclosures will reveal. But what they tell or reveal are what is presumed to be known about Heidegger – the man. Remarks he made, effects on others, views expressed, statements written, writings published, etc. – all inscribe the life, constitute the memory, mark off the line between the man and the memory, the difference between the life and the life story (the life as written).

One might ask then: what is the bottom line? The answer cannot be other than: living, living on, and living on in memory, disclosing (in the ontico-ontological difference) what must not be forgotten. This is doubtless why Derrida has taken on the task of writing, *in memoriam*, of Jacques Ehrmann, Roland Barthes, and Paul de Man. In each case, the memories are real.[16] They mark the life as relived in memory, memory that when narrated – as in Plutarch's *Lives*, as in Dante's *Vita Nuova*, as in Vasari's *Lives of the Artists*, as in Boswell's *Johnson*, as in Derrida's own account of Plato or even Heidegger – makes the life 'come alive' again. In each case, memory as narrated is written. The writing of memory, memory of one no longer with us, is a writing sometimes without a 'by'-line – just an obituary, a remembering of one no longer living. The bottom line then is living on – in writing, in narrated memory, in philosophy – on the line.

Derrida's pro-gram is not to offer biographies, critical studies, or analyses of texts. Rather his task is to offer readings of texts, to work through a text or network of texts such that the boundaries and limits are respected, the borders marked off, and the margins carefully delineated. Derridean readings mark edges, barriers, or obstructions to the smooth passage through the text(s) in question. They also highlight places of indecidability: hinge elements that separate off and bring together at the same time. In short, Derridean readings mark lines, membranes, hymens, bars, and borders. There is no attempt to claim itself as an alternative philosophy, nor is it an effort at analyzing or offering arguments implicit in what is read. Derridean deconstruction moves to the line between synthesis and analysis, between system-building and critical breaking-down, between construction and destruction. In Heideggerian terms, it does not operate at the ontic level of beings, nor does it attempt to give an account of Being. Rather it is performed or enacted at the very place of difference in what Heidegger would call the Being of beings, the place of truth, of unconcealment, of disclosure. For Derrida, the place of difference is a line, a line between, a pairing and separating. For Derrida, deconstruction will provide an accounting of the very textualities of a text, its lines of demarcation and its lines of contrition, its lines of marginality and its lines of delimitation. The textualities of the text are differential considerations, features that identify and mark as different, that present and postpone the meaning(s) of the text, that clarify and obscure what is happening in the text.

III The between line

In conclusion – so that it will not be necessary to read between the lines – consider the juxtaposition of Heidegger's text and Derrida's text. Mark off the relation between the difference in the Being of beings and the difference in the living on (surviving) and the being – overcome – by death (by drowning), between the 'essence of man' (*Menschenwesen*) and living – on (*Survivre*). Together – juxtaposed – in relations – at the place of difference – between Derrida and Heidegger – is the time of the line, the time of difference, the time of the inscription of living – particular living – as marked out in a reading of the two texts – in short, the time of textuality.

But what are the characteristics of this line between Heidegger and Derrida, this line between which marks off the two in their respective regions of discourse and philosophical practice? In order to provide something like an answer, consider Jacques Lacan's account of the line between the signifier and the signified. In Lacan, reading Saussure with his obsession for anagrams, the very bar between the two aspects of the sign is telling. Lacan shows that in distinguishing and bringing together the binary pair of signifier and signified, word and concept, Saussure offers an example. He wants to demonstrate not only the binary character of the sign but also its arbitrary nature. Saussure's example is that of *l'arbre* or 'tree'. For the signifier, he offers the word '*arbre*.' For the signified, he draws a picture of a tree. But the anagram of '*arbre*' is *barre*. Saussure's unconscious is at work selecting the very example of that word which distinguishes itself from its concept by designating the line between, the '*barre*' between the signifier and the signified. Hence the sign, a unit which gets its identity only from its *difference* from all other signs, is itself compromised by Saussure's very example. For not only does the word for 'tree' in French designate that which separates that word from its concept, but also *l'arbre* becomes *l'arbitraire* – the arbitrary nature of the sign itself. The tree proliferates and also designates the place between the word and its concept: it marks the bar or barrier between and calls that relation 'arbitrary.' The tree, then, becomes the sign that makes the difference, that marks the line between, that is alive with multiplicity: it branches off and is disseminated in many directions – all at the place of difference. Hence like the difference between the signifier and the signified, which together constitute the oppositional sign unit, the difference between Heidegger and Derrida itself marks the bar, the limit, the barrier between the German tradition and the French tradition and yet two traditions whose common border both establishes difference and builds a common market, economic strategy, and intellectual collaboration. Identity and difference – elements of the line, the signifier and the signified of the between – line which cannot be other than their respective texts brought into juxtaposition, brought into confrontation with one another at the line, at the Rhine, the river between, the place where they meet, the place where their respective philosophies come alive. The line therefore is not only a theoretical line, a critical line, a philosophical line, but also a political and textual line, a line that marks all sorts of differences between Heidegger and Derrida while at the same time bringing them together into a vital relation.

The reading of the line that inscribes particular living is also the mark of the line that inscribes the remembering of living. Living that was, living that should be remembered or that cannot be forgotten, living that mattered, living that meant something, living that is distinctly not mine but not unrelated to mine, living that lives on in remembering. The reading of the line of difference marks not just living, but also remembering. Living is not dying. Dying distinguishes itself from living. Dying makes remembering possible. Remembering another is retrieving the other from obscurity, making the other live again – in memory. Marking that memory not only with a memorial, a tombstone, an epitaph, an obituary, a biography, a testimonial, a recollection, or a prayer but also with a reinscription of the line of difference between living and dying as the line of difference between dying and remembering.

The line of difference between Derrida and Heidegger marks other lines of difference. This one line proliferates other lines of difference. If the bottom line is difference and 'living on' – and living marks off dying – and dying marks off remembering, and remembering overcomes forgetting, and forgetting makes way for truth as disclosure, and truth as disclosure occurs along political lines, and political lines are set according to different ways of thinking, then the bottom line for the line of difference is repeated differently, repeated between philosophy and non-philosophy, between thematic and theoretical practice, between the text and its textualities. The bottom line is a shifting line, a line drawn in many places for the purpose of distinction, specification, clarification, identity . . . As a shifting line, the bottom line is repeatable (differently), unfathomable, and without end. Others will live on, others will die, others will be remembered, others will write, others will frame texts. Inscribing the line of difference is not only the marking off of a philosophy of the text, but also a philosophy of life. Like a palmist reading the lines in a client's hand, the text is both a fortune and fortunate. Without it, the lines could not be read. With it, one can, must, will live on – if not in life, then in the differences marked by the text . . .

And thus the final line of each text – *and now there are three*: Two from Derrida: (i) 'I take this unhappiness on myself and I am immeasurably glad of it and to that thought I say eternally, "Come," and eternally it is there.'[17] *And* (ii) 'Not without repeating it, and that goes without saying.'[18] And (iii) – that is, one from Heidegger: this time it is the time with which he ends his letter, whose last line reads: 'I send you my hearty greetings.'[19] The time of the letter has become *literally* the time of the line – with greetings that are sent – not in time – but which will return eternally . . .

Chapter 10

DERRIDA AND SARTRE: HEGEL'S DEATH KNELL

Christina M. Howells

Ils ne savent pas qu'en fait ils décapitent, pour ainsi dire, l'hydre. (Jacques Derrida, *Glas*, p. 118)

Derrida and Sartre spend much of their philosophical energy in a (vain?) attempt to decapitate the Hegelian hydra. Derrida also spends some time in occasional parricidal attacks on Sartre. Both see Hegel as a serious threat, but Sartre tends to confront it directly, through philosophical argument (albeit of a paradoxical and 'continental' variety), whereas Derrida's rebuttal is both more oblique and also more explicit. Both are well aware that the dialectic engulfs contradiction and recuperates any other attempt at subversion as error that will be transcended.

> If one thinks what the *logos* means, if one gives thought to the words of the *Phenomenology of Mind and the Logic*, for example, there is no way out of the absolute circle. In any case that is what the discourse of the *Sa* [Absolute Knowledge] means. To believe one can get out of it, or attempt to, is pure verbalism: one is not thinking what one is saying, one does not realize the meaning of the words which therefore remain empty. (*Glas*, p. 253)[1]

> If you want to burn everything, you must also consume the fire, avoid keeping it alive like a precious presence. So you must extinguish it, keep it in order to lose it (really) or lose it in order to keep it (really). (*Glas*, p. 269)

How to prevent the fire in which Absolute Truth and Values are consumed from becoming, in its turn, an Absolute? How to interrupt the operation of the *Aufhebung*, to manipulate a negative which is more than a mere moment in an all-embracing

169

process, how to escape the perpetual reversal entailed in any oppositional system of thought? As Derrida asks elsewhere: 'What would be the nature of a negative which could not be transcended [relevée]?' (*Marges*, p. 126). It is far from certain whether the ambiguous status of Derrida's parenthetical 'really' (*'vraiment'*) or the vehemence of his rejection of all originary or teleological thinking can ensure his own immunity from Hegel's transformative logic. Far from certain, either, whether Sartre's assertion that 'We must insist against Hegel that being *is* and that nothingness *is not*'[2] can ultimately protect his *néant* against the charge of hypostatization that has been levelled at it.[3] As Derrida and Sartre would (or should?) be the first to admit.

Glas constitutes Derrida's most intensive study of Hegel whom he op-poses (literally) to Jean Genet. And his commentary on Genet is set up, at least in part, as a critical response to *Saint Genet, comédien et martyr*, Sartre's seminal study published over twenty years earlier.[4] Direct reference to Sartre is limited to a few relatively brief passages, but the precursor text underlies much more of *Glas* than Derrida is perhaps prepared to acknowledge. *Glas* might be considered an example of what Harold Bloom would call *Tessera*, a work of 'completion and antithesis',[5] for Derrida certainly 'misreads' *Saint Genet*, creating a most remarkable work of his own in the process. The two main accusations he levels against Sartre's reading of Genet are that it is 'thematic' criticism (*Glas*, p. 181), and that it purports to provide a 'key' (*Glas*, p. 36) to the interpretation of Genet's works. It is true that Sartre does occasionally use the terms *thème* and *clé* (studiously eschewed by Derrida who prefers *foyer, question, champ, chaîne*, etc.), but not in any sense that would make his account either 'thematic' or reductive. Sartre argues that 'Genet is a child who has been convinced that, in his inmost depths, he is *an Other than himself*' (*SG*, p. 47; *Glas*, p. 37). Derrida interprets this as being no more than a rephrasing of the notion that the ego is synthetic and transcendent, in other words a universal phenomenon, not specific to Genet:

General enough to serve as an introduction to the transcendental structures of the ego, it was as efficient and undifferentiated as a *passe-partout* (master-key), as a

universal key slipping into all the lacunae of meaning.
(*Glas*, p. 37)

In fact, Sartre's point is that Genet's 'self' is not merely transcendent like the ego of us all, it is also *experienced* as alienated, 'Other than itself.' An analogous difference is seen as constituting Genet's relations to the imaginary which he envisages not as a *pis-aller* to the real, but rather as a superior order *because of* its very unreality.

Glas probably represents Derrida's most concerted attack on intentional authorial meaning and textual unity: *Saint Genet* also marks the point at which Sartre comes closest to abandoning his attempt to preserve the authority of the subject. Genet is *pensé*, *parlé* (thought, spoken), his words are stolen from him, he cannot *use* language which belongs to the bourgeois so he tries to manipulate *la part du diable* ('the devil's share,' that is, language as it escapes its user) in a refusal of communication which none the less risks being deviated in its turn. But Derrida is singularly unsympathetic to Sartre's discussion of Genet's language, dismissing as 'vague Mallarmeism' (*Glas*, p. 21) his analysis of the ' "vibratory disappearance" of signification' (*SG*, p. 564; *Glas*, p. 21), though the phrase is certainly no more metaphoric than Derrida's own reference to 'the knell . . . [which] marks the end of meaning, sense and the signifier' (*Glas*, p. 39). It is disquieting and intriguing to see Derrida resort to critical sleight of hand of a kind he would certainly castigate in others: he reduces a fascinating and lengthy discussion of a passage from *Notre Dame des Fleurs* which he later examines himself, to the decontextualized (and, according to Derrida, self-verifying) statement that, 'The structure of the poetic phrase reflects very precisely the ontological structure of sainthood' (*Glas*, p. 21; *SG*, p. 563), without giving any indication of the analysis of self-destroying signification of which Sartre's proposition forms part.

But it would be inappropriate in this context to do more than give a few pointers towards Derrida's *misrepresentation* of Sartre. For the 'misreading' is of course no accident – the extent of Derrida's familiarity with *Saint Genet* may be deduced from his use of the text as seminar material at the Ecole Normale[6] – and the reasons behind it will become progressively clearer. More significant, perhaps, than the direct criticisms, are the ways in which *Glas* may be read as an unacknowledged response to Sartre's work, whether by opposing it, striking off obliquely from it, expanding it, or even imitating it. Of course, *Glas* and *Saint Genet* remain radically different in many vitally important respects. Derrida's elaborate treatment of death or of flowers, for example, Sartre's exploration of the 'themes' of sainthood, evil, or the Medusa-like stare of the 'Other' undeniably establish the specificity of their works. And furthermore, certain similarities may be attributed not to any version of 'influence,' however complex, but rather to the way in which the criticism of both philosophers appears to embrace so closely the characteristics of the text under scrutiny.

Like Sartre, Derrida is uncomfortably aware of the hostility his reading would arouse in Genet, who might be amused to be called a '*machine à draguer*' (*Glas*, p. 229), but who would hate to be understood, mastered, or made to serve a 'worthwhile' (anti-)philosophical cause. But whereas Sartre overtly *betrays* Genet by interpreting him and suggesting a possible 'good use' for his texts, Derrida hopes that his fragmentary and 'preliminary' study (*Glas*, p. 229) will obviate the risk of seeming to totalize the writer. However, he realizes that even the least pedantic comments – the least 'hermeneutic and doctoral' (*Glas*, pp. 239–40) – may still become a 'matrix' or a 'grammar' (*Glas*, p. 229), and that Genet would certainly not be reassured by the plea of good intentions:

> He will hate me for it. . . . And in every case. If I support or valorise his text he will see this as a kind of approbation, or even appropriation – masterful, scholarly, paternal or maternal. (*Glas*, p. 223)

Paternal or maternal – for sexual difference, its elision and inversion, forms much of the stuff of Genet's texts. It also appears as intimately if obscurely related to the vexed question of signification. Baudelaire's *Thyrse*, and its 'astonishing duality' is clearly the precursor text here, picked up by both Sartre and Derrida.

> The stick is your will, upright, strong and unshakeable; the flowers are the wanderings of your fantasy around your

will; they are the feminine element executing around the male its prestigious pirouettes. Straight line and arabesque, intention and expression, firmness of will, sinuosity of the Word, unity of aim, variety of means, all-powerful and indivisible amalgam of genius, what analyst will have the hateful courage to divide and separate you?[7]

Sartre's commentary on Genet's use of the image of the thyrse forms part of his discussion of pansexualism:

When it is a matter, for Genet, of marking the relations of a 'queen' with a male, a comparison always comes back to his pen: that of a spiral twisting around a rigid upright pole. And this image evolves to the point of becoming a sexual motif reproduced everywhere in Nature; here it is, first of all, as a *spectacle*:
'The queens chat and twitter around the males who are upright, still, vertiginous, still and silent as branches.'
Then as a *gesture*:
'All the queens imparted to their bodies a spiral movement and tried to entwine the handsome man and wrap themselves around him.'
Then as a metaphor:
'Around some of them, more upright and solid than the others, coil clematis, ivy, nasturtiums, little pimps too, entwining.'
Finally the sexual schema flows over into perception itself: the sky in the midst of the palaces becomes 'the column of azure that marble entwines around.' (*SG*, p. 125)

Derrida takes over the metaphor to describe the way in which 'Genet's sentences wind themselves around a direction like ivy along a truncated column' (*Glas*, p. 87).[8] Further, he imagines Genet's feeling of entrapment within *Glas*'s critical commentary in similar terms: 'He would already feel entwined. Like a column, in a cemetery, eaten away by ivy, a parasite arriving too late' (*Glas*, p. 228).

Sartre's theoretical vocabulary remains close to that of the nineteenth-century poet: he speaks of the inseparability of 'sense' and 'expression' (*SG*, p. 193) even when he is remarking not on a successful act of communication but rather on its inevitable failure in the 'infernal circle' (*SG*, p. 193). Derrida, as we have seen, announces the death of 'meaning,' 'sense,' and the 'signifier' (*Glas*, p. 39), because, in part, of the (false) oppositional system on which they are based. He has argued elsewhere[9] that his attention to the *signifier* does not indicate any ultimate privileging of that element of the binary and hierarchized signifier/signified opposition which he deems to be itself metaphysical, but rather forms part of the reversal phase of the deconstructive enterprise. 'GLAS' is primarily neither signifier nor signified, not simply the death-toll of 'meaning' and 'theme' which remain to haunt any textual analysis, nor yet merely the phonetic decomposition of language into its formal elements. Derrida's tracing of *Gl* through Genet's texts is intended to subvert the form/content opposition which it cannot, none the less, overthrow entirely. Hence the proliferation of puns which depend on the interplay of phonic resonance and meaning, and the neo-Cratylic etymologizing which has the effect of bestowing on the word an autonomy and personal history which appear self-destructive in the immensity of their pretensions. *Glas* represents Derrida's most radical attempt to date to get beyond the infernal interdependence and inevitable failure of semanticism and formalism (*Glas*, p. 165), empiricism and metaphysics (*Glas*, pp. 252–3). 'The complicity of formalism and empiricism is confirmed yet again' (*Glas*, p. 220). Sartre has made a similar point about the complicity of realism and idealism (*SG*, pp. 69–70). Intriguingly, but perhaps on reflection inevitably, both philosophers return the question of oppositions and their ultimate connivance and falsehood to that of sexual difference. When Sartre discusses the pederasty of Genet's texts he is not referring solely to their homosexual content, but rather to the system of inversions, illusions, and betrayal which the texts establish. 'Poetry risks becoming treachery' (*SG*, p. 206); 'He steals a word, just one, and the reader notices that he *is spoken*. . . . Genet's poetry is the vertiginous flight of meanings towards nothingness' (*SG*, pp. 560, 572). 'He forces others to support, in his place, the false against the true, Evil against Good, Nothingness against Being' (*SG*, p. 575). By a quite different route, and as part of his meditation on Hegel, Derrida comes to a similar conclusion about the relationship of difference and opposition to the sexual sphere. Infinite difference is ultimately self-negating.[10] 'Non-existent and infinite difference would thus be sexual difference *as opposition*. . . . And if it transcends [*relève*] difference, opposition, conceptuality itself, is homosexual' (*Glas*, p. 249).

And it is in their relation to Hegel that *Saint Genet* and *Glas* have most in common, for Genet serves both Sartre and Derrida as an ideal foil to Hegelian totalitarianism. But if Derrida owes much to Sartre in his choice and treatment of Genet as an opponent to Hegel, the debt is an unacknowledged irony, for Derrida has been pleased to represent Sartre as some kind of neo-Hegelian interested only in synthesis and totalization. As I have shown elsewhere,[11] Sartre, contrary to Derrida's assertions,[12] persistently refuses to identify being and presence, maintaining that 'the in-itself cannot be present' (*EN*, p. 165), and rejecting the Hegelian notion that 'only the present is,'[13] arguing that, precisely, 'the present is not' (*EN*, p. 168), it is *néant* rather than *être* (*EN*, pp. 164–5). Moreover, he anticipates Derrida's deconstruction of Husserl's *Logical Investigations* in *La Voix et le phénomène* (1967) in his analysis of the presence-to-itself of the *pour-soi* which he sees as a measure of its non-identity: 'If it is present to itself, that means it is not completely itself,' it is a 'way of . . . escaping identity' (*EN*, p. 119). Sartre's *pour-soi* is not Being in any recognizable sense of the term, it is rather the 'nihilation of being' (*EN*, p. 712). The whole argument of *L'Etre et le néant* is to insist 'against Hegel that being *is* and nothingness *is not*' (*EN*, p. 51). Hegel's transformation of negation into affirmation is vigorously resisted by both Sartre *and* Derrida in so far as it risks obliterating difference and reducing the power of the negative to negate. The negative moment of the Hegelian dialectic is precisely that: a moment which will be transcended. Hegel dissolves difference in the eventual unity of being and non-being, presence and absence. Derrida refers repeatedly to the inescapability of the *Aufhebung*, or speculative dialectic, referring to it as an 'inexhaustible ruse'[14] which *différance* sets out to elude:

> If there was a definition of *différance* it would be precisely the limiting, the interruption, the destruction of the Hegelian dialectic *everywhere* it operates.[15]

Sartre's own attack on Hegel is three-pronged – through the

ontology of *L'Etre et le néant* which maintains being and nothingness as radically distinct; through Marxism in the *Critique de la raison dialectique* – for Marx, according to Sartre, never tried to dissolve the reality of human initiative in the welter of historical process; and finally in *L'Universel singulier* where he argues that from Kierkegaard we learn that failure is a subjective reality which cannot be explained away as an objective 'relative positivity.'[16] It is through failure that human subjectivity proves inassimilable to '*le savoir objectif.*' Derrida's response to Hegel necessarily shares a similar focus: an opposition to Hegelian ontology through *différance*; a reflection in *Glas* on Marx's *Theses on Feuerbach* and their attempt to come to terms with the dialectic (see pp. 222–31); and third, a discussion of the struggle by Bataille and Kierkegaard to escape Hegelian totalization through 'a-theology'[17] and a version of Christian mysticism respectively. It is the mystical valorization of failure which exercises a perverse fascination over both Sartre and Derrida (as indeed over Bataille),[18] but which they feel to be ultimately untenable because, as a form of *loser-wins*, it risks becoming inauthentic in Sartre's terms, metaphysical in Derrida's. Kierkegaard faces the same danger as anyone tempted by negative theology: that of falling back into precisely the trap he set out to evade and transforming negation into affirmation. 'Universal negation is equivalent to the absence of negation.'[19] Furthermore, Hegel has already confronted Kierkegaard's argument in advance: absolute singularity is, by its very absoluteness, part of the universal, ultimately sacrificed and thereby preserved: 'It is "saved" at the same time as lost as a singularity. . . . It . . . renounces its singular freedom. . . . "Singularity is absolute singularity, infinity, the immediate contrary of itself" ' (*Glas*, p. 160, quoting Hegel). Negative theology, for Sartre and Derrida, is not truly negative: both philosophers cite Eckhart to illustrate what Derrida calls ontotheology: 'When I said that God was not a being and was above being, I was not thereby contesting his being, on the contrary I was attributing to him a higher being' (*ED*, p. 398).[20] Their objections to negative theology are the same as their objections to Hegel: it is a sophistical reaffirmation of Being parading as negation. It also bears what they recognize to be an uncanny – but strongly resisted – resemblance to their own versions of paradoxical logic. Indeed

Derrida's forceful repudiation of the similarity might be interpreted as *dénégation*: 'This description of *différance* is not theological, not even of the most negative order of negative theology. . . . *Différance* is . . . irreducible to any ontological or theological . . . reappropriation' (*Marges*, p. 6). The vehemence of his rejection of Sartre is perhaps explicable in terms of a similarly close but resisted parallel between his own attempt to undermine Being and that of existential 'nihilism.'

Moreover, it is not simply Kierkegaard whom Hegel has subsumed in advance. As Derrida points out, any 'misreading' of Hegel – including necessarily Sartre's and his own – is always already inscribed within Absolute Knowledge if it does not fall by the way-side 'as a remainder' (*Glas*, p. 259). Hegel has confounded both Sartre and Derrida by enclosing them within the sceptic's perennial dilemma. For if Sartre denies the possibility of absolute, objective truth,[21] and Derrida its desirability, as philosophers (of whatever sort), they are caught in the paradox of necessarily appearing to espouse in practice the truth-claims they are in theory rejecting. This perhaps in part explains their fascination with Genet who seems to slip out of the all-embracing hands of the recuperative dialectician precisely because he has no interest in Hegel, absolute knowledge, or even truth, and refuses to enter the debate except in a parodic mode. For he is evidently familiar with the paradoxes and inversions of negative theology and its Hegelian resonances:

> To want to be nothing is a phrase one often hears. It is Christian. Should we understand by it that man seeks to lose, to allow to be dissolved, that which in some fashion gives him a banal singularity, that which gives him his opacity, so that, the day of his death, he may present to God a pure transparency, not even iridescent? I don't know and I don't care.[22]

Genet may not care but Sartre and Derrida certainly do. And this is the nub of their shared anxiety about 'betraying' the arch-traitor; and perhaps also part of the explanation of their tendency to 'idealize' him by accepting his own self-portrait as villain; for Sartre appears to recognize a degree of authenticity in the simple ethical inversions he condemned five years earlier in his study of Baudelaire, and Derrida writes with unconcealed admiration of Genet's choice to follow a path of danger, terrorism, and revolution (*Glas*, p. 45). Both Sartre and Derrida may *use* Genet to try to get outside Hegelian totality through loss, failure, fragmentation, or some kind of 'remainder', but it is clear that he has not (really) *failed* in the eyes of either of them. Genet's technique of inverting hierarchized oppositions – the most evident, perhaps, those of hetero- and homosexuality, good and evil, real and imaginary, original and copy, fidelity and treachery,[23] communication and non-communication, truth and lies – fascinates Sartre by its unconventional, paradoxical, anti-bourgeois nature, and Derrida, one might surmise, by its proximity to the reversal phase of deconstruction. In *theory*, Genet does not go far enough for either philosopher, he remains stuck at the level of inversion, but in *practice* he perhaps goes further than either, especially as this lack of interest in either synthesis or truth saves him from falling back (or forwards) into either seriousness or metaphysics. His use as a foil to Hegel lies then not so much in a duplication of the Kierkegaardian project, but rather in the way he lends himself to both the Sartrean and the Derridian enterprises: to undermine the overweening Truth-claims of the totalizing dialectic. Derrida focuses primarily on its *telos*, Absolute Knowledge, *le Savoir Absolu*, *le Sa* (*Sa* is, of course, also the abbreviation for the *signifiant* [signifier] and thus an ironically (in)appropriate way of expressing what would certainly fit the label of Transcendental Signified); Sartre on its *process*: thesis, antithesis, synthesis. It is this pattern of negation and recuperation that Sartre uses to *parody* Hegel, for if Genet appears to mimic a dialectical mode of procedure, it is only to undermine it in a sequence of spiralling *tourniquets* which never come to rest in synthesis or totalization. Sartre sets Genet's shot-silk textual and sexual contradictions up against the totalitarian clarity of Hegel's *Logic*, for they lead only to a dizzying repetition of the same self-destroying reversals.

> The dialectical progression . . . curves round to become a circular movement. (*SG*, p. 171)

> A work of Genet's, like Hegel's phenomenology, is a consciousness which sinks down into appearances, discovers itself at the peak of its alienation, recovers itself and relegates things to the rank of *its objects*. (*SG*, p. 145)

Sartre describes Genet derealizing himself in the realm of appearances, in a celebration of falsehood and the imaginary, in a defiance of God and his 'goods':

Nothing on earth belongs to this waking dreamer except lies, falsity and imitations. He is the lord of pretences, con tricks and *trompe-l'oeil*. Wherever objects appear as what they are not, do not appear as what they are, he is king. Fake king, king of fakes. And what is a fake, but the counterfeiting of being? (*SG*, p. 402)

But Genet only imagines his bad taste, it is anti-humanist, an inversion of 'real' bad taste: 'For Genet a taste for the false becomes false bad taste' (*SG*, p. 406). In Derrida's account, similarly, Genet's preference for the *ersatz*, for galalith over marble (*Glas*, pp. 140, 225) is seen as a form of studied inversion related to the pattern of loser-wins: 'The worst is the best, but you must not get it wrong, the worst is not the least good . . . You need to be a connoisseur of fakes' (*Glas*, p. 226).

Genet's preference for the fake subverts the hierarchy of original/copy, but stops short of the kind of radical contesting of origin to be found in Derrida or Deleuze[24] and which has become a *topos* of contemporary thought. For Genet, *toc* still takes its value by opposition to the 'real.'[25]

In his study of the *Aufhebung*, Jean-Luc Nancy cites Ernest Hello: 'Pride, Satan and Hegel give the same cry: Being and Nothingness are identical.'[26] The assimilation of Hegel and Satan throws light on the reasons underlying Genet's 'misappropriation' of the dialectic: 'We have left behind the aporias of Being only to fall into those of Non-Being' (*SG*, p. 173). 'For the Being of Evil is at once the Being of Non-Being and the Non-Being of Being' (*SG*, p. 177).

Genet provides a non-serious opponent to Hegel, for his obscene practical demonstrations of dialectical reversal cast the lofty abstract philosophical theorizing in a comic mode. Sartre's examples are treachery: 'For treachery is not a return to the Good: it is Evil doing evil to itself; two negations do not make an affirmation: they are lost, coiled one with the other, in the demented night of the no' (*SG*, pp. 195–6). And sodomy: Genet's admiration for the homosexual who takes the active role is undermined in a parody of the transformative dialectic which is also a form of self-parody:

> The Tough-Guy is, to speak like Hegel, Evil transformed into the absolute-subject. (*SG*, p. 135)

> 'It was a little later . . . that he understood that his cry, that evening, had been wrong: "A male who screws another male is a double male."' A male who screws another is not a double male: he's a female who doesn't realize it. (*SG*, p. 152)

It is this means of undermining any pretension to a stable truth by a series of reversals which refuses to privilege even its own position, that Derrida has focused on in his choice of initial text for *Glas, Ce qui est resté d'un Rembrandt déchiré en petits carrés bien réguliers, et foutu aux chiottes*[27] in which Genet proceeds by an ostentatious rejection of definitive conclusions:

> To want to be nothing is a phrase one often hears. It is Christian: Should we understand that man seeks to lose . . .? I don't know and I don't care. . . . It goes without saying that everything I have just said only has any importance if one accepts that everything was more or less false. . . . And it goes without saying that the entire works of Rembrandt have a meaning – at least for me – only if I know that what I have just written was wrong. (*Rembrandt*, pp. 22, 25, 28)

The *Rembrandt* text, published in 1967, is clearly full of parodic allusions to the (Hegelian/)Sartrean notion of the universal singular, and verbal echoes of *La Nausée* and *Les Mots*:

> A whole man, made of all men and who is worth all of them and whom anyone is worth. (*Les Mots*, p. 214)[28]

> I had the revelation that every man *is worth* every other. . . . I was incapable of saying how I passed from the realization that every man is like every other to the idea that every man is all other men. (*Rembrandt*, pp. 21, 26)

It also, one may assume, gives Derrida the idea of juxtaposing two contrasting but interrelated columns of text, a technique he used previously in *Marges* (1972). The textual interplay between

Hegel, Genet, Sartre, and Derrida would be too complex even to start to unravel.[29] *Glas* is precisely *not* Derrida's attempt to totalize Hegel, Sartre, and Genet. It is intentionally fragmentary and open-ended, but no more than any other writer can he control the meaning and reception of his own text. *Glas* escapes Derrida in at least two ways: precisely because it appears to *master* the texts he is decomposing, juxtaposing, and deconstructing; and ironically and perhaps more seriously, by in fact constituting the unreadable text he seems to have set out to attempt. As Derrida admits, '*il bande double*' (*Glas*, p. 77), he wants to have it both ways, but above all to be irrecuperable. He approaches Genet in a way which is explicitly *intended* to alienate 'the archeologists, philosophers, hermeneuts, semioticians, semanticians, psychoanalysts, rhetoricians, poeticians, perhaps even all readers who still believe in literature or in anything' (*Glas*, p. 50). If *Glas* is unreadable but not irrecuperable, Derrida has surely failed (really) on all scores.

But when all else fails, magic comes into its own. If Sartre and Derrida are confounded, like Hercules, in their attempt to behead the Hegelian hydra, Genet perhaps succeeds like Iolaus who decapitated it with fire not sword, by dint of lateral prestidigitation: 'Since that kind of operation could not succeed through dialectics, I had recourse to magic' (*Glas*, p. 276, quoting Genet). And like all good conjurors, Genet's final trick is to vanish into thin air, taking with him the magic carpet on which his left-wing philosophical admirers had been standing: the so-called *révolté* who had abandoned literature, published posthumously one last work denying the very title of revolutionary which had earned him such unlikely reverence. *Un captif amoureux*[30] describes revolution as a game – the result of dreams which cannot be lived out (*CA*, pp. 142, 227, 312); his own involvement in the Palestinian struggle as purely artistic and poetic (*CA*, pp. 16, 455), the war as *comédie* (*CA*, p. 202). Genet uses the autobiographical mode to meditate on marginality (*CA*, pp. 203, 350), simulation (*CA*, p. 206), derealization (*CA*, pp. 206, 421), commitment, language, and writing (*CA*, pp. 279, 346, 372, 401). Has the *tourniquet* twisted its final spiral? Should we decide that Genet's 'mémoires' ratify the theories of Sartre and Derrida or parody them in their turn? Like the philosophers, the critic is left empty-handed.

Chapter 11

DERRIDA, LEVINAS, AND VIOLENCE

Edith Wyschogrod

War is both king of all and father of all, and it has revealed some as
gods, others as men; some it has made slaves, others free.

(Heraclitus of Ephesus)

In the field of texts whose signatures are respectively Jacques
Derrida and Emmanuel Levinas,[1] a cut is made which separates
their writing from previous western thought by – as Levinas
remarks of Derrida – bringing to an end 'a naivety, an unsuspected dogmatism that slumbered in the depths of' recent philosophy.[2] Just as Kantianism divided dogmatic from critical
thought, their work breaks with Hegelian philosophy not by
standing it on its head or by reflecting on what remains
unthought in it but by a radical act of secession. Far from
criticizing the theoretical grounds of systematic philosophy, for
such criticism is often reabsorbed by the system, Levinas calls
the sphere of history itself as the domain of violence and war
into question. While Marx and Engels offer a political and economic criticism of Hegel they still envision the possibility of an
intellectual grasp of the totality, a theoretical comprehension of
the movement of history as a whole.[3] Levinas believes that
recourse to the alterity of the other person who resists incorporation into the totality offers a way for transcending the structures of totalization. 'Transcendence in immanence,' Blanchot
remarks. 'Levinas is the first to inquire into this strange structure' which defies the dialectical sublation of transcendence.[4]
Derrida criticizes Hegel for the imperialism of the *logos* which
is to be breached not by a quest for an otherness that transcends
logocentric language but by way of transgression, thus exposing
its diffractions and unmasking its pretensions to certainty and

truth. I hope to explore this difference between transcendence and transgression as it bears on violence and war, a task made easier by the comments each has written of the other's work. Perhaps there is to be found here a bequeathing, a chain of filiation itself born of a breaching of totality.[5]

I From anonymous being to warring totality

Levinas's account of violence is linked to his description of an emergent self. Differences in ontic framework enable the self to acquire its complexity and range from the primordial setting in which it attains separate existence to an ambience in which habitation, work, and cognition appear. Levinas does not provide a genetic account of the self's development but subjects the phenomenological data to free variation. By ignoring some of the self's functions in a given context others are brought to light: the meaning of existence as a separate being, the enjoyment of what one lives on, habitation. The self's distinctive activities reveal a correspondingly amorphous calculus of violence: the wrenching free from undifferentiated being, absorption of the alterity of world and object through cognizing acts, as well as the generally acknowledged violence of murder and war. At each level there is a specific opening for transcendence although once transcendence appears it is traduced by the very framework it pierces.

Derrida's treatment of Levinas to which I shall turn in detail later is heedful of these contrasts which are, in turn, reflected in his own version of the repressive character of the *logos* and the turbulence of writing.

For Levinas, the most primordial manifestation of violence occurs in connection with being-in-general, the *il y a*, that which is before there are separate existents. It is the sphere of the absence of transcendence since there are no apertures through which the traces of transcendence could make their way. Maurice Blanchot interprets the *il y a*, 'one of Levinas's most fascinating concepts,' as an effort to describe the obverse of transcendence.[6] Thus the *il y a* is not the precursor to the God of revelation who will emerge from it in the course of being's self-development. Contrary to Hegel's account of the evolution of the absolute, the *il y a* remains present in the absence of things as a field of forces, an ontological 'black hole,' the sheer fact of being when there is nothing at all. Yet, *before* there is alterity and negation, the *il y a* is seething with the promise of violence. Anonymous and faceless, its being is the being of the end of the world as it is described in apocalyptic literature.[7] In 'Violence and Metaphysics' Derrida contests details of this description but in his own writings on apocalypse, to be considered later, Derrida interprets Levinas as an apocalyptic thinker whose text is a series of imperatives demanding the recognition of the Other. Levinas then becomes central to his own comparison of the temporalization of apocalypse to the time-scheme of writing.

Levinas describes the impact of the *il y a* upon individuals and social collectivities even if, strictly speaking, individuality and collectivity do not exist in the undifferentiated darkness of being-in-general. Because the *il y a* is a kind of pleroma from which there is no exit, the existent encounters it in horror. The only relief from its impingement is sleep but even this can be uncertain because sometimes consciousness balks at sleep. Detached both from objects and human presence, the consciousness of insomnia is depersonalized, experienced not as individual wakefulness but as the wakefulness of being. Consciousness cannot get rid of itself: the weight of its unending presence is experienced as engulfment by the *il y a*.[8]

The only exit from anonymous being is the mastery of being by the upsurge of a consciousness which discriminates, rupturing the anonymous vigilance of the *il y a*, a wrenching free that is itself a movement of violence. More, in taking charge of its own existence, the subject does not overcome violence but enters a new ontic framework in which violence will be differently expressed. But the separated self born with the birth of consciousness as a solitary self exerts a mastery over the fatality of being and can become receptive to the encounter with alterity.

Collective participation in the *il y a* is expressed as the worship of pagan gods which, for Levinas, remains a perpetual human possibility rather than a historical type rooted in the Graeco-Roman world. The separated being that emerges from the *il y a*, 'lives on' the world but still remains at the edge of the *il y a*. The ethos of paganism expresses this precarious existence. It is lived 'at the frontier of a night . . . an ever new depth of absence, an existence without existent . . . outside of being and the world, [the] mythical. The nocturnal prolongation of the element is the reign of mythical gods' (*TI*, p. 142).

Levinas specifically identifies this form of existence with National Socialism and with Heidegger's philosophy.

> When Heidegger draws attention to the forgetting of being
> . . . when he deplores the orientation of intelligence
> towards technology, he maintains an order of power more
> inhuman than technocracy. . . . (It is not certain that
> National Socialism . . . does not rest on a peasant
> rootedness. . . .) It is a question of an existence that accepts
> itself as natural. . . . It is a question of *pagan* existence.[9]

Paganism's potential for violence is different than that of history, for historical violence operates within a framework of war and peace, even if this peace is not that of messianic eschatology. Although war reduces the individuality of human beings and reaches into the *il y a*, it remains a phenomenon of history and politics. 'The art of foreseeing war and of winning it by every means [is] politics,' Levinas writes (*TI*, p. 21). By contrast, the destruction inherent in being-in-general could only be pure and total destruction, an apocalyptic end of human existence.

Despite the paucity of reference to the holocaust of the Second World War, as the abyss of violence, its apocalyptic character for Levinas and its centrality for his thought can scarcely be doubted. As an event of total destruction, it lies beyond phenomenality, swallowed up by the *il y a* on the one hand, and because it aims at faces, belongs to totality on the other. But it is Blanchot, rather than Levinas himself, who tries to forge a language of holocaust by 'a writing of the disaster.'[10] Blanchot refers to the holocaust as 'the *absolute* event of history – which is a date in history – that utter-burn where all history took fire, where the movement of Meaning was swallowed up,'[11] and as 'that which does not have the ultimate for a limit, but bears the ultimate away in the disaster.'[12] For Blanchot, the disaster is also beyond history, the recurrent primal scene of the loss of thought and language. In an interview with Philipe Nemo, Levinas identifies his analysis of the *il y a* with Blanchot's descriptions of the disaster. He writes:

In Blanchot it is no longer being, and it is no longer 'something,' and it is always necessary to unsay what one says – it is an event which is neither being nor nothingness. . . . Blanchot called this 'disaster' which signifies neither death nor an accident, but as a piece of being which would be detached from its fixity of being, from its reference to a star, from all cosmological existence, a *dis-aster*. He gives an almost verbal sense to the substantive disaster. [In this work of Blanchot] the ideas which I hold today are still sought. (*EI*, pp. 50f.)

It is not only Levinas's writing but Blanchot's writing of Levinas's concealed writing of the disaster that is taken up by Derrida, a writing that demolishes both the book and writing and calls for an arche-writing that writes outside the framework of the *logos* and, like the disaster, can restart itself.

II   The violence of economy and polity

The self, now separated from the *il y a*, exhibits a twofold character. On the one hand it is a being that enjoys what it lives on, that dwells and labors; on the other it is integrated into a totality that comprises economic and political functions. History, the account of what no longer lives, rather than sheer separation, constitutes the self of totality, integrating the self into a whole only after death. In its capacity as a living self, separated being exists as interiority, inaugurating a dimension closed to history and therefore also to totalization (*TI*, p. 55). The self of interiority 'lives on' the world in an environment Levinas calls the elemental. Earth, sea, sky, and light which present themselves as surface without underside are examples. Lying half way between blind participation in the *il y a* and cognition, participation in the elemental is experienced as pleasure, as the love of life. The separated self also shelters itself by appropriating some fragment of the elemental earth for habitation so that the self-reflexiveness of interiority can emerge fully and open the way for cognitive representation.

Work also transforms the elemental by altering nature so that things, as distinct from environments, can come to presence (*TI*, p. 133). The primordial model of labor is the hand that simultaneously seeks and takes hold of a goal and is subject to missing its aim on any given try. The end is not represented first but is a result of the process itself. 'The hand is by essence groping and emprise. Groping is not a technically imperfect action, but the condition for all technique' (*TI*, p. 167). Work is the corporeal effort, the foray of the hand in its attempt to subdue nature.[13]

Unlike the philosophies of subjectivity beginning with Kierkegaard that counterpose interiority to system, to a self-aggrandizing totality, Levinas interprets both totality and at least one aspect of subjectivity, its capacity to reduce the otherness of what is not self, as power. Thus, for Levinas, violence is not only expressed as force exerted by the totality against interiority, since the totality seeks to penetrate the space of interiority, but also as the self's reduction of the other to the Same (*EI*, p. 78). Just as history objectifies and engulfs the lives it synthesizes, so too interiority in its relations to need, labor, and habitation reduces alterity. But interiority also initiates the movement towards responsibility for the other. Thus, when asked about the relation between ethics and politics, Levinas replies:

> Politics must always be criticized starting from the ethical.
> This . . . would render justice to that secrecy which for
> each is his life . . . a secrecy . . . which does not . . . isolate
> some rigorously private domain of a closed interiority, but
> [one] which holds to the responsibility for the Other. (*EI*,
> pp. 80f.)

This is a responsibility whose source, Levinas believes, is inaccessible and is therefore 'the principle of an absolute individuation' (*EI*, pp. 81f.).

Not only is the action of the separated self an exercise of power, but, Levinas claims, cognition interpreted as representation is also implicated in violence. Levinas argues that the being that represents is conditioned by already belonging to the world of life prior to its representing acts but that representation appears to constitute the very being in which it is implicated. In fact the representing act substitutes itself *after the event* for the earlier reality. Thus there is an inherent diachronicity that is suppressed in representation, a point that is significant for understanding Levinas's importance for Derrida's discussion of *différance.* More critical for Levinas than the time-boundedness of representation is its reduction of the other to the Same, the dissolution of alterity by consciousness to a content of consciousness. Levinas writes:

> Philosophy is produced as a form through which refusal of commitment to the other shows itself, as waiting in preference to action, as indifference with regard to others, as the universal allergy [an inimical response to alterity] of the first infancy of philosophers. The itinerary of philosophy remains that of Ulysses whose adventure in the world has only been a return to his native isle – an accommodation to the Same, a misunderstanding of the Other. (*HAH*, p. 40)

Levinas most often interprets knowledge in terms of the trans-cendental constitution of its objects. This view, characteristic of the German idealist tradition from Kant to Husserl, takes intelligibility as the end-point of the acts of a consciousness that correlates one thing or datum with another. Sometimes Levinas describes knowledge in Merleau-Ponty's terms as the insepar-ability of thought and expression for an incarnate existent. In either case the alterity of the other is reduced or ignored. More, the much vaunted freedom of action of western humanism is based upon this model of knowledge (*HAH*, p. 13).

While representation reduces alterity, it can just as easily be argued that representation withdraws from the represented, does not alter it and provides an extra-territorial vantage-point for gaining access to it. If action is immobilized in knowledge, why should Levinas regard knowledge along with action as a form of violence? And if representation is a form of power, what can be substituted for it in regulating society? These ques-tions can only be answered by considering the incursions of alterity into totality.

III   The face and violence

The movement of the self thus far described, a self-propulsion towards the non-self that ends in a return to self, establishes the self as an egoism. A break with egoity requires an intentional structure of the separated being that seeks its satisfaction else-where than in the domain of being. Desire provides the requisite condition for escaping the totalizing power of consciousness. Need, a cycle of emptiness and repletion that exemplifies the self's egoity, is distinguished from desire which presupposes a satisfied being and is directed towards other persons. This tropism towards the Other breaks into the self's sovereign existence and puts its own being into question. The presence of the Other precedes all collaborative cultural creations and is the necessary condition for signification.[14]

The Other is given first in a cultural context, but the significance of alterity breaks through this complex of appearances and is manifested as an abstract presence that cannot be integrated into any ontic framework. For Levinas, there is nothing apart from the Other's self-presentation, nothing in addition to the form given to vision. But alterity pierces the nexus of cultural and visible forms by way of the visible world through the phenomenon that announces it, the human face. When it appears in a conjuncture alongside other phenomena, the face is discrete, 'an epiphany,' 'a visitation.' Breaking through its visible form, 'the face speaks. The appearing of the face is primordial speech' (*HAH*, pp. 47f.). The face appears as nude, as without form, as destitute and strange. Because it cannot be incorporated by the self, it challenges egoity and opens the dimension of responsibility for the Other. To be a self in the light of the presence of the Other means being unable to get rid of being answerable for the Other.

Selfhood is now envisaged in moral rather than cognitive or productive terms. This moral self is divested of two features John Locke and others have attributed to it: continuity of memory stream and of body. The first feature reduces alterity to a content of present consciousness; the second allocates to one's own body rather than the other's a deciding condition of selfhood. In rejecting these determining criteria, Derrida continues Levinas's critique of traditional views of self. We shall see that while the existence of an ethical agenda is not obvious in Derrida's work, it is by no means absent. His attack on the subject is linked to a transgressive analysis of truth and certainty that entails moral consequences: 'Deconstruction . . . is not *neutral*. It *intervenes*. . . . [But] there is no *effective* and *efficient* position, no veritable force of rupture without a minute, rigorous and extended analysis' (*P*, p. 93).

With the advent of the social dimension of existence expressed as the desire for the Other, a new possibility for violence is opened up for Levinas. The negation existing at earlier ontic levels – the destruction of things or animal life – falls within the framework of domination and expresses the power of the self. But annihilating other persons is a quantum leap over earlier forms: the killing of the other is murder, an attack on transcendence, on what lies outside the sphere of ontology. The face is in the trace of transcendence, the beyond from which the face comes and which issues from an immemorial past that cannot be converted into the origin of the face. 'Murder exercises a power over that which escapes power. . . . The alterity that is expressed in the face provides the unique 'matter' possible for total negation' (*TI*, p. 198). Because the Other lies outside the self's power, he or she exceeds that power infinitely and 'paralyzes the power of power' (*TI*, p. 198). The fact that murder is committed all the time indicates that what opposes the self is not a superiority of force but the Other's transcendence, 'the resistance that has no resistance – the ethical resistance' (*TI*, p. 199).

Murder which aims at the face must be distinguished from war. Although it is a central motif in his thought, nowhere does Levinas provide a sustained discussion of war. Its phenomenological distinctiveness must be pieced together from numerous scattered remarks in his work. War is at its most primordial level the law of being: 'We do not need obscure fragments of Heraclitus to prove that being reveals itself as war' (*TI*, p. 21). Levinas does not merely claim that war affects being but asserts far more radically that it is the very truth of being. When separated beings move into the objective arrangements of economy, they enter an order in which force is the test of the real. Here violence is not only killing *tout court*, but alienation, 'making [people] play roles in which they no longer recognize themselves' (*TI*, p. 21). Everyone is implicated in the order war inaugurates.

It might be expected that Levinas would identify war with the order of the Same, the reduction of alterity by a consciousness that represents, but he does not do so. It is no surprise that war does not manifest exteriority, but Levinas makes a stronger claim: 'It destroys the identity of the Same' (*TI*, p. 21).

Why does Levinas not hold that war is the *law* of the Same? Because the Same is ruled by representation which is in complicity with war but belongs to a different ontic framework. Representation conceals, while pretending to reveal, the seething turbulence of being. Like Nietzsche, Levinas thinks that war is the king of all, but the 'truth' of representation conceals this and is therefore a hypocritical truth: 'War rends the images that dissimulate reality,' so it cannot be one with these images (*TI*, p. 21). How then does war at this primordial level show itself? 'It is fixed in the concept of totality, which dominates Western philosophy' (*TI*, p. 21). Within totality individuals are governed by forces they do not understand and the meaning of their existences is derived from the totality.

If war is the dark underside of the True, and the Good is the natural concomitant of the True, then the roots of the Good are also concealed in violence. But this is impossible because the Good is by its very nature non-violence, the proscription against killing. Only a hypocritical civilization would conceal from itself the violence of being and link goodness to a truth thus established. This confusion leads to mistaking ethics, which, for Levinas, is the rule of alterity, for rules of prudence that hold sway in the totality. This gesture of concealment by truth of its violent underside is precisely what Derrida will track down in his account of *différance*, dissemination, and the logic of substitution.

IV Derrida, writing and the same

The difference between Derrida and Levinas is the breach between speech and writing, a writing which is itself fissured by spatial and temporal difference. For Levinas, the face, in the track of transcendence, is always already language, a primordial an-iconic speech. This speech is always the same, the silent appeal of the Other to resist murder and to become accountable for the Other in his or her destitution. But it is also an identity in difference, for each and every *differing* face beseeches the self, although in the *same* way. If this speech is to break into language, if it is to 'circulate' within the totality, it must itself become conceptual and not silent speech. Only divine speech realizes itself without defect, while all other speech is a fallen speech. But, for Levinas, speech, and not writing, is pre-eminently language. In a crucial passage describing his differences with Levinas, Derrida comments: 'The aspect of living and original speech *itself* which Levinas seeks to save is clear. Without its possibility, outside its horizon, writing is nothing. In this sense writing will always be secondary' (*WD*, p. 102).

But a close reading of Derrida's account of *différance* may show a pattern of *conformation* to Levinas's view of speech and may serve to disclose surprising affinities between Levinasian speech and Derridian writing. The by now familiar 'concept' of *différance* must be invoked in a context where it is linked to the trace, the track or spoor of that which is absent.[15] Derrida writes:

> *Différance* is the systematic play of differences, of the traces of differences, of the *spacing* by means of which elements are related to each other. This spacing is the simultaneously active and passive (the *a* of *différance* indicates this indecision as concerns activity and passivity . . .) production of the intervals without which the 'full' term would not signify. . . . It is also the becoming-space of the spoken chain – which has been called temporal or linear; a becoming-space which makes possible both writing and every correspondence between speech and writing, every passage from the one to the other. (*P*, p. 27)

For Derrida, the time-design of *différance* precludes the possibility of any element of discourse signifying in and of itself. Each element acquires meaning only through a play of differences, the intersignificative relations to one another of elements which themselves lack self-present meaning. Each element is so interwoven with every other that it is constituted only by the traces within it of the other bits in the chain or system. There are no independent meanings but only 'traces of traces.'

For Levinas, the face, too, signifies in the absence of an origin. Derrida can argue that, for Levinas, the face is in the trace of an originary transcendence, the *fons et origo* of all meaning. But if transcendence is always already past, can never be brought into plenary presence, it is a non-origin. Moreover, as I noted earlier, each and every face signifies the same proscription against murder, although each and every face is unique. This identity in difference opens out into a chain of virtually infinite substitutions in the absence of an origin. Derrida's web of language replicates within language the temporal pattern of ethics.

Still, the model of language proposed by Levinas privileges spoken discourse, whereas Derrida turns to writing. Would Levinas, too, not be better served by writing than by speech? Does writing not neutralize the demands of economy better than speech? Moreover, 'does not the writer who [deprives] himself of the *enjoyments* and effects of his signs . . . more effectively renounce violence?' (*WD*, p. 102). Why does Levinas, Derrida asks, choose speech? Because the face is an an-iconʟ *imago dei* existing in the trace of a fully present divine speech. In this context Derrida claims that, for Levinas, 'The limit between violence and non-violence is perhaps not between speech and writing but within each of them. . . . [The trace] is not to be confused with the letter or with speech' (*WD*, p. 26). The *logos* attributed to Levinas's conception of spoken discourse is a 'broken' *logos*, one already profoundly infiltrated by writing.

In an interview with Julia Kristeva, Derrida comes close to appropriating this conflation of speech and writing as his own position. In the context of the trace, speech and writing appear to function according to the same rules. 'Phoneme or grapheme are constituted on the basis of the trace' (*P*, p. 26), and *'différance* is also the becoming-space of the spoken chain' (*P*, p. 27), Derrida writes. Now, writing is other than graphematic and other than phonetic, and the trace is a kind of contaminant occluding the 'purity' of both speech and writing as well as blurring their boundaries.

If discourse is quasi-scriptic, quasi-grammatological for Levinas as it is for Derrida, is there a moral dimension in Derrida's account of language and being? To be sure, Derrida, like Levinas, criticizes the self-certifying character of truth as a lie discourse tells itself. But is this all? If so, then Derrida would merely appeal to a higher truth, that of *différance* which would become a master concept useful for undermining the lie. But Derrida, like Levinas, renounces the possibility of an anchoring concept embedded of necessity in the *logos* of a self-present speech. Logocentric speech untainted by writing is 'an auto-affection. . . . The subject can hear or speak to himself and be affected by the signifier he produces, without passing through an external detour, the world, the sphere of what is not "his own.'"[16] Is this description of the spoken word not also a condemnation of the monological character of speech? Does the living voice not place the world at the self's disposal rather than the self at the disposal of the other? But even if 'substitution, supplementarity, the-one-for-the-other . . . in its decisive suspension of the for itself' reflect this condemnation, they still fall short of ethics in Levinas's sense as the 'for-the-other of my responsibility for the other person.'[17]

V 'The rotten sun'[18]

Because philosophical language is, for both Levinas and Derrida, metaphorical, and, for Derrida, nothing apart from this metaphoricity guides signification, it is essential to dismantle the key metaphors of western thought (*WD*, p. 92). Both Husserl's phenomenology and Heidegger's philosophy of being depend on the metaphor of light. Whether bringing into view an object for a subject or ushering what lies concealed out of concealment, light is an essential condition for truth. Derrida suggests it may be impossible to philosophize in the absence of light.

Light is necessary for the repressive violence of thought, but language, even the primordial language of the face, without light is also inconceivable. Can there be a common source for the illumination of the *logos* that determines theoretical comprehension on the one hand and the radiance of epiphany on the other? Levinas turns to the Platonic sun which doubles as the source of light that illuminates being and as the Good beyond being, a sun that both creates and destroys the relation of thought and language to being. In his early work, Levinas thinks of this movement as an ex-cendence from being to the Good, from light to sun. This view takes account of two aspects of solar power, illumination and destructive immolation. This duplicitous character of the solar metaphor is a central motif in the work of George Bataille:

> The sun from the human point of view (. . . as it is confused with the notion of noon) is the most *elevated* conception. It is also the most abstract object, since it is impossible to look at it fixedly at that time of day. [For those compelled to

emasculate the noon day sun] that sun must be said to have
the poetic meaning of mathematical serenity and spiritual
elevation. If on the other hand one obstinately focuses on it
. . . it is no longer production that appears in light but
refuse or combustion.[19]

This is 'the rotten sun' that 'loves the night' and directs its
violence. Bataille's metaphor opens the possibility for a black
sun, a lightless orb that is still sun. In *Totality and Infinity* the
sun remains a metaphor for 'heliopolitics' but is also the sun
that stood still for Joshua (a frequently cited reference), a dark
orb like Bataille's but, unlike it, beyond the light of being and
thought and expressing a goodness that is otherwise than
power. Derrida suggests that the controlling metaphor for transcendence in *Totality and Infinity* is no longer the sun as the
neutral Good, but the Good as fecundity and generosity. This
shift may have occurred when, for Levinas, the link of light to
ontology was seen to predominate and only a 'dark' sun could
express an extra-ontological Good.

It is clear to Derrida that the renunciation of the light of
theoretical intelligence is a difficult move for Levinas because
rationality appears to be the natural counterforce to the violence
of the *il y a* and of history. Instead, Levinas posits the complicity
of all three, interpreting the relation of theoretical intelligence
and communion in the *il y a* as 'a premetaphysical unity of one
and the same violence' (*WD*, p. 87). I suggested earlier that
these are linked for Levinas in National Socialism as a 'religion'
of blood and soil that represents a primordial violence of the *il
y a* but also aims at faces, for without the explicit presence of
faces there could be neither murder nor war.

The question of whether infra-historical violence or supra-
historical peace as Levinas interprets them are possible is not
only the focus of differences between Derrida and Levinas, but
opens new perspectives on Derrida's own account of language.
Derrida's strategy is to dissolve the being-in-general and transcendence of Levinas into time-bound or intra-historical functions. This dissolution in turn is achieved by showing that
signification arises as difference, the difference between God
and the world, between being-in-general and the face. I shall
consider each of these in turn.

Levinas, Derrida argues, takes it as axiomatic that infinity cannot be violent but that totality, on the other hand, must be finite as well as the scene of violence. Were it not for God, totality would be a world of unmitigated savagery. But the fact is, it is not. The only condition under which totality would manifest unrestrained violence would be that of a one-person world, one in which there is only a single naked man. In the absence of the single man constraint, if there is more than one person, transcendence enters the world and alters the field of violence. But if per contra there is only a single individual, there can be no war for there is no face, no relation between self and other. In short, in a world where the face is fully respected (a post-eschatological world) there can, by definition, be no war, and, in a world where there is no other, no epiphany of the face, there can be no war (*WD*, pp. 106ff.).

Derrida's point is that war is present in a world in which God is always already speaking, always already implicated in war (*WD*, p. 107). 'We can have a relation to God only within such a system. Therefore war – *for war there is* – is the difference between the face and the finite world [the only 'site' for the divine speech] without a face' [*WD*, p. 107]. But has not the world always been thought of as the site of the absence and presence of God, as constituted by their difference? And is it not only from the site of the world that we are able to think 'the essence of God'? What is crucial for Derrida's own position is his conclusion that 'in a sense our language . . . accommodates poorly, the play of the world that precedes God' (*WD*, p. 107). Transcendence is caught in the web of the world. Derrida can now stand Levinas's claim that we are in the trace of transcendence on its head: perhaps, Derrida suggests, God '*is an effect of the trace.*' The dissolving of transcendence has opened the way for an exclusionary move against all that is outside the field of writing and difference. There remains only the task of showing that self-identical and infra-historical being, the being of the *il y a*, can never be the scene of violence. Only the time and space of event and history can become the arena in which violence occurs.

To show that pure being cannot be the locus of violence, Derrida argues that first, pure violence and pure non-violence are both equally impossible, and second, pure Being is itself an unviable notion. In the first case violence could not occur before there are faces so that a relationship between beings without face is non-violent. (Derrida seems to argue for something like a Lockean state of nature without proscriptive conditions.) But, paradoxically, this non-violence is violence because the condition for violence is absence of relation to the Other, a condition that obtains in pure being without distinction. Without the face there can be neither the initiation nor the ceasing of violence.

On the second point – whether pure being is possible – Derrida appeals to Heidegger's notion of the ontological difference, the difference between being and beings. On the one hand, for Levinas there must be being because without being there is no opening for the face. *Pure* being is pure violence or non-violence, each impossible as we have seen. But as Heidegger has shown, being cannot be an entity apart from beings. In manifesting itself, being always appears as the being of beings and is therefore caught up in history and language and therefore in a certain violence: 'A Being without violence would be a Being that would occur outside the existent; nothing; nonhistory; nonoccurrence; nonphenomenality' (*WD*, p. 147).

Similarly, a language from which the verb to be is absent is a non-language. But this is just the language Levinas seems to favor, 'a nonviolent language . . . a language of pure invocation, pure adoration, proffering only proper nouns in order to call to the other from afar' (*WD*, p. 147). Such a language would exist in a kind of pre-ontological silence; but would not such silence open the danger of 'the worst violence' which would 'silently cohabit the idea of peace.' (*WD*, p. 147)? The silence of peace is a limited silence protected by the violence of language, Derrida claims.[20] Thus, and the point is crucial for Derrida's account of language, 'the violence of war is inescapable' (*WD*, p. 147).

VI   The language of peace

If a purely irenic language is ruled out, is there none the less an 'impure' language of peace? What must such a language be like if it is to express the difference between history and peace within history itself? Does such a language inaugurate a new time and, if so, in what sense is it an apocalyptic language? And how is the end-time of apocalypse related to the end of philosophy described in his own work and that of Levinas? It may be useful to consider the last question first because it provides an entering wedge into Derrida's interpretation of Levinas as, in important respects, an apocalyptic thinker.

In his work on apocalypse, Derrida compares the pronouncement of the end of days in *The Apocalypse of John* with Kant's excoriating of those who pronounce the end of philosophy, the mystagogues who place themselves above reason. Such persons, Kant declares, listen to a private voice, a polysemic voice of pleasure (*TAP*, pp. 31ff.). Such a voice deranges and maddens in contrast to the true voice that speaks clearly to all, that of the moral law (*TAP*, pp. 34ff.). Kant's opponent sees reason as emasculated, but Kant counters that it is the mystagogues who in their anti-rational defiance 'seize the robe of Isis' as if to disrobe the goddess herself (*TAP*, pp. 44, 49). Kant's worry is that the end of philosophy will be brought about by mystification, by the 'tone of apocalypse' (even if Kant almost never invokes the word) that threatens the purity of practical reason.

This apocalyptic tone, if we can imagine it as definable, is characterized by the polysemy of language, by 'grafts' and 'intrusions.' It opens the possibility for another tone other than that of philosophy or 'the tone of another' which interrupts the smooth surface of language and philosophy (*TAP*, pp. 67ff.). The truth of apocalypse is not some content other than end-time itself (*TAP*, p. 69). The truth of apocalypse is apocalypse itself. Derrida's view is well summarized in T.S. Eliot's pub-closing phrase, 'Hurry up now, it's time.' Can we nevertheless abandon the canons of reason? Not altogether, as Derrida stresses throughout his work, because we are 'each one of us today . . . [both] the mystagogue and *Aufklärer* of an other' (*TAP*, p. 53).

The extreme urgency of tone of apocalyptic writing *is* its point. The apocalyptic text summons – when the Lamb opens a seal, one of the Four Horsemen of the Apocalypse says 'Come' – to a destination that is unclear (*TAP*, p. 88). This is because there is no destination: 'The event of this, "Come," precedes and calls forth the event' (*TAP*, p. 91). The call to 'transcend' philosophy is an apocalyptic summoning to inaugurate what philosophy cannot contain. This is precisely, Derrida claims, what Levinas (and Blanchot) have introduced into philosophy. Temporalized as a past without present, the call comes from elsewhere. Because it is without content it is a dangerous call, one that can lead to the violence of authoritarian discourse or the peace of messianic eschatology (*TAP*, p. 94). Distinguishable only by tone, it may be an invitation to go beyond being that does not issue from an egological center and is not addressed to an egological self.

But if apocalypse is a call without issue or goal, is the risk not run of endless apocalypse, an apocalypse without actualization, an imminence that falls short of the end? There would be nothing outside apocalypse, endlessly restarting itself. Does not the transcendental structure of writing reflect this time-design of apocalypse itself (*TAP*, p. 79)?

We are now prepared to examine the extent to which his reflections on apocalypse lead Derrida towards a *rapprochement* with Levinas's conception of an irenic language. If the appeal to alterity is intrinsic to the apocalyptic situation of writing, then writing is itself 'commanded' by alterity and the Other proscribes violence. Derrida's essay on apocalypse is sparked by the essay written in honor of Levinas (*TAP*, p. 79) and reflects a shift from his earlier and more critical essay on violence in which Heidegger is used as a counterpoise to Levinas's anti-ontological stance. In the later essay, Derrida concedes the importance of Levinas's analysis of language for his own view of writing: 'Its force is not that of writing in the current sense of the term; it constrains writing by alone making it possible' (*TEL*, p. 36). Derrida conveys a sense of this imperative by using the familiar *tu*, thereby strengthening the sense of personal address and urgency.

The entire essay ('En ce moment même . . .') can be read as a meditation on the question, 'Who is Emmanuel Levinas?'. The books of Levinas can have no theses, cannot *be* books since they invite the reader to consider him or her self as he (Levinas) presents himself: 'Here am I for the Others' (*TEL*, p. 43). Levinas's text itself will always already have constrained. But whom?[21] Not Jacques Derrida nor the reader, because if Levinas has succeeded, the reader, become hostage for the other, is no longer an egoity. The rejection of egoity is, in this context, extended to include even the natural right of the self to persevere in its own existence. Derrida dislocates the protocols of voice and speech by subjecting himself, the 'author' of an essay on Levinas, to the constraints of Levinas's language of responsibility, to a passivity beyond passivity. 'Here I am,' Derrida writes. Responding to the pressure of alterity, to the text that is and is not Levinas's text, Derrida, who is not Levinas but also is no longer Derrida, issues the call of apocalyptic writing: 'Here I am, now, for the other. Come.'

Chapter 12

DERRIDA AND FOUCAULT: MADNESS AND WRITING

Bernard Flynn

The objections and hesitations expressed by Derrida concerning the very possibility of the project enunciated by Foucault in *Histoire de la folie*[1] (and particularly upon the relationship between madness and the practice of philosophy) are the focus of this essay. Derrida's critique concerns the site – the relationship between interiority and exteriority – that madness and philosophy occupy in relation to one another. Ultimately it is a question of reason and its other. Derrida's objections will, in part, take the form of a problematization of both Foucault's reading of Descartes's *First Meditation*, and the historical significance which Foucault attributes to the *Meditations* in the philosophical project of excluding and silencing the voice of madness.[2] We shall, then, consider the Foucault article which responds to Derrida, or more precisely, which responds to Derrida's critique of his reading of the First Meditation, since this is the only aspect of Derrida's critique that Foucault explicitly responds to. With this article the exchange is terminated; the tone of the last page of Foucault's response hardly invites further dialogue. Afterwards I will attempt to construct a further stage of this discussion by drawing upon other works of Derrida.

The basis of Derrida's critique of Foucault is hardly the pedantic concern that Descartes's *First Meditation* may have been misread in a passage that occupies less than 4 pages of a 673-page book. As is often the case in Derrida's textual practice, a small section of the text is read as the place where fundamental assumptions of work are revealed, or perhaps less successfully concealed, as for example in *Speech and Phenomena*, his reading of the few preliminary distinctions in Husserl's voluminous

Logical Investigations.[3] This practice is similar to the psychoanalytic interpretation of a dream by means of 'irrelevant details' which are produced by displacement and offer a road from the manifest to the latent content. As in the dream, placement offers a clue to significance. Foucault places his reflections on Descartes at the beginning of the chapter entitled 'The Great Confinement.' Here he writes:

> Madness, the voices of which were liberated in the Renaissance but whose violence it had already mastered, will be reduced to silence in the Classical Age by a strange act of force. . . . In the road of doubt, Descartes encounters madness on one side of the dream and all forms of error.[4]

In the transition from the Renaissance to the Classical Age – the transition from Montaigne to Descartes – 'an event happened.'[5] This characterization of an event as *in* history, Derrida contends, constitutes the very condition of the possibility of Foucault's project in the *Histoire de la folie*. Therefore, before turning to Foucault's reading of Descartes, let us evoke Derrida's reflections upon this alleged event which enables Foucault to historicize the confinement of madness by reason, first, in the *Meditations* of Descartes and then in the Hôpital Général of Paris.

Why does the datable event of the confinement of madness constitute the condition of the possibility for Foucault's discourse on madness? As we know, for Foucault, the Hôpital Général – itself not a medical institution – will give rise, by a series of transformations, to 'The Birth of the Asylum'; that is to say, to the medicalization of madness and the birth of psychiatry, thereby constituting a radical silencing of the voice of madness.

> The language of psychiatry, which is a monologue of reason about madness, has been established only on the basis of such a silence. . . . I have not tried to write the history of that language, but rather the archaeology of that silence.[6]

If the confinement of madness by reason gives rise to the language of psychiatry, then it would appear that it would be sufficient to put out of play the psychiatric discourse – 'this monologue of reason' – in order to be able to speak of madness itself. By a sort of condensation, the psychiatrist and his discourse have become the incarnation of the rational and political order which confines madness. But, Derrida argues, 'The psychiatrist is but the delegate of this order, one delegate among others.'[7] One cannot escape the language of order and reason by putting in brackets the language of psychiatry.

All our European languages, the language of everything that has participated, from near or far, in the adventure of Western reason – all this is the immense delegation of the project defined by Foucault under the rubric of the capture or objectification of madness.[8]

Derrida contends that all those who speak this language, including Foucault, participate in this objectification of madness. He thereby implicates Foucault in the very 'crime' that he denounces. This crime is a crime for which there can be no trial, because the very ordered procedure of the trial would repeat the crime itself. For the same reason that the trial is impossible, it would seem that Foucault's project also is impossible, or if not impossible, possible only on the basis of *another project*, not enunciated but enacted and presupposed by Foucault. His book could only be written from a position prior to the division – or using Foucault's word, the decision – separating reason and madness.

Foucault himself acknowledges many of the difficulties that Derrida has evoked, nevertheless as Derrida reminds us, to acknowledge a difficulty is not to overcome it. If Foucault's project presupposes a site prior to the division of reason and madness, he leaves this discussion 'in the shadows' and this is 'bothersome' for two reasons. The first reason concerns and problematizes the privilege accorded by Foucault to the Classical Age in terms of the exclusion of madness. In the Preface to *Madness and Civilization* he writes:

The Greeks had a relation to something that they called *hybris*. This relation was not merely one of condemnation; the existence of Thrasymacus or of Callicles suffices to prove it, even if their language has reached us already enveloped in the reassuring dialectic of Socrates. But the Greek Logos had no contrary.[9]

If the Greek *logos* without contrary reaches us only 'in the reassuring dialectic of Socrates,' then it is not the Classical Age and the discourse of Descartes which have mastered and objectified madness, but rather the dialectic of Socrates is not reassuring, since it also participates in a *logos* without contrary. Foucault cannot have it both ways. In his later work, Foucault will draw this discussion 'out of the shadows'; it would appear that he rejects the radical disjunction that he claimed for the Classical Age and which Derrida criticizes. We shall return to this theme later.

The second reason is more significant in that it is here that Derrida implicates Foucault's discourse – a discourse that would claim to operate at a distance from, and in opposition to, the discourse of reason – within the fundamental gesture of metaphysics designated as a thought of presence whose destiny is to enthrone Reason as the very structure of Being. Foucault wishes to write the history of the division of reason and madness; however, at the same time he states:

> *The necessity of madness*, throughout the history of the West, is linked to the deciding gesture which detaches from the background noise, and from its continuous monotony, a meaningful language that is transmitted and consummated in time; briefly, it is linked to the *possibility of history*.[10]

This connection between the division of reason and madness and the very possibility of history – a connection which Derrida calls profound and which he pursues in his own reflection – none the less presents two problems for him. On the one hand, it evokes again his first objection, namely, if the exclusion of madness is co-extensive with the very possibility of history, then madness cannot have been excluded in the determinate historical epoch of the Classical Age. Is the Classical Age simply an example of this exclusion, and if so, what is its specificity? On the other hand, and more seriously, how can one write the history of the very possibility of history, the history of historicity? If history, tradition, and reason are constituted by the division of reason and madness – sense and nonsense – must not the discourse on this division have situated itself in a region prior to this division? Must not the reason that charts this division be a reason 'more profound than that which opposes and determines itself in a historically determined conflict. Hegel again, always.'[11] It is exactly the work of the 'we-subject,' the philosophical subject, of Hegel's *Phenomenology of Spirit* to see the common root of the divisions that are lived in the determinate forms of consciousness as irreducible and ultimate.[12] The history of the division of madness and reason can only be written by a reason which encompasses the division itself.

> The attempt to write the history of the decision, division, difference runs the risk of construing the division as an event or a structure subsequent to the unity of an original presence, thereby confirming metaphysics in its fundamental operation.[13]

Derrida is not demanding that Foucault give a transcendental deduction of his categories, but rather that he reflect upon the site from which his discourse emanates. Inasmuch as Foucault's reflections on madness and the discourse of order, although by no means identical, are none the less similar to other such discourses – for example, Szasz, Deleuze, Guattari – Derrida suggests, but does not pursue this theme, that perhaps the provocation is an event within psychiatric discourse itself; however, since Foucault has bracketed on principle this discourse on madness, he is forced to utilize a popular and equivocal notion of madness. 'But everything transpires as if Foucault *knew* what "madness" means.'[14] We shall return to this later, but for the moment it suffices to suggest that the pre-comprehension of the meaning of madness perhaps makes Foucault's discourse itself reassuring.

Having shown that Derrida's difference with Foucault is not simply based upon an interpretation of the *First Meditation*, but on the contrary, that his contestation of the reading of this meditation actually illustrates a more general critique, let us now turn to Descartes. Foucault contends that when Descartes evokes all the reasons to doubt – illusions, errors, dreams, and madness – he deals with the latter in a way which is fundamentally different from the manner in which he deals with the former.

> And how could I deny that these hands and this body are mine, were it not perhaps that I compare myself to certain

persons, devoid of sense, whose cerebella are so troubled and clouded by the violent vapours of black bile, that they constantly assure us that they think they are kings when they are really quite poor, or that they are clothed in purple when they are really without covering, or who imagine that they have an earthenware head or are nothing but pumpkins or are made of glass. But they are mad, and I should not be any less insane were I to follow examples so extravagant.[15]

When dealing with dreams, Foucault points out that for Descartes the illusion of the dream is overcome within the dream itself, since the dream, like the imagination of the painter, is limited to arbitrary rearranging but does not create 'corporeal nature in general and its extension.'[16] Thus the intelligible natures remain true even in sleep.

Neither sleep peopled with images, nor the clear consciousness that the senses can be deceived is able to take doubt to the extreme point of universality, let us admit that our eyes deceive us, 'let us assume that we are asleep,' nevertheless truth will not slip entirely into the night.[17]

Truth is the condition of the possibility of the dream. There is a nucleus of truth which is unaffected by the state of dreaming. In the dream, illusion is dispelled from the side of the object of thought; this is not so with madness, where it attaches itself not to the object of thought but to the subject who thinks. Mad thoughts are produced by a subject whose 'brain is clouded by the violent vapours of black bile.' Madness is not constituted by believing in something which is not true, for example that I am sitting in front of the fire when I am in fact in bed. Madness is the impossibility of thought. 'I should not be any less insane were I to follow examples so extravagant.' Foucault writes:

In the economy of doubt, there is a fundamental disequilibrium between madness on the one hand, and dreams and error on the other. Their situation is different in relationship to the truth and to the one who seeks it: dreams and illusions are surmounted in the very structure of truth; but madness is excluded by the subject who doubts.[18]

Descartes exiles madness; for although there are in fact madmen, nevertheless, 'thought, as the exercise of the sovereignty of a subject who puts himself in the service of the perception of truth, cannot be insane.'[19] Just as Descartes exiles madness from thought, the police will intern one out of every hundred inhabitants of Paris in the Hôpital Général.

Derrida objects to Foucault's reading of Descartes on a number of grounds. Let us now attempt to distill the basis of his objections from the details of his commentary. First, he points out that in fact Descartes does not surmount within the structure of truth anything which is subject to 'natural doubt.' Only those things which are subject to doubt by means of metaphysical doubt – doubt for which there is no natural motive – are surmounted by the *cogito* and the veracity of God. Derrida is quite correct when he writes that Descartes 'does not ever set aside the possibility of total error for *all* knowledge gained from the senses or from imaginary constructions.'[20] Things that are simple and intelligible are not affected by natural doubt but only by metaphysical doubt, and it is only they that are, for Descartes, genuine objects of knowledge. All 'ideas' having sensory origin are excluded from the truth; and madness is also excluded, since 'madness is only a particular case, and, moreover, not the most serious one of the sensory illusions which interests Descartes at this point.'[21]

Second, Derrida sets up Descartes's rejection of madness in terms of an imaginary dialogue with a non-philosopher who can appreciate that one might reasonably doubt the senses with regard to things seen at a great distance, but would balk at the idea of doubting that 'these hands and this body are mine,' since the only way one could do that would be to follow the example of the madman. 'Oh! have it your way,' says the imaginary Descartes, 'we would indeed be extravagant to pretend that we are mad; but let me point out to you another experience which is much more common and that will not appear to you as at all extravagant, *dreams*.' Derrida has Descartes proceed in a manner similar to Freud's in his movement from the *Studies on Hysteria*[22] to *The Interpretation of Dreams*.[23] The same non-philosopher might ask Freud: 'How can you generalize your theories and apply them to normal people inasmuch as you derive them from people who are crazy?' Freud might respond: 'Let me point out to you another experience which is much more common, etc . . . *dreams.'*

Returning to Descartes, it is important to note that by altering the pretext for doubt from madness to dreams, Descartes has not only assuaged the fears of the non-philosopher, he has also discovered not simply a more common case of sensory error but in fact a much more serious one. For the dreamer 'is madder than the madman.'[24] The madman is never mad enough, he is not always wrong, whereas the dreamer is always wrong to believe what he 'sees.' However, Descartes must even further radicalize the doubt, for neither the madman nor the dreamer is mad enough for his purpose, since in the dream and in madness the simple and intelligible natures remain. Both the madman and the dreamer know that when two more demons join the three who have been tormenting them, there will now be five demons; thus Descartes's fiction of the evil genius.

According to Derrida, the arrival on the scene of the evil genius gives rise to a situation madder than any madman – total deception, including simple natures – 'how do I know that . . . I am not deceived every time I add two and three?'[25] Derrida also undercuts two other ways in which it might be said that Descartes has interned madness – namely, that of making it an affair of the body, the black bile; or of the will, a moral fault – by pointing out that the evil machinations of the wicked genius affect even purely intellectual operations, for example counting, and that they are visited upon one in such a way that one bears no responsibility for them. Thus Derrida concludes that Descartes has not excluded madness in the manner in which Foucault claims that he has.

> Thus, ideas of neither sensory nor intellectual origin will be sheltered from this new phase of doubt, and everything that was previously set aside as insanity is now welcomed into the most essential interiority of thought.[26]

At this point we rejoin that aspect of Derrida's critique of Foucault which preceded the conflict over the reading of the *First Meditation.* Indeed Descartes has not interned madness in the manner claimed by Foucault, rather he has in fact interned, or excluded, it in another way – a way that is not specific to him but which is coextensive with language as such. Descartes illustrates, or enacts, but does not originate an exclusion of madness:

> to wit, if discourse and philosophical communication (that is, language itself) are to have an intelligible meaning, that is to say, if they are to conform to their essence and vocation as discourse, they must simultaneously in fact and in principle escape madness. . . . By its essence the sentence is normal.[27]

Derrida argues that this escape from madness is not the product of a determinate moment in history, it is rather that which opens history, and speech in general. Let us attempt to illustrate what this means by presenting Derrida's reflections on Descartes. For Foucault, there is a relationship of exteriority between madness and philosophy, and this opposition is engendered by an act of force. Whereas for Derrida, there is a philosophical moment in which madness and philosophy envelop one another, a madness at the interior of philosophy itself: 'the Cogito escapes madness only because at its own moment, under its own authority, it is valid *even if I am mad*, even if my thoughts are completely mad.'[28] The certainty of the *cogito* is not attained by the imprisonment of madness, rather it is accomplished 'within madness itself.' Descartes's hyperbolic doubt and the *cogito* offer a haven for madness because they are gestures that 'exceed the totality' in the direction of infinity or nothingness. If *everything*, including the contents of my thoughts, is false or nonexistent, 'I still think, I am *while* I think.'[29] The *cogito*, even if it is deceived about everything, precisely in this gesture exceeds everything. Derrida says 'that it can be defined only in relation to a precomprehension of the infinite and undetermined totality.'[30] For Derrida this moment of excess, of lack of determination, absence of work, this uneconomical gesture is madness.

Before proceeding to Derrida's conception of the moment of Descartes's confinement of madness, let us evoke the essence of Derrida's critique of Foucault. It is that Foucault's structuralist method, called totalitarian by Derrida, is only capable of dealing with determination; and that it is itself a moment of confinement of madness, to the extent that it reduces this moment of radical indeterminacy, of excess, to an aspect of a specific historically determined totality. Derrida writes, 'I think, therefore, that (in Descartes) everything can be reduced to a determined historical totality except the hyperbolical project.'[31] According to Derrida, philosophy – all philosophy – and not simply that of the Classical period, is constituted by the difference between hyperbole and determination, excess and limitation, the economical and the uneconomical, and ultimately between language and silence. 'Like nonmeaning, silence is the work's limit and profound resource.'[32] It is a silence perhaps like the one Merleau-Ponty writes about in *The Visible and the Invisible*: 'this silence will *not be the contrary* of language.'[33] Derrida does not propose this opposition as an essential structure that would subtend all philosophy as a sort of *philosophia perennis*, since the very notion of essence resides on the side of determinacy. It is none the less for him an escape from historicism; however, the difference is not one between essence and history, but the difference between historicity and history. It is this difference which opens history.

> I believe that historicity in general would be impossible without a history of philosophy, and I believe that the latter would be impossible if we possessed only hyperbole, on the one hand, or, on the other, only determined historical structures, finite *Weltanschauungen*. The historicity proper to philosophy is located and constituted in the transition, the dialogue between hyperbole and the finite structure, between that which exceeds the totality and the closed totality, in the difference between history and historicity; that is, in the place where, or rather at the moment when, the Cogito and all that it symbolizes here (madness, derangement, hyperbole, etc.) pronounce and reassure themselves then to fall, necessarily forgetting themselves until their reactivation, their awakening in another statement of the excess which also later will become another decline and another crisis.[34]

Returning to Descartes, according to Derrida, the moment in which hyperbole falls reassuringly into the determinate is the moment when Descartes reflects and pronounces the *cogito*, inscribing it in a system of deductions and finally guaranteeing its stability across time by the veracity of God. Ultimately the *cogito* is stabilized by its entry into a language which is finalized toward communication. The moment when madness is excluded is not that of the *cogito*, but rather the moment when the *cogito* appears as such for another. The *cogito* can function as the basis of the Cartesian system only when its duration is stabilized by divine veracity, and this is clearly specific to the philosophy of Descartes. For Derrida, the moment when philosophy as such constitutes itself as a barrier against madness is the moment when hyperbole becomes discourse – a moment in which the silence, which like madness is the absence of work, comes to be inscribed in communication, in a work: '*At its height* hyperbole, the absolute opening, the uneconomic expenditure, is always reembraced by an *economy* and is overcome by economy.'[35] And this applies to Foucault's discourse as well. The liberation of yesterday's madman is co-substantial with the gesture by which the madness within us is interned and silenced.

Now let us turn to Foucault's response to Derrida's critique. Foucault chose to respond only to Derrida's critique of his reading of the *First Meditation*, but implicitly his response contains a more general reproach concerning the nature of philosophical discourse, and its relation to other discourses. Foucault's response is powerful and interesting. Perhaps it is even more interesting as an adumbration of the trajectory of his later work than as a response to Derrida. As with our presentation of Derrida's critique of Foucault's Descartes interpretation, we will not follow each moment but try to present the general thrust of his response. For me, the center of gravity of Foucault's response is a distinction that he locates in the heart of the *Meditations*, and which we enter by means of Foucault's reflection on the title of Descartes's work.

We must keep in mind the very title of 'meditations.' Any discourse, whatever it be, is constituted by a set of utterances which are produced each in its place and time, as so many discursive events. If it is a question of a pure demonstration, these utterances can be read as a series of events linked one to another according to a certain number of formal rules; as for the subject of the discourse, he is not implicated in the demonstration: he remains, in relation to it, fixed, invariable and as if neutralized. On the other hand a 'meditation' produces, as so many discursive events, new utterances which carry with them a series of modifications of the enunciating subject: through what is said in meditation, the subject passes from darkness to light, from impurity to purity, from the constraint of passions to detachment, from uncertainty and disordered movements to the serenity of wisdom, and so on. In meditation, the subject is ceaselessly altered by his own movement; his discourse provokes effects within which he is caught; it exposes him to risks, makes him pass through trials or temptations, produces states in him, and confers on him a status of qualification which he did not hold at the initial moment.[36]

As readers of *Discipline and Punish* know, Foucault has done a study of the spiritual writings of Jean-Baptiste de La Salle and Ignatius Loyola.[37] In his response to Derrida, he proceeds to read the *Meditations* as a spiritual exercise, the goal of which is the transformation of the meditating subject. A meditation, or spiritual exercise, does not simply establish a truth, rather it engenders a subject who is capable of seeing the truth that it has established. The meditation produces effects which either enable the subject to continue to pursue the meditation, or which disqualify him from proceeding any further. Foucault divides Descartes's *Meditations*; he shows that within them there are indeed passages which are intelligible as a 'systematic stringing together of propositions – moments of pure deduction.'[38] According to Martial Guéroult's classic commentary on Descartes, *Descartes' Philosophy Interpreted According to the Order of Reasons*,[39] as the title would indicate, all the propositions in the *Meditations* can be construed as such. However, Foucault argues that there is also a dimension of the *Meditations* which is an exercise 'by which each reader must be affected, if in turn he wants to be the subject enunciating this truth on his *own behalf*.'[40] He claims that between these two dimensions there is a 'chiasma,' a crossing over of the two forms of discourse; and the place of this intersection is the opposition between madness and dreaming.

Descartes proposes a practical syllogism: I must distrust any source of information that has ever deceived me; in fact I must treat as false any information that comes to me from a source which had ever deceived me. Since the senses are clearly such a source of information, in that I have been deceived by them in the past, I must therefore reject all sense knowledge. But there are perceptions that 'one can not rationally doubt.'[41] Why can one not rationally doubt certain perceivable things, when we have just established a binding and rational syllogism the conclusion of which was that *all* sense knowledge was subject to doubt? It is at this point that the dimension of the *Meditations* as an exercise enters the text. The subject simply cannot bring himself to doubt things that are perceived up close – for example, that he has a body, etc. The subject cannot make himself a universally doubting subject, even though we have concluded from the above syllogism – a syllogism which links propositions according to formal rules and excludes the subject and its capacities – that everything is dubious. This incapacity to doubt marks 'the point of intersection of the two discursive forms – that of system and that of the exercise.'[42] In order to become capable of doubting everything, the subject will have to undergo a modification because although the things are already dubious, the subject is incapable of doubting them. The obstacle to doubt is the suspicion that if I were to doubt that I am sitting here by the fire, etc., then my enterprise would no longer be rational. Why? Because there are in fact people who are deluded or confused about their actual state – they believe that they are kings when they are poor, that they are dressed when they are naked, etc. – Foucault argues that implicitly a test, an exercise, is proposed: if I were to follow their example I would be able to doubt my state of actuality, I would constitute myself as a subject capable of calling everything into doubt, but in so doing I would disqualify myself as a rational subject in search for truth, I would be as 'extravagant' as they. The test is proposed but dropped. The resistance of actuality to the exercise of doubt is reduced by too strong an example: the possibility of madness annuls the very possibility of valid meditation. The two qualifications, 'doubting subject' and 'meditating subject,' are not in this case simultaneously possible.

Foucault notes that Descartes uses the Latin word *insanus* to characterize people whose brains are clouded by the vapors of black bile. This term has a medical connotation. Whereas when he admonishes us not to follow their example, he uses the term *demens*, a term which has a juridical rather than a medical connotation. These people are disqualified when it comes to 'speaking, promising, pledging, signing, starting a legal action, etc.';[43] and Foucault adds, they are also disqualified as subjects of a meditation finalized toward truth. At this point Descartes proposes another test, another attempt to modify the subject in such a way as to become a subject capable of universal doubt. He evokes sleeping and dreaming; they are not qualities of other people but rather virtualities of any subject; they are frequent occurrences and are accessible by memory. Dreaming also, like madness, renders dubious my state of actuality: am I sitting here dressed or in bed naked? Like the invocation of the example of madness, thinking about dreaming is an exercise, a risk, a modification of the subject, a stupefaction at not knowing whether one is awake or asleep.

> But in modifying him, in making him a subject uncertain of being awake, thinking about dreams does not disqualify him as meditating subject: even though transformed into a 'subject supposedly asleep,' the meditating subject can safely pursue the progression of his doubt.[44]

As we have seen, for Derrida the transition from madness to dreaming has two motives: first, it has a pedagogic advantage – it does not frighten off our interlocutor; second, it is a more radical problematization of sense perception – the dreamer is madder than the madman. Derrida effects this transformation by what Foucault calls 'inventing voices beneath the text.' For Derrida it is in response to the objection by the non-philosopher that Descartes moves from madness to dreaming. Foucault's objection to this procedure is important for it bears on the status of philosophical discourse as such. Derrida, as we have shown above, sees in philosophy a moment of excess, a moment that exceeds the totality of being and a 'fall' into determinacy. If this is the case, there can be no question of excluding madness, or anything else. There is no 'outside' of philosophy. There is rather an outside within philosophy, in fact Derrida has argued that the notions of 'inside' and 'outside' are fundamental meta-physical concepts. If this is so, then Foucault's use of the notion of excluding, a putting outside, is well within the providence of metaphysical discourse. Foucault's objections can be summarized as follows: first, the argument that we have just presented in which Foucault tries to show the radical disjunction between madness and dreaming; second, that Derrida imagines that madness is excluded by a non-philosopher; third, that Derrida removes any philosophical status from exclusion by characterizing it as 'naive and rustic.' What is at stake is not simply the question whether madness is exterior to philosophy, but rather by implication whether or not there is an exterior of philosophy. Let us deal quickly with the second and third of Foucault's objections, then turn to his treatment of the evil genius, and finally return to the basic argument by which madness is excluded by Descartes. It seems to me that the second and third objections depend upon the first. In Derrida's presentation, it is not the non-philosopher who excludes madness, it is rather that he presents Descartes with a motive to move on to a better and more radical example. (If, in fact, a more radical example is what is in dispute.) Besides 'non-philosophers' who talk to Descartes quickly become philosophers. As for the third objection, there is a question of denying philosophical status to Foucault's exclusion only if dreaming is not a more radical example than madness, and again this is what is in dispute.

The status of dreaming notwithstanding, the man subjected to the machinations of the evil genius would seem to be further removed from the truth than any madman. Foucault points out that there is an opposition between the figure of the madman – who believes what he should not, believes that he is a king when he is poor – and the man beset by the evil genius who cannot believe anything whatsoever. However, it is unclear to me what Foucault makes of this, since both the madman and the evil genius enter the text of Descartes only to provoke doubt; and reflection on the madman and the evil genius both, in different ways, does this. Foucault's basic problem with Derrida's use of the evil genius is that he does not note the extent to which 'the episode of the evil genius is a voluntary, controlled exercise, mastered and carried out from start to finish by a meditating subject who never lets himself be surprised.'[45] There is a distinct difference between Foucault's treatment of

215

the hypothesis of the evil genius and his two earlier tests – namely, madness and dreaming, where the one is excluded, the other enacted. Both modify the subject, the one to the point of disqualifying it, the other enabling it to continue. For him this hypothesis appears not to modify the subject at all. Indeed it is voluntary and controlled, but so are the other two tests. Descartes at no point proposes that I become mad, he only states that 'perhaps I might compare myself to certain persons etc.'. This act of comparison is voluntary and controlled, and no less so than the fiction of the evil genius. It seems to me that this is very much Derrida's point: within a reasonable conversation madness could only be evoked as a fiction which would have no more disorienting power than the fiction of the evil genius; and in fact, if Derrida is right, it would be less disorienting.

Now let us return to the heart of Foucault's objections to Derrida; it involves Foucault's attempt to read the *Meditations* as an exercise. As was noted above, Derrida never replied to Foucault concerning this issue. This being the case, I will nevertheless attempt to construct a possible response to Foucault based on Derrida's writings; of course I am not claiming to speak in Derrida's voice, a project that would make readers of his work wince or chuckle. What does it mean to read the *Meditations* as a criss-crossing of 'pure demonstration' in which the subject is not implicated, and as a series of discursive events in which the subject is modified? Is not Foucault suggesting that this second dimension of the work must be read in terms of Descartes's *intention* to produce modifications in the subject? The question is: is such a form of writing possible, can one read a text in terms of the intentions of its author? A spiritual exercise orchestrates itself in terms of an attempt to link, to weld, writing to experience – to the presence of a subject. Devotional writing aims at implicating a particular subject, or engendering a particular type of subject; it tries to specify a context, to link writing to the structure of an event. As Foucault writes: 'But above all, differences at the level of what happens in the meditation, at the level of the *events* which follow one another, *acts* carried out by the meditating subject . . . *effects* produced in the meditating subject . . . the qualification of the meditating subject.'[46]

What we are suggesting is that Foucault is reading the *Medi-*

tations in terms of a theory of the success or failure of performative utterances. Let us quote Austin, as cited by Derrida in 'Signature Event Context':

> Speaking generally, it is always necessary that the *circumstances* in which the words are uttered should be in some way, or ways, *appropriate*, and it is very commonly necessary that either the speaker himself or other persons should *also* perform certain *other* actions, whether 'physical' or 'mental' actions or even acts of uttering further words. Thus, for naming the ship, it is essential that I should be the person appointed to name her, for (Christian) marrying, it is essential that I should not be already married with a wife living, sane and undivorced, and so on.[47]

Might we not continue Austin's series of examples by adding: for being a meditating subject searching after truth, it is necessary that I not be *demens*. Against this attempt to link writing to a specific event or context, let us evoke all that Derrida has written concerning the radical de-contextualizing quality of writing as such.

> this unity of the signifying form is constituted only by its iterability, by the possibility of being repeated in the absence not only of its referent, which goes without saying, but of a determined signified or current intention of signification, as of every present intention of communication. This structural possibility of being severed from its referent or signified (and therefore from communication and its context) seems to me to make of every mark, even if oral, a grapheme in general, that is . . . the nonpresent *remaining* of a differential mark cut off from its alleged 'production' or origin.[48]

What we are claiming is that Foucault has credited Descartes with having achieved a form of writing which is impossible. Writing, according to Derrida, entails the 'disqualification or the limit of the concept of the "real" or "linguistic" context, whose theoretical determination or empirical saturation are, strictly speaking, rendered impossible or insufficient by writing.'[49] The essentially iterable character of writing dis-joins it, not from all context, but from any specific context or singular event. Indeed

Derrida has shown us throughout the course of his writings that the desire to occult the essential iterability of writing, thereby rendering it indissolubly linked to the event of self-presence, is the constitutive, if impossible, desire of metaphysics. Foucault reads Descartes as if he had fulfilled this desire when he links the meaning of Descartes's text to 'the series of events (acts, effects, qualifications) which the discursive practice of meditation carries with it.'[50]

It is true that the project of the writer of spiritual exercises is to link his writing to events in the experience of a subject, to a passage 'from darkness to light, from impurity to purity, from the constraint of passions to detachment';[51] however, this desire is thwarted by the divine (as Hegel would have it) or demonic nature of language. It is frustrated because the essential iterability of writing carries with it the possibility of a re-contextualization without reference to the signifying intentions of the author, the context of its production, or the event in the experience of a subject from which it would proceed or to which it would give rise. For example, the pious spiritual exercises of a Jean-Baptiste de La Salle or an Ignatius Loyola may become texts read by a non-religious French philosopher writing a book on the origins of the disciplinary society. To my mind, Foucault, in linking the meaning of Descartes's text to the context in which it would count as a performative success, and to the events that it must engender, has produced a deeply metaphysical reading of Descartes which fundamentally never replies to Derrida's problematization of the possibility of his discourse on madness – his project 'to speak madness itself.'

If it is impossible to qualify or disqualify a discourse in terms of its relation to a specific context, then the intersection of discourse and madness must be thought not at the juncture of specific discourses and their contexts, but rather at the intersection of discourse and silence. It is as such that Derrida reads the writings of Antonin Artaud. In 'La Parole soufflée,'[52] he reads the 'work' of Artaud as a work which promises, and defers, its withdrawal into silence.

NOTES

Introduction

1 Some will wish to contest our selections themselves. We include Freud among the philosophers, and those who are wont to worry whether Nietzsche or Foucault are really philosophers will be demonstrating more about their own prejudices than what is really at issue. Our concern has not been canonical but rather philosophical: how does contemporary continental thinking constitute itself and establish its historical (or in some cases, neo-historical) formations? Here philosophizing involves rethinking history as well. Reading the history of philosophy is also a rereading of the contemporary age.

2 See for example: Irene Harvey, *Derrida and the Economy of Différance* (Bloomington, Indiana University Press, 1986); Christopher Norris, *Deconstruction: Theory and Practice* (London, Methuen, 1982) and *Derrida* (London, Fontana Modern Masters, 1987); Hugh J. Silverman and Don Ihde, eds, *Hermeneutics and Deconstruction* (Albany, SUNY Press, 1985); John Sallis, ed., *Deconstruction and Philosophy* (Chicago, University of Chicago Press, 1987); Rodolphe Gasché, *The Tain of the Mirror: Derrida and the Philosophy of Reflection* (Cambridge, Harvard University Press, 1986); Hugh J. Silverman, *Inscriptions: Between Phenomenology and Structuralism* (London and New York, Routledge & Kegan Paul, 1987).

3 Currently moving into successive final stages of preparation are CP-III: *Postmodernism in Philosophy and Art*; CP-IV: *Gadamer and Hermeneutics*; CP-V: *Questioning Foundations*.

Chapter 1   Plato's *Pharmakon*: between two repetitions

1 This statement of Derrida's was made during a discussion that followed the delivery of his lecture 'Différance' at the Sorbonne in

1968. It appears in D. Wood and R. Bernasconi, eds, *Derrida and Différance* (Evanston, Northwestern University Press, 1988), pp. 83–95.

2 Jacques Derrida, *Dissemination*, trans. Barbara Johnson (Chicago, University of Chicago Press, 1981), p. 98. Henceforth (*D*).

3 Jacques Derrida, *Positions*, trans. Alan Bass (Chicago, University of Chicago Press, 1981), pp. 43ff. On contradiction and dialectics, see also his *Writing and Difference*, trans. Alan Bass (Chicago, University of Chicago Press, 1978), pp. 246ff. Henceforth (*WD*).

4 Plato, *Statesman*, 277d–e. On the difference between Derrida's and Plato's notion of weaving (*symploke*), see Rodolphe Gasché, *The Tain of the Mirror: Derrida and the Philosophy of Reflection* (Cambridge, Mass., Harvard University Press, 1986), pp. 95ff.

5 Plato, *Phaedrus*, in E. Hamilton and H. Cairns, eds, *The Collected Dialogues of Plato* (Princeton, Princeton University Press, 1969), 235a. Henceforth cited by Dialogue and Stephanus number).

6 Ronna Burger's excellent book, *Plato's Phaedrus: A Defense of a Philosophic Art of Writing* (Montgomery, University of Alabama Press, 1980), has an important discussion of this speech that takes Derrida's work on Plato into account.

7 Jacques Derrida, *Of Grammatology*, trans. Gayatri Chakravorty Spivak (Baltimore, Johns Hopkins University Press, 1980), p. 160.

8 John Sallis has an important discussion of this issue in his major work on Plato: *Being and Logos: The Way of Platonic Dialogue* (New York, Humanities Press, 1987).

9 For example, in Book X of the *Republic* and in the discussion of writing and painting towards the end of the *Phaedrus*.

10 cf. (*D*), p. 16.

11 (*D*), p. 85. In Egyptian mythology, Thoth (Theuth), the god of writing is assigned to replace the absent sun god at night. Thus Thoth is the moon god. See (*D*), p. 89.

Chapter 2   Mysticism and transgression: Derrida and Meister Eckhart

1 I use the following abbreviations to the works of Derrida:
  ED *L'Ecriture et la différence* (Paris, Editions de Seuil, 1967).
  Mdp Marges de la philosophie (Paris, Editions de Minuit, 1972).
  MoP Margins of Philosophy, trans. Alan Bass (Chicago, University of Chicago Press, 1982).
  WD *Writing and Difference*, trans. Alan Bass (Chicago, University of Chicago Press, 1978).

2 I use the following abbreviations to the works of Eckhart:

Q   *Meister Eckhart: Deutsche Predikte und Traktate*, ed. J. Quint (München, Carl Hanser Verlag, 1963).

C-M *Meister Eckhart: The Essential Sermons, Commentaries, Treatises, and Defense*, trans. Edmund Colledge and Bernard McGinn (New York, Paulist Press, 1981).
In this text, I employ Alan Bass's translation from the French, which seems to me a fair rendering of Eckhart's German.

3 Mark Taylor, *Erring: A Postmodern A/Theology* (Chicago, University of Chicago Press, 1984).

4 Derrida clearly dissociates himself from any outright denial of reference in 'Limited Inc., a b c', trans. Samuel Weber, *Glyph* 2 1977, pp. 192–8. See also Derrida's interview 'Deconstruction and the Other,' in Richard Kearney, ed., *Dialogues with Contemporary Continental Thinkers* (Manchester, Manchester University Press, 1984), especially p. 123.

5 See my *The Mystical Element in Heidegger's Thought* (Athens, Ohio University Press, 1978; reprint: New York, Fordham University Press, 1986), pp. 228–35. See 'Idolatry and Metaphysics,' the 'Introduction' to the Fordham reprint, for another discussion of deconstruction and mysticism.

6 The best discussion of this is Bernard McGinn, 'Eckhart's Condemnation Reconsidered,' *The Thomist* 44, 1980, pp. 390–414.

7 I have discussed this point in detail in my 'The Nothingness of the Intellect in Meister Eckhart's *Parisian Questions*,' *The Thomist* 39, 1975, pp. 85–115.

8 In 'Neoplatonic Henology as an Overcoming of Metaphysics,' *Research in Phenomenology* 13, 1983, pp. 25–42, Reiner Schürmann distinguishes Eckhart's 'negative theology' (the doctrine of God as a highest being, the subject matter of onto-theo-logic) from his 'henology' (the Godhead as a process of coming to be, *Wesen*, *Anwesen*), arguing that the latter, as a non-entitative experience of Being as process, overcomes metaphysics. This point also applies to Plotinus (see *MdP*, pp. 187, 206; *MoP*, pp. 157, 172). I will touch upon this dimension of process and overflow in Eckhart in the third part of this study.

9 See Frank Tobin, *Meister Eckhart: Thought and Language* (Philadelphia, University of Pennsylvania Press, 1986), pp. 76–77.

10 ibid., pp. 171–9. See also Michel de Certeau, 'Mystic Speech,' in his *Heterologies: Discourse on the Other*, trans. B. Massumi (Minneapolis, University of Minnesota Press, 1986), pp. 80–100.

11 There is thus even a Marxist interest in Eckhart: see A. Hans, 'Maitre Eckhart dans le miroir de l'idéologie marxiste,' *La vie spirituelle* 124, 1971, pp. 62–79.

12 John D. Caputo, *Radical Hermeneutics: Repetition, Deconstruction and the Hermeneutic Project* (Bloomington, Indiana University Press, 1987). See chapter 9, 'An Ethics of *Gelassenheit*', pp. 265–6.

13 In the time since I completed this essay, Derrida has published 'Comment ne pas parler? Dénegations,' in *Psyché: inventions de l'autre* (Paris, Galilée, 1987), pp. 535–96, which is an exciting discussion of negative theology *vis-à-vis* the work of the Catholic theologian and philosopher Jean-Luc Marion.

Chapter 3   Derrida and Descartes: economizing thought

1 This can be seen in Jacques Derrida's critique of Foucault in 'Cogito and the History of Madness,' and in his allusions to Foucault in his later essay 'Sign, Structure and Play in the Human Sciences,' in *Writing and Difference*, trans. Alan Bass (Chicago, University of Chicago Press, 1976), henceforth (*WD*); references to Michel Foucault are from *Folie et déraison: L'Histoire de la folie à l'age classique* (Paris, Gallimard, 1966), henceforth (*HF*).

2 Jean-Luc Marion examines the relation of fiction to certainty by considering the self-made character of science in *Sur la théologie blanche de Descartes* (Paris, Presses Universitaires de France, 1981), pp. 231–340. His analysis is elucidated and critiqued by Marjorie Grene in *Descartes* (Minneapolis, University of Minnesota Press, 1985), pp. 78–85. Both Marion and Grene focus on Descartes's use of fiction in his elaboration of hypothetical discourse, rather than focusing on its figurative and rhetorical character.

3 The effort to read Descartes 'intertextually,' to use Kristeva's term, is intended as a critique of the traditional way of reading the Cartesian text according to an ascending hierarchy that culminates in the *Meditations*, and which is supposed to reflect according to Guéroult the 'order of reasons,' in his 'Introduction' to *Descartes and The Order of Reasons* (Evanston, Northwestern University Press, 1985).

4 All the references to Descartes are from *The Philosophical Works of Descartes*, trans. Elisabeth S. Haldane and G.R.T. Ross (Cambridge, Cambridge University Press, 1969), vol. 1. Henceforth (*HR*).

5 Foucault interprets the performative aspects of the Cartesian text as further proof for the exclusion of madness. See Appendix II to (*HF*).

6 This interpretation of language and its elaboration into a theory of representation is based on Kristeva's reading of Bakhtin, in 'The Word, the Dialogue and the Novel,' in *Desire and Language*, trans.

L. Roudiez and A. Jardine (New York, Columbia University Press, 1980), pp. 64–89.

7 Foucault, *L'Archéologie du savoir* (Paris, Gallimard, 1969), pp. 31–43.

8 For an analysis of the problem of language for the baroque and the emergence of Classical discourse, see my *Subjectivity and Representation in Descartes: The Origins of Modernity* (Cambridge, Cambridge University Press, 1988), chapter 1.

9 One of the major ambiguities in Derrida's reading of Descartes is his explicit re-use of Foucault's terminology of madness, which results in overemphasizing the role of madness, while attempting to put its exclusionary logic into question.

10 For Derrida's critique of humanism, which elaborates Heidegger's critique, see 'The Ends of Man,' in *Margins of Philosophy*, trans. Alan Bass (Chicago, University of Chicago Press, 1982), pp. 109–36.

11 For a historical analysis of the paradoxical centrality of God in Pascal, and man's place, see Lucien Goldmann's elaboration of *deus absconditus* in *Le Dieu caché: étude sur la vision tragique dans les pensées de Pascal et dans le théatre de Racine* (Paris, Gallimard, 1959), pp. 32–49, 71–94.

12 Blaise Pascal, *Les Pensées*, ed. L. Lafuma (Paris, Seuil, 1963), pp. 550–1; Pascal interprets Descartes's mathematical certitude as inconclusive, since for him mathematics as a game of man-created rules cannot provide the metaphysical grounding that Descartes is seeking. For Pascal's critique of mathematics, see *De l'esprit géométrique et de l'art de persuader* (Paris, Seuil, 1963), pp. 348–59.

13 Pascal, *Les Pensées*, 1963, p. 551 (my translation).

14 Although Derrida refers explicitly to the notion of game in Lévi-Strauss, his elaboration of play as a theoretical concept is based on the Nietzschean interpretation of play as we can see in his discussion in 'Sign, Structure and Play,' in (*WD*), pp. 289–92.

15 Derrida's critique of the concept of economy is elaborated in his reading of Bataille, 'From Restricted to General Economy: A Hegelianism without Reserve,' in (*WD*), pp. 271–2.

Chapter 4   Derrida, Kant, and the performance of parergonality

1 Immanuel Kant, *Critique of Judgment*, trans. J.H. Bernard (New York, Hafner Press, 1951), p. 61. Henceforth (*CJ*).

2 Jacques Derrida, *La Vérité en peinture* (Paris, Flammarion, 1978). See 'Parergon,' pp. 19–168. Henceforth (*LVP*).

3 Jacques Derrida, 'Economimesis,' in *Mimesis des articulations*, ed. Sylviane Agacinski (Paris, Aubier-Flammarion, 1975). In this essay,

Derrida examines the relation between a productive, originating economy and the processes of repetition, interability, and production as mimesis in and beyond Kant's work. The issue of analogy as it relates to exemplarity is also discussed in more detail there.

4 For more on this issue as it relates to the question of the foundations of metaphysics, see my *Derrida and the Economy of Différance* (Bloomington, Indiana University Press, 1986). See in particular the introduction entitled 'Derrida's Kantian Affiliation or Prolegomena to the Deconstruction of Metaphysics and the Recognition of *Différance*,' pp. 1–22.

5 For instance, Derrida speaks of the example as a particular in the following (*LVP*, p. 60): 'Le jugement réflechissant ne dispose que du particulier et doit remonter, faire retour vers la généralité: *l'exemple* (c'est ce qui nous importe ici) y est donné *avant la loi* et permet la découvrir dans son unicité même *d'exemple*' (my emphasis). Further, he speaks of examples as illustrations, for use in pedagogy (*LVP*, p. 60): 'Le discours scientifique ou logique courant procède par jugements déterminants, *les exemples* suivent pour déterminer ou, dans un dessein pédagogique, pour *illustrer*.' It is worthy of note that Kant, in explaining the difference between determinant and reflective judgment, uses the term 'particular' (*Besondere*). See *Kants Werke, Akademie Textausgabe V* (Berlin, Walter de Gruyter, 1968), p. 179.

6 Kant's usage of exemplarity, despite his lack of a theory of the same, is also in evidence in the third *Critique* with reference to the problem of education of the genius (*CJ*, pp. 150–63). There is no evidence, however, that this notion of exemplarity (presupposed), articulated somewhat in terms of the exemplifier that defies an exemplified, that calls forth yet defies any mimetic relations, is the same as the notion of exemplarity being analyzed presently: namely, exemplarity as parergonality.

7 Immanuel Kant, *Critique of Pure Reason*, trans. Norman Kemp Smith (New York, St Martin's Press, 1965), p. 178 (my emphasis).

8 The development of this notion is most extensively articulated by J.L. Austin in *How to do Things with Words* (Cambridge, Mass., Harvard University Press, 1962), pp. 4–11. His now classic examples of performatives include: '(a) "I do (sc. take this woman to be my lawful wedded wife)" – as uttered in the course of the marriage ceremony; (b) "I name this ship the *Queen Elizabeth*" – as uttered when smashing the bottle against the ship; (c) "I give and bequeath my watch to my brother" – as occurring in a will; and (d) "I bet you sixpence it will rain tomorrow".' John R. Searle also

elaborates and further analyzes this notion in *Speech Acts* (Cambridge, Mass., Cambridge University Press, 1969), p. 68: 'some utterances were not sayings, but doings of some other kind.'

9 In his early work on Rousseau, Derrida makes the distinction between 'declared' and 'described' statements; the former being made explicitly as stated intentions or themes of the text, the latter being movements which the text manifests but which, however, remain at the level of the unthought or the unthematized within the text. See *Of Grammatology*, trans. Gayatri Chakravorty Spivak (Baltimore, Johns Hopkins University Press, 1974), pp. 97–316.

10 Derrida claims: 'en m'autorisant de cette brisure réflechissante, je commence ma lecture de la troisième *Critique* par des exemples.' Further: 'Cette docilité est-elle perverse? Rien ne permet encore d'en décider' (*LVP*, p. 60).

11 Derrida (*LVP*), pp. 24–5 (my translation).

12 This 'logic' is discussed in detail in Derrida's reading of Rousseau via the term 'supplement', which forms an analogy to his reading of Kant here via the term 'parerga'. The reading of Rousseau is found in Derrida's *Of Grammatology*, 1974.

13 Kant (*CJ*), p. 62.

14 Derrida's discussion of this reliance as enframing of the third *Critique* by the *Religion* text is extensive. He illustrates how the division of the problem into a quaternary also parallels the text on *Religion* as well as how the underlying presuppositions Kant relies on in the analysis of judgment have been secretly borrowed from Christianity. This discussion by Derrida takes place most notably in (*LVP*), pp. 64–6.

15 Derrida's discussion of this point connects the privileging of the category of quantity over quality in Kant's analysis of the sublime. Since the definition of sublimity entails something beyond the largest quantity, beyond quantitative measure, Derrida questions the usage of quantity at all as the frame in which to articulate the sublime, as opposed to quality. This privilege is found to be emanating from the first *Critique*, notably from the table of categories. Derrida's analysis of this issue occurs mainly in (*LVP*), pp. 155–7.

16 Derrida (*LVP*), pp. 58–9, 71–3.

17 Derrida (*LVP*), p. 73 (my translation).

18 The issue of entitling, as naming, as setting up a frame around the text, as its concept, arché, or telos is an abiding theme in Derrida's work and he once again problematizes the issue in the opening remarks of his essay, 'Parergon.' He suggests numerous possible titles for the paper before announcing in the text that his title will be

'the circle and the abyss' (p. 28). The actual title remains, however, distinct from this, as 'Parergon,' and without an explicit explanation given.

19 Derrida (*LVP*), p. 32.
20 Derrida (*LVP*), p. 49 (my translation and emphasis).
21 Derrida (*LVP*), p. 49.
22 For the most extensive discussions by Husserl, as he develops this notion, see his *Logical Investigations II*, trans. J.N. Findlay (London, Routledge & Kegan Paul, 1970), pp. 552–93. See also Husserl's *Ideas*, trans. F. Kersten (The Hague, Martinus Nijhoff, 1982), pp. 199–210, where he discusses the centrality of this concept for all phenomenological studies.
23 Kant, *Critique of Pure Reason*, 1965, p. 178.
24 Derrida's analysis of Kant clearly focuses on more than the issue of exemplarity and indeed in some respects does not address this issue at all, at least not in explicit terms of parergonality. But his focus is concerned with a hidden layer or layers within Kant's text, his strategic moves within his overt and explicit intentions, which connect his work with fundamental presuppositions which in turn originate in Christianity on the one hand and in a doctrine of humanism on the other. It is this layer which we have not addressed here, although it is not unrelated to our topic, but it is more distant and less directly related than that of parergonality itself.

Chapter 5   Derrida, Hegel, and the sign

1 Jacques Derrida, 'Positions,' an interview with Jean-Louis Houdebine and Guy Scarpetta in *Positions*, trans. Alan Bass (Chicago, University of Chicago Press, 1981), p. 61. Henceforth (*PO*).
2 Jacques Derrida, *Of Grammatology*, trans. Gayatri Chakravorty Spivak (Baltimore, Johns Hopkins University Press, 1978), pp. 3–140. Henceforth (*OG*); 'Semiology and Grammatology,' in (*PO*), pp. 15–36.
3 Jacques Derrida, *Writing and Difference*, trans. Alan Bass (Chicago, Chicago University Press, 1978), p. 281. Henceforth (*WD*).
4 ibid.
5 (*OG*), p. 3.
6 (*OG*), p. 4.
7 (*PO*), p. 22.
8 Jacques Derrida, *Margins of Philosophy*, trans. Alan Bass (Chicago, University of Chicago Press, 1982), pp. 69–108. Henceforth (*MP*).
9 G.W.F. Hegel, *The Encyclopedia of the Philosophical Sciences*, trans. M.J. Petry (Dordrecht and Boston, D. Reidel Publishing Company,

1977), sections 445–60, pp. 103–208. Henceforth cited by section number.

10 ibid., p. 91.

11 (*MP*), p. 74.

12 (*MP*), p. 81.

13 (*MP*), p. 82.

14 ibid.

15 (*MP*), pp. 82–3.

16 (*MP*), pp. 80–1.

17 (*MP*), p. 74.

18 (*WD*), pp. 256–7. For a provocative argument concerning the 'idealizing mastery' issue, see Joseph C. Flay, 'Hegel, Derrida and Bataille's Laughter,' in W. Desmond, ed., *Hegel and his Critics* (Albany, SUNY Press).

19 (*PO*), p. 44 (my emphasis).

20 (*PO*), pp. 42–5.

21 Jacques Derrida, *Dissemination*, trans. Barbara Johnson (Chicago, University of Chicago Press, 1981), pp. 269–71. This point has been forcefully argued by Rodolphe Gasché in *The Tain of the Mirror: Derrida and the Philosophy of Reflection* (Cambridge, Mass., Harvard University Press, 1986). See especially pp. 102–40 and pp. 204–40.

22 My analysis of contradiction has benefited greatly from Thomas J. Bole's excellent 'Contradiction in Hegel's *Science of Logic*,' *Review of Metaphysics* 40, 1987, pp. 515–34. Henceforth (*CH*).

23 G.W.F. Hegel, *Hegel's Science of Logic*, trans. A.V. Miller (New York, Humanities Press, 1976), p. 43. Henceforth (*SL*).

24 Thomas J. Bole (*CH*), and Klaus Hartmann, 'Zur neuesten Dialektik-Kritik,' *Archiv für Geschichte der Philosophie* 55, 1973, and 'Hegel: A Non-Metaphysical View,' in *Hegel: A Collection of Critical Essays*, ed. A. MacIntyre (New York, Anchor Books, 1972), pp. 101–24.

25 (*CH*).

26 (*PO*), p. 44.

27 (*SL*), p. 385.

28 (*SL*), p. 389.

29 (*SL*), pp. 393–478.

30 (*CH*).

31 (*SL*), p. 433.

32 ibid.

33 ibid.

34 ibid.

35 (*SL*), p. 435.

36 Hence, in the 'Lesser Logic' of the *Encyclopedia*, Hegel does not discuss contradiction within the logic of essence.

37 (*SL*), pp. 825–6.
38 (*CH*).
39 (*PO*), p. 101.
40 Moreover, the very distinction between the thematic and methodological senses of contradiction can only be made on the basis of the sort of logical interpretation followed in this paper. Cf. (*CH*).
41 For the detailed argument regarding this point, see my 'Hegelian Dialectic and the Limits of Representation,' in *Postmodernism and Continental Philosophy*, eds Hugh J. Silverman and Donn Welton (Albany, SUNY Press, 1987).

Chapter 6 Drawing: (an) affecting Nietzsche: with Derrida

1 Friedrich Nietzsche, *Sämtliche Werke, Kritische Studienausgabe*, 15 volumes, eds Giorgio Colli and Mazzino Montinari (Berlin, Walter de Gruyter, 1980), volume 3. Henceforth (*KSA*) followed by volume number, notebook number (in italics), and fragment number.
Compare the '*Vorschrift*' in (*KSA*) 14, p. 269.
All translations from either German or French are mine unless otherwise indicated.
2 See, for instance, Peter Szondi, *Poetik und Geschichtsphilosophie* (Frankfurt, Surkhamp Verlag, 1974), vol. 1, chapters 11–12 and the bibliography.
3 See Martin Heidegger, *Kant und das Problem der Metaphysik* (Frankfurt, Klosterman, 1965), section 34, for the first incisive topology of self-affection; and see further, Jacques Derrida, *La Voix et le phénomène* (Paris, PUF, 1972), pp. 92–7. Henceforth (*VP*). The English translation is unreliable: witness its title, *Speech and Phenomena* (Evanston, Northwestern University Press, 1973). A reading of Kant's *Opus Posthuman* (Berlin, Cassirer, 1918), convolutes I, VII and X, would be required reading to show the *critical* space of self-affection in the self-deconstruction of Kant's *Critique*.
4 See Jacques Derrida, *Otobiographies: l'enseignement de Nietzsche et la politique du nom propre* (Paris, Galilée, 1984), especially sections II, III, and IV. Henceforth *Otobiographies*). English translation by Avita Ronell, 'Otobiographies,' in *The Ear of the Other* (New York, Schocken, 1985), pp. 1–38. Henceforth (*E*).
5 Martin Heidegger, *Nietzsche I, II* (Pfullingen, Neske, 1961), especially 'Nietzsche's Metaphysics,' pp. 257–334, vol. II. Henceforth cited as (*N* I) and (*N* II).
6 See especially David F. Krell, *Postponements: Woman, Sensuality and Death in Nietzsche* (Bloomington, Indiana University Press, 1986), in

the Index under 'distance,' and the corresponding discussions and notes. Add (*KSA*) 10, 7, 106, 129, and (*KSA*) 12, *1*, 7, 10, *2*, 13, to his references, among many others. In (*KSA*) 10, 7 we hear of an 'affect of distance.'

7 Cf. (*N* I), p. 70, and Heidegger's discussion in general throughout (*N* I) and (*N* II) of Nietzsche's will. But see also (*KSA*), 9, *6*, 119, 193, 314; 10, 7, 77, 81, 210, 226, 266; 10, *9*, 39, 48; 10, *12*, 30, 35, *16*, 20, *24*, 11, 12, 20; 11, *25*, 185, 380, 389, 436, *27*, 2, 19, 24.

8 See in general, Pierre Klossowski, *Nietzsche et le cercle vicieux* (Paris, Mercure de France, 1969), and especially chapters 2 and 4, and the 'Additional Note to Nietzsche's Semiotics,' pp. 357–67. This work is the essential one for Nietzsche's doctrine of the 'eternal return' and is here, as in Derrida's dealing with Nietzsche, presupposed.

9 Equivalent to Friedrich Nietzsche, *Der Wille Zur Macht* (Stuttgart: Alfred Kröner, 1964), section 556. Henceforth (*WM*).

10 Consult also Rodolphe Gasché, 'Autobiography as *Gestalt*: Nietzsche's *Ecce Homo*,' *Boundary* 2, 1981, pp. 271–90.

11 See *Otobiographies*, pp. 40–1, (*E*), pp. 5–6, for the issue of that border.

12 ibid.

13 For more on this border-structure, see particularly Jacques Derrida's 'Survivre,' in *Parages* (Paris, Galilée, 1986). Henceforth (*P*).

14 Cf. *Otobiographies*, (*E*), p. 45, a portion of a roundtable held on autobiography, where Derrida says: 'that the eternal return of the same is selective . . . within a differential relation of forces. What returns is the constant affirmation "Yes, Yes" . . . a selective return *without* negativity or which *reduces* negativity through affirmation, alliance or hymen' (my emphasis). This 'return' via the affirmative and the exclusion or reduction – sublimation? cancellation? – of 'negativity' cannot exclude the surface effects of the *guarde* or the prophylactics of protection within the dissemination of the impossible exposure, which always reconstitutes a consciousness *après-coup*.

15 See Jacques Derrida, 'Le Facteur de la vérité,' in his *La Carte postale* (Paris, Aubier-Flammarion, 1980); English translation by Alan Bass, *The Post Card* (Chicago: University of Chicago Press, 1987). Henceforth (*CP*), with French and English paginations following respectively.

16 *Otobiographies*, pp. 53–4, (*E*), pp. 11–12; see also (*CP*), 'Envois,' and Jacques Derrida, *Schibboleth: Pour Paul Celan* (Paris, Galilée, 1986), especially pp. 47ff.

17 See section III of *Otobiographies*, 'De l'état – le signe autograph,' where Derrida insists on the implication of Nietzsche's text with

Nazism, especially in pages 92–9. I should say that the texts Derrida comments on would require scrutiny in combination with later more critical texts where Nietzsche seems aware of the dangers of his earlier expressions. The category of textual guilt remains to be elaborated.

18 See (*CP*), 'Spéculer – sur "Freud," ' where the pseudo-concept 'life death' comes under elaboration.

19 See Karl-Otto Apel, *Transformation der Philosophie* (Frankfurt, Surkhamp Verlag, 1976), vols I and II, for an elaboration, dispersed through many articles, of Appel's important position.

20 See (*P*) for an elaboration of this in relation to Blanchot.

21 See also (*KSA*) 9, 11, 125. All these fragments belong to 1881, the year of the discovery of the eternal return.

22 See the subtitle of *Ecce Homo*. To grant or give myself time, *me donner du temps*, is to be inserted by self-affection into temporality, to be self-inscribed into self-projected time.

23 (*VP*), p. 92.

24 I am here alluding to Heidegger's *Sein und Zeit* and its discussion of *Zeitlichkeit* and *Temporalität*.

25 Compare Nietzsche's famous fragment recapitulating his metaphysics for which Heidegger takes him to task in (*N* II), p. 288: (*KSA*) 12, 7, 54, or (*WM*), section 617, which begins: 'Recapitulation: to *imprint* the character of being upon becoming – that is the *highest will to power.*'

26 I am referring to Blanchot's *oeuvre* and his analyses and treatments of death.

27 (*CP*), p. 381, (*E*), p. 359.

28 'Projection' here in both a Nietzschean and Heideggerian sense at once; 'wounded' metaphorically meant.

29 Jean-Luc Nancy, *L'Imperatif catégorique* (Paris, Flammarion, 1983), henceforth cited as (*IC*).

30 See Klossowski, *Nietzsche et le cercle vicieux*, 1969, for a general semiotic analysis of the affects in Nietzsche. One may also wish to consult Gilles Deleuze, *Nietzsche et la philosophie* (Paris, PUF, 1973, 4th edn), especially chapter 2.

31 See works cited above for Klossowski and Deleuze for further connections between the drives, the affects, and the will, and also Heidegger in (*N* I).

32 Heidegger in (*N* I) *Übermächtigung*, for which see his crucial explication of the will once again.

33 See also Jacques Derrida, *Disseminations* (Paris, Seuil, 1967) for the 'hymen,' while again referring to *Parages*, note 13 above, for the 'border structure.'

34 Heidegger in (*N* I, II) speaks of the 'true' Nietzsche. Here the 'himself' crosses itself out in narrating its own life death, which requires dating and signing the text as well.

35 See Emmanuel Levinas, *En découvrant l'existence avec Husserl et Heidegger* (Paris, Vrin, 1974) among other works for his conception of an 'immemorial past.'

36 See Paul de Man, *Allegories of Reading* (New Haven and London, Yale University Press, 1979), chapter 11: 'Promises.' See also, Jacques Derrida, *Mémoires: For Paul de Man*, trans. C. Lindsay, J. Culler, and E. Cadava (New York, Columbia University Press, 1986).

37 See the roundtable on autobiography in *Otobiographies*, English edition.

38 Nietzsche's posthumous life, even if politically 'highlighted' by the Nazi association, has been tumultuous, from his reception soon after his madness to his existentialist influence upon Heidegger and Jaspers to his resurrection in 1960s France by the radical left, so that the 'story' is both long and complicated. Derrida has focused upon the Nazi association, because it must not be slurred over.

Chapter 7 '*Ça cloche*'

1 The translator wishes to thank Sarah Kofman for her invaluable suggestions and Aurora Wolfgang for her expertise and friendship. The title itself announces the complexity of the translation process. For this text, then, it functions as a reminder of the issue of translation as well as the resting place for the language of the 'original.' '*Ça cloche*' can be translated as a colloquial expression: something is not right, off kilter, doesn't ring true. But it is also a phrase that expands or unfolds exponentially as the author plays with rhyme and reference. The most obvious examples concern the shorthand 'Sa' for the Hegelian concept of absolute knowledge and 'ça,' the French term for the Freudian id. The most resounding pun is upon the title of Derrida's *Glas*, another term of infinite gloss. Kofman's essay abounds with ringing bells and death knells as she puns and corresponds with Derrida's subject(s). The result is a delightfully dense contextual web. As title and text '*Ça cloche*' remains untranslatable at crucial junctures.

2 '*Ça cloche*' was first delivered at the 1980 Cerisy colloquy, 'Les fins de l'homme.' Published among the conference papers in 1981, the essay was reprinted in Sarah Kofman's *Lecteurs de Derrida* (Paris, Galilée, 1984), pp. 117–51. [TN]

3 Jacques Derrida, 'The Ends of Man,' in *Margins of Philosophy*, trans.

Alan Bass (Chicago, Chicago University Press, 1982), pp. 111–36.
[TN]

4 Jacques Derrida, *Glas* (Paris, Galilée, 1974). [TN]

5 *Relever* plays on the French translation of the Hegelian concept of *Aufheben* (to sublate, to relieve). It refers here to the relationship between two terms where one both erases and elevates the other. [TN]

6 Hegel, cited in Derrida, *Glas*, 1974, p. 130.

7 ibid., p. 130.

8 For the ends of Freud, cf. Sarah Kofman, *Énigme de la femme, la femme dans les textes de Freud* (Paris, Galilée, 1980); *Woman's Enigma, Woman in Freud's Texts* (Ithaca, Cornell University Press, 1985). Derrida has noted this operation step by step in his 'Spéculer sur Freud,' in *La Carte postale* (Paris, Aubier-Flammarion, 1980); 'Speculations on Freud,' *Oxford Literary Review* 3, 1978, pp. 78–97.

9 Sigmund Freud, 'Three Essays on Sexuality' (1924), *Standard Edition* 7:200.

10 Sigmund Freud, 'The Taboo of Virginity,' *Standard Edition* 11:205–6.

11 Cf. Freud, 'Jokes and Their Relationship to the Unconscious,' *Standard Edition* 8:62: 'A. borrowed a copper kettle from B. and after he returned it was sued by B. because the kettle now had a big hole in it which made it unusable. His defense was: "First, I never borrowed from B. at all; secondly, the kettle had a hole in it already when I got it from him; and thirdly, I gave him back the kettle undamaged." Each one of these defenses is valid in itself, but taken together they exclude one another. A. was treating in isolation what had to be regarded as a connected whole. . . . We might also say: "A. has put an 'and' where only an 'either-or' is possible." ' See also: Freud's dream of Irma in *The Interpretation of Dreams* (I), *Standard Edition* 4:119–20. [TN]

12 Sigmund Freud, 'Femininity,' *Standard Edition* 22:131.

13 ibid., pp. 131–2.

14 ibid., p. 130.

15 Freud, 'The Taboo of Virginity,' p. 206.

16 ibid.

17 Cf. Sigmund Freud, 'Fetishism,' *Standard Edition* 21:153: 'What happened, therefore, was that the boy refused to take cognizance of the fact of his having perceived that a woman does not possess a penis. No, that could not be true: for if a woman has been castrated, then his own possession of a penis was in danger; and against that there rose in rebellion the portion of his narcissism which Nature has, as a precaution, attached to that particular organ. In later life a grown man may perhaps experience a similar panic

when the cry goes up that Throne and Altar are in danger, and similar illogical consequences will ensue.' [TN]

18 Following Freud's argument in 'Fetishism,' 'homosexual' in this text (as in *Glas*) almost exclusively refers to a masculine sexual economy and solution. [TN]

19 Sigmund Freud, 'On the Universal Tendency to Debasement in the Sphere of Love,' *Standard Edition*, 11:185–6.

20 Cf. Jean Genet, *The Thief's Journal*, trans. Bernard Frechtman (Harmondsworth, Penguin Books, 1967), p. 5: 'My excitement is the oscillation from one to another.' [TN]

21 Cf. Freud, 'Fetishism,' pp. 156–7:

> there are many and weighty additional proofs of the divided attitude of fetishists to the question of the castration of women. In very subtle instances both the disavowal and the affirmation of the castration have found their way into the construction of the fetish itself. This was so in the case of a man whose fetish was an athletic support belt which could also be worn as bathing drawers. This piece of clothing covered up the genitals entirely and concealed the distinction between them. Analysis showed that it signified that women were castrated and that they were not castrated; and it also allowed of the hypothesis that men were castrated, for all these possibilities could equally well be concealed under the belt. . . . A fetish of this sort doubly derived from contrary ideas, is of course especially durable. [TN]

22 ibid., pp. 155, 156.

23 ibid., pp. 152–3.

24 '*La double bande*': The translation of *bande* as 'erection' chooses the sexual connotation in English since there is no corresponding double entendre from the French *bande* (slang, like 'hard-on'). In this text bandaging, wrapping, and binding are equivalent to and different from rising and erecting. In translation *contrebande* also loses the complexity of counter, inverse, contra, and banded – bound – as well as the allusion to the *Ersatz*, false, illegal (against boundaries) and the play with the sexual connotation. Thus, the reader should note the absence of binding and bandaging in the choice of the purely sexual allusion represented by 'erection.' [TN]

25 A play on *sein* (breast, fold) and *seing* (signature) as well as a reference to *Sein* (being) with a further resonance in the rhyme with *ceindre* (enclose, strap, band).

26 Cf. Derrida, 'The Double Session,' in *Dissemination*, trans. Barbara Johnson (Chicago, Chicago University Press, 1982), pp. 173–286; '*La double séance*,' in *La Dissémination* (Paris, Seuil, 1972); 'Restitutions of

Truth to Size,' trans. John P. Leavey, *Research in Phenomenology* 8, 1978, pp. 1–44, and 'The Parergon,' *October* 9, 1979, pp. 3–40; *La Vérité en peinture* (Paris, Flammarion, 1978). [TN]

27 Stilitano is the castrated object of Genet's oscillating desire in *The Thief's Journal*. *M'ec* cites Genet's *'Ce qui est resté d'un Rembrandt déchiré en petits carrés,'* the following passage in particular: 'Qu'est-ce donc qui s'était écoule de mon corps – je m'ec.' *Mec* can easily be recognized as the colloquial expression for a common type, any 'guy,' but *m'ec* plays into both a generalized equivalence and a singular action: eq/ec . . . equivalence and economy of me/m' – the oscillation is between self and other as in 'every man is all other men. . . . No man was my brother: each man was myself, but isolated temporarily in his particular skin.' Cf. Genet (Paris, Gallimard, 1968), pp. 23–7. *M'ec* writing, therefore, is a methodical disintegration *and* affirmation of doubled distinctions – or, (tongue in cheek) some guy's writing. [TN]

28 Kofman's final citations are from Maurice Blanchot's *Le Dernier Homme* (Paris, Gallimard, 1957). [TN]

29 This debate, transcribed by Sarah Kofman, appears after the text of *'Ça cloche'* in the published accounts of the 1980 Cerisy conference. The original is included in *Les Fins de l'homme* (Paris, Galilée, 1981).

Chapter 8   On Derrida's 'Introduction' to Husserl's *Origin of Geometry*

1 Jacques Derrida, 'Introduction' in Edmund Husserl's *L'Origine de la géométrie* (Paris, PUF, 1962); English translation by John P. Leavey, *Edmund Husserl's Origin of Geometry: An Introduction* (New York, Nicolas Hays Ltd, 1978). Henceforth (*I*).

2 Jacques Derrida, 'The Time of a Thesis: Punctuations,' in A. Montefiore, ed., *Philosophy in France Today* (Cambridge, Cambridge University Press, 1983), pp. 39ff.

3 Cf. in particular *La Carte postale de Socrate à Freud et au-delà* (Paris, Aubier-Flammarion, 1980) with the chapter headings 'Envois' and 'Le Facteur de la vérité,' and also 'Signature événement contexte,' in *Marges de la philosophie* (Paris, Editions de Minuit, 1972), pp. 365–93. English translation by Alan Bass in *Margins* (Chicago, University of Chicago Press, 1982), pp. 309–30.

4 In particular cf. Derrida, 'Signature événement contexte,' 1972, and 'Limited Inc a b c . . .,' in *Glyph* 2, 1977, pp. 162–254.

5 Cf. for more details on this, Rudolf Bernet, *'Differenz und Abwesenheit: Derridas und Husserls Phänomenologie der Sprache, der Zeit, der Geschichte, der wissenschaftlichen Rationalität,'* in *Studien zur*

neueren französischen Phänomenologie: Phänomenologische Forschungen 18, 1986, pp. 88–99.

6 This analysis also permits a better understanding of the difficult passage in *La Voix et le phénomène* (Paris, PUF, 1967), pp. 104ff., where Derrida describes the (potential) death of the author or speaker as a necessary condition of the meaning of the text or statement (and even of the use of the pronoun 'I'); English translation by David Allison, *Speech and Phenomena* (Evanston, Northwestern University Press, 1973), pp. 93ff.

7 However, a quite different analysis of the 'book' can already be found in Derrida's *De la grammatologie* (Paris, Editions de Minuit, 1967); English translation by Gayatri Chakravorty Spivak, *Of Grammatology* (Baltimore, Johns Hopkins University Press, 1974). The first chapter of this book bears the significant title, 'The End of the Book and the Beginning of Writing.'

8 In Derrida's *Speech and Phenomena* this idea is taken up anew in the context of a radical critique of the ideal of a purely expressive language. The sixth chapter is significantly entitled 'The Voice that keeps Silence' (p. 70). Derrida's critique of Husserl's ideal of a purely expressive language is considered in detail in Bernet's '*Differenz und Abwesenheit,*' 1986, pp. 68–76.

9 Husserl's entire analysis of historicity suggests on the contrary that there is no truth 'without a veil.' See also Derrida's later reflections on this subject in *Eperons: les styles de Nietzsche* (Paris, Flammarion, 1978); English translation by Barbara Harlow, *Spurs: Nietzsche's Styles* (Chicago, Chicago University Press, 1978). In this seductive text Derrida orientates himself in particular to the beginning of Nietzsche's *Beyond Good and Evil*: 'If we suppose that truth is a woman . . .'

10 Cf. Bernet, '*Differenz und Abwesenheit,*' 1986, pp. 105–111.

11 See, for example, the relation between thought and language, (*I*), p. 70, note 66; the relation between writing as proper spiritual body and as sensible body, (*I*), pp. 92, 97; the relation between the magnitude of a project and the extent of its burial, (*I*), p. 118, note 129; the relation between idealization and the intuition of essence, (*I*), p. 135; the determination of imagination as a capacity which is creative and reproductive at the same time, (*I*), p. 125, note 141; the relation between the power of reason as a subjective capacity and the historical impotence of philosophy, (*I*), pp. 144ff.

Chapter 9 Derrida, Heidegger, and the time of the line

1 Martin Heidegger, *The Question of Being*, trans. Jean T. Wilde and William Kluback (New Haven, College and University Publishers, 1958).

2 Jacques Derrida, 'Living On: Border Lines,' in Harold Bloom *et al.*, eds, *Deconstruction and Criticism* (New York, Seabury, 1979).

3 Michel de Montaigne, 'Of Experience,' in *The Complete Essays*, trans. Donald M. Frame (Stanford, Stanford University Press, 1957).

4 Francis Bacon, *Essays* (New York, Penguin, 1986).

5 Jacques Derrida, *Of Grammatology*, trans. Gayatri Chakravorty Spivak (Baltimore, Johns Hopkins University Press, 1976).

6 See Hugh J. Silverman, *Inscriptions: Between Phenomenology and Structuralism* (London and New York, Routledge & Kegan Paul, 1987) esp. chapters 5–9. And see the whole orientation of *Continental Philosophy-I* devoted to *Philosophy and Non-Philosophy since Merleau-Ponty*.

7 Friedrich Nietzsche, *Thus Spoke Zarathustra*, trans. R. Hollingdale (New York, Penguin, 1969).

8 See Heidegger, 'Time and Being,' in *On Time and Being*, trans. Joan Stambaugh (New York, Harper & Row, 1972), and Derrida, 'Ousia and Grammé,' in *Margins of Philosophy*, trans. Alan Bass (Chicago, University of Chicago Press, 1982).

9 See, for instance, Albert Hofstadter, 'Enownment,' *Boundary 2*, 4, 1976, pp. 357–77, and his translator's introduction to Martin Heidegger, *Poetry Language Thought*, trans. Albert Hofstadter (New York, Harper & Row, 1971). Henceforth (*PLT*).

10 See Silverman, *Inscriptions*, especially chapters 2–4.

11 Heidegger, 'The Origin of the Work of Art,' in (*PLT*), pp. 72–8.

12 Heidegger, 'What Are Poets For?' in (*PLT*), pp. 91–142. Although delivered on the twentieth anniversary of Rilke's death in 1946, the essay was first published in *Holzwege* (Frankfurt, Klostermann, 1950).

13 Derrida, 'Survivre,' in *Parages* (Paris, Galilée, 1986), pp. 117–218.

14 Maurice Blanchot, *L'Arrêt de mort*. English translation by Lydia Davis as *Death Sentence* (New York, Station Hill, 1978).

15 Derrida, *De l'esprit* (Paris, Galilée, 1987).

16 In this connection, I should like to remember Professor Philip Rhinelander (Professor Emeritus of Philosophy and Humanities at Stanford University), who died on 20 March 1987 at the age of 79.

17 Derrida, 'Living On: Border Lines,' 1979.

18 ibid.

19 Heidegger, *The Question of Being* (New Haven, Conn., College and University Press, 1958), p. 8.

Chapter 10   Derrida and Sartre: Hegel's death knell

1 Jacques Derrida, *Glas* (Paris, Editions Galilée, 1974).
2 Jean-Paul Sartre, *L'Etre et le néant* (Paris, Gallimard, 1943). Henceforth (*EN*).
3 See Robert Champigny, *Stages on Sartre's Way* (Bloomington, Indiana University Press, 1959).
4 Jean-Paul Sartre, *Saint Genet, comédien et martyr* (Paris, Gallimard, 1951). Henceforth (*SG*).
5 See Harold Bloom, *The Anxiety of Influence* (London, Oxford, and New York, Oxford University Press, 1973).
6 See my 'Derrida l'insoumis,' *Le Nouvel Observateur*, 9 September 1983, pp. 62–7.
7 Charles Baudelaire, 'Le Spleen de Paris,' in *Oeuvres complètes* (Paris, Edition de la Pléiade, 1961), p. 285.
8 See also Derrida, *Glas*, 1974, p. 35.
9 Jacques Derrida, *Positions* (Paris, Editions de Minuit, 1972), p. 110. Henceforth (*P*).
10 Jacques Derrida, *De la grammatologie* (Paris, Editions de Minuit, 1967), p. 191.
11 See my 'Sartre and Derrida: qui perd gagne,' *Journal of the British Society for Phenomenology* 13, 1982, pp. 26–34.
12 See Jacques Derrida, 'Les Fins de l'homme,' in *Marges de la philosophie* (Paris: Editions de Minuit, 1972). Henceforth (*M*).
13 G.F.W. Hegel, *Philosophy of Nature*, vol. 1, ed. and trans. M.J. Petry (London, Allen & Unwin, 1970), section 259, p. 235.
14 (*M*), p. 339.
15 (*P*), p. 55.
16 Jean Paul Sartre, 'L'Universel singulier,' in *Situations IX* (Paris, Gallimard, 1972), p. 166. See also *Critique de la raison dialectique* (Paris, Gallimard, 1960), p. 103: 'The conflict between Hegel and Kierkegaard finds its resolution in the fact that man is neither signified nor signifier, but both signified-signifier and signifying-signified.'
17 See Jacques Derrida, *L'Ecriture et la différance*, 'Points Edition' (Paris, Seuil, 1967), chapter 9.
18 ibid., pp. 399–400.
19 Jean-Paul Sartre, 'L'Engagement de Mallarmé,' *Obliques* 18–19, numéro spécial, Sartre, ed. M. Sicard, p. 94. See also *Glas*, p. 225:

'The critique (of a logic) which reproduces in itself (the logic of) what it criticizes will always be . . . an idealist gesture.'

20 See also (SG), p. 229, note 1.

21 See, for example, *Situations IX*, p. 148, and *Critique de la raison dialectique*, p. 741.

22 Jean Genet, 'Ce qui est resté d'un Rembrandt,' in *Oeuvres complètes*, vol. IV (Paris, Gallimard, 1968).

23 Echoes of this inversion are to be found towards the end of Sartre's *Les Mots* (Paris, Gallimard, 1964).

24 See, for example, Gilles Deleuze, 'Platon et le simulacre' and 'Klossowski ou les corps-langage,' in *Logique du sens* (Paris, Editions de Minuit, 1969).

25 See also *Saint Genet*, pp. 209–10.

26 Jean-Luc Nancy, *La Remarque spéculative: un bon mot d'Hegel* (Paris, Editions Galilée, 1973), p. 33.

27 Genet, *Ce qui est resté d'un Rembrandt*, 1968.

28 Sartre, *Les Mots*, 1964, p. 214.

29 For an uneven but occasionally brilliant study of *Glas* which attempts to enter into its textual web rather than unravel it, see, of course, Geoffrey Hartman, *Saving the Text* (Baltimore, Johns Hopkins University Press, 1981).

30 Genet, *Un captif amoureux* (Paris, Gallimard, 1986).

Chapter 11 Derrida, Levinas, and violence

1 The principal texts cited in connection with Emmanuel Levinas's analyses of violence are: *Totality and Infinity*, trans. Alphonso Lingis (Pittsburgh, Duquesne University Press, 1969) – henceforth (*TI*); *Humanisme de l'autre homme* (Montpellier, Fata Morgana, 1972) – henceforth (*HAH*); *Ethics and Infinity*, trans. Richard A. Cohen (Pittsburgh, Duquesne University Press, 1984) – henceforth (*EI*). The main texts in which Derrida comments on Levinas or which are relevant to the theme of violence in Levinas are: 'Violence and Metaphysics,' in *Writing and Difference*, trans. Alan Bass (Chicago, University of Chicago Press, 1978) – henceforth (*WD*); *Positions*, trans. Alan Bass (Chicago, University of Chicago Press, 1981 – henceforth (*P*); 'En ce moment même dans cet ouvrage me voici,' in *Textes pour Emmanuel Levinas*, ed. François Laruelle (Paris, Galilée, 1980) – henceforth (*TEL*); *D'un ton apocalyptique adopté naguère en philosophie* (Paris, Galilée, 1983) – henceforth (*TAP*). Page references for these volumes appear in parentheses in the body of the text. Essays other than those mentioned but that appear in collections listed are separately noted. Additional works by Levinas and

Derrida are cited fully in the notes. The English translations of citations from works in French for which published translations are unavailable are my own.

2 Emmanuel Levinas, 'Jacques Derrida: tout autrement,' in *Les Dieux dans la cuisine: vingt ans de la philosophie en France*, ed. Jacques Brochier (Paris, Aubier, 1978), p. 105. Originally published in *L'Arc*, 54, 1973. Also reprinted in *Noms propres* (Montpellier, Fata Morgana, 1975).

3 Martin Jay, *Marxism and Totality* (Berkeley, University of California Press, 1984), p. 13. Because this study focuses on recent Marxist conceptions of totality, there is only passing reference to Levinas.

4 Maurice Blanchot, 'Notre compagne clandestine,' in *Textes pour Emmanuel Levinas*, ed. François Laruelle (Paris, Jean Michel Place, 1980), p 85. Levinas has published a collection of essays and interviews on Blanchot, *Sur Maurice Blanchot* (Montpellier, Fata Morgana, 1975) that underscore the importance of Blanchot for his thinking.

5 References to the relation of father and son abound in Derrida's work. *Glas* (Paris, Galilée, 1974) offers sustained commentaries on Hegel's explorations of paternity in classical Christian doctrine. For Hegel, it is claimed (p. 41): 'The life of spirit as history is the death of the father in the son.' The relation of speech to writing in terms of paternity is described in 'Plato's Pharmakon,' in *Dissemination*, trans. Barbara Johnson (Chicago, University of Chicago Press, 1981), pp. 65–155. King Thamus, the father of speech, asserts his authority over Theuth, the father of writing, but writing is the bastard child of speech. Levinas connects the relation of father to son with messianic eschatology. It is tempting to think of Derrida as the 'son' who is trickster/transgressor of the *logos* and Foucault for whom the paternal self transcends itself by breaking free from itself by means of the son as father. The son's relation to the father as one of 'rupture and recourse' could account for the identities in difference of their work.

6 Blanchot, *Textes pour Emmanuel Levinas*, 1980, p. 86.

7 Emmanuel Levinas, *De l'existence à l'existent* (Paris, Vrin, 1947), pp. 25–6.

8 Emmanuel Levinas, 'Le temps et l'autre' in *Le Choix, Le Monde, L'Existence*, Cahiers du Collège Philosophique (Paris, Arthaud, 1949), p. 136.

9 Emmanuel Levinas, *En découvrant existence avec Husserl et Heidegger* (Paris, Vrin, 1949), p. 170. See also his 'Heidegger, Gagarine et nous,' in *Difficile Liberté* (Paris, Albin Michel, 1963), pp. 255–60.

10 This phrase is close to the title of the work by Blanchot, *The Writing of the Disaster*, trans. Ann Smock (Lincoln, University of Nebraska

Press, 1986). For an extended analysis of the relations of Levinas to Blanchot and Bataille, see Joseph Libertson, *Proximity: Levinas, Blanchot, Bataille* (The Hague, Nijhoff, 1982).

11 Blanchot, *The Writing of the Disaster*, 1986, p. 47.

12 ibid., p. 28.

13 In an unpublished translation by John Leavey of a 1981 seminar by Derrida, '*Geschlecht* II: The Hand of Man According to Heidegger,' Derrida says of Heidegger and his predecessors: 'The hand will be the (monstrous [in the sense of that which shows]) sign, the proper of man as (monstrous) sign.' It will distinguish man from every other species and 'above all from the ape.'

14 For an account of the Other by way of the contrasting approaches of transcendental constitution and the philosophy of dialogue, see Michael Theunissen, *The Other: Studies in the Social Ontology of Husserl, Heidegger, Sartre and Buber*, trans. Christopher Macann (Cambridge, Mass., MIT Press, 1984). Although Levinas is not considered, many of Levinas's criticisms of Husserl as well as Derrida's arguments against Levinas are treated in the context of the relations of Husserl to Martin Buber.

15 An account of the move from language as a web of signifiers to the thematics of the trace is found in Shira Wolosky, 'Derrida, Jabès, Levinas: Sign-Theory as Ethical Discourse,' in *Prooftexts* 2, 1982.

16 Jacques Derrida, 'The Voice that Keeps Silence,' in *Speech and Phenomenon and Other Essays on Husserl's Theory of Signs*, trans. David Allison (Evanston, Northwestern University Press, 1973), p. 78.

17 Levinas, *Les Dieux dans la cuisine*, 1978, p. 110.

18 'Rotten Sun' is the title of a piece by George Bataille. See *Visions of Excess: Selected Writings, 1927–1939*, vol. 14, in the series *Theory and History of Literature* (Minneapolis, University of Minnesota Press, 1985), pp. 57–9.

19 ibid., p. 57.

20 In my *Spirit in Ashes: Hegel, Heidegger and Man-Made Mass Death* (New Haven, Yale University Press, 1985), I argue that the language of concentration and slave-labor camps is parodic and deconstructive, reducing ordinary signification to silence. Elaine Scarry in a study influenced by deconstruction, *The Body of Pain: The Making and Unmaking of the World* (Oxford, Oxford University Press, 1985) confirms the view that, in the case of torture, it is essential to develop a language of pain because in the absence of language the discourse of the torturer or the regime is imposed on the victim.

21 In 'En ce moment . . .' Derrida considers the 'who' from a feminist perspective in terms of woman as alterity. See also Catherine

Chalier, *Figures du feminin* (Paris, La Nuit Surveillée, 1982) for a feminist account of Levinas.

Chapter 12   Derrida and Foucault: madness and writing

1 Michel Foucault, *Histoire de la folie à l'age classique* (Paris, Gallimard, 1972).
2 René Descartes, *Meditations of First Philosophy*, in *Philosophical Works of Descartes*, trans. E.S. Haldane and G.R.T. Ross (New York, Dover Publications, 1931).
3 Jacques Derrida, *Speech and Phenomena and other Essays on Husserl's Theory of Signs*, trans. David Allison (Evanston, Northwestern University Press, 1973).
4 Foucault, *Histoire de la folie*, 1972, p. 56 (my translation).
5 ibid., p. 58.
6 Michel Foucault, *Madness and Civilization*, trans. Richard Howard (New York, Pantheon Books, 1965), p. x.
7 Jacques Derrida, *Writing and Difference*, trans. Alan Bass (Chicago, University of Chicago Press, 1978), p. 35. Henceforth (*WD*).
8 ibid.
9 Foucault, *Madness and Civilization*, 1965, p. x.
10 Quoted in (*WD*), p. 42.
11 (*WD*), p. 43.
12 G.W.F. Hegel, *Phenomenology of Spirit*, trans. A.V. Miller (New York, Oxford University Press, 1979).
13 (*WD*), p. 40.
14 (*WD*), p. 41.
15 Descartes, *Meditations of First Philosophy*, 1931, p. 145.
16 Foucault, *Histoire de la folie*, 1972, pp. 56–7.
17 ibid., p. 57.
18 ibid.
19 ibid., p. 58.
20 (*WD*), p. 48.
21 (*WD*), p. 50.
22 Sigmund Freud, *Studies on Hysteria*, trans. James Strachey (New York, Penguin Books, 1978).
23 Sigmund Freud, *The Interpretation of Dreams*, trans. James Strachey (New York, Avon Books, 1972).
24 (*WD*), p. 51.
25 (*WD*), p. 53.
26 (*WD*).
27 (*WD*), pp. 53–4.

28 (WD), p. 55.
29 (WD), p. 56.
30 (WD).
31 (WD), p. 57.
32 (WD), p. 54.
33 Maurice Merleau-Ponty, *The Visible and the Invisible*, trans. Alphonso Lingis (Evanston, Northwestern University Press, 1968), p. 179.
34 (WD), p. 60.
35 (WD), pp. 61–2.
36 Michel Foucault, 'Cogito Incognito: Foucault's "My Body, This Paper, This Fire,"' *Oxford Literary Review* 4, 1979, pp. 5–28.
37 Michel Foucault, *Discipline and Punish: The Birth of the Prison*, trans. Alan Sheridan (New York, Pantheon, 1977).
38 Foucault, 'Cogito Incognito,' 1979, p. 19.
39 Martial Guéroult, *Descartes' Philosophy Interpreted According to the Order of Reasons*, trans. Roger Ariew (Minneapolis, University of Minnesota Press, 1984).
40 Foucault, 'Cogito Incognito,' 1979, p. 19 (my emphasis).
41 ibid., p. 20.
42 ibid.
43 ibid., p. 16.
44 ibid., p. 13.
45 ibid., p. 26.
46 ibid., p. 18.
47 Jacques Derrida, 'Signature Event Context,' in *Margins of Philosophy*, trans. Alan Bass (Chicago, University of Chicago Press, 1982), p. 323.
48 ibid., p. 318.
49 ibid., p. 316.
50 Foucault, 'Cogito Incognito,' 1979, pp. 18–19.
51 ibid., p. 19.
52 Jacques Derrida, 'La Parole soufflée,' in (WD), pp. 169–96.

BIBLIOGRAPHY

I Texts by Jacques Derrida

1962

Edmund Husserl's Origin of Geometry: An Introduction. Ed. David B. Allison, trans. John Leavey. York Beach, ME, Nicholas Hays, 1978.
L'Origine de la géométrie. Paris, PUF, 1962.

1967

Of Grammatology. Trans. Gayatri Chakravorty Spivak. Baltimore, Johns Hopkins University Press, 1975.
De la grammatologie. Paris, Minuit, 1967.
Speech and Phenomena and Other Essays on Husserl's Theory of Signs. Trans. David Allison. Evanston, Northwestern University Press, 1973, 1979.
La Voix et le phénomène: introduction au problème du signe dans la phénoménologie de Husserl. Paris, PUF, 1967, 1972, 1976, 1979, 1983.
Writing and Difference. Trans. Alan Bass. Chicago, University of Chicago Press, 1978; London, Routledge & Kegan Paul, 1978.
L'Ecriture et la différance. Paris, Seuil, 1967, 1969.

1972

Dissemination. Trans. Barbara Johnson. Chicago, University of Chicago Press, 1981; London, Athlone Press, 1981.
La Dissémination. Paris, Seuil, 1972.
Margins of Philosophy. Trans. Alan Bass. Chicago, University of Chicago Press, 1982; Hassocks, Harvester Press, 1982.
Marges de la philosophie. Paris, Minuit, 1972, 1975.
Positions. Trans. Alan Bass. Chicago, University of Chicago Press, 1982; London, Athlone, 1982.
Positions. Entretiens avec Henri Ronge, Julia Kristeva, Jean-Louis Houdebine, Guy Scarpetta. Paris, Minuit, 1972, 1975.

1973

The Archeology of the Frivolous: Reading Condillac. Trans. John Leavey. Pittsburgh, Duquesne University Press, 1980.
Introduction to Condillac, *Essai sur l'origine des connaissances humaines.* Paris, Galilée, 1973. Republished separately as *L'Archéologie du frivole.* Paris, Gonthier-Denoel, 1976.

1974

Glas. Trans. John Leavey and Richard Rand. Lincoln, University of Nebraska Press, 1986.
Glas. Paris, Galilée, 1974; Gonthier-Denoel, 1982.

1975

Adami. Paris, Galerie Maeght, 1975.
'Economimesis.' *Diacritics,* vol. 11, no. 2, 1981, pp. 55–93.
  'Economimesis.' In *Mimesis des articulations.* Paris, Aubier-Flammarion, 1975.

1976

Spurs: Nietzsche's Styles. Trans. Barbara Harlow. Chicago, University of Chicago Press, 1979. Bilingual edition.
Eperons. Les styles de Nietzsche. Venice, Corbo e Fiori, 1976 (Quadrilingual edition). Paris, Flammarion, 1978.
' "Fors." The English Words of Nicolas Abraham and Maria Torok.' Trans. Barbara Johnson. *The Georgia Review,* vol. 11, no. 1, 1977, pp. 64–116.
Cryptonymie: le verbier de l'Homme aux loups. Paris, Aubier-Flammarion, 1976.
'Ou commence et comment finit un corps enseignant.' In Dominique Grisoni, ed., *Politiques de la philosophie.* Paris, Grasset, 1976.
'Entre crochets.' *Digraphe,* no. 8, 1976, pp. 97–114.

1977

Limited Inc., a b c . . . Trans. Samuel Weber. Baltimore, Johns Hopkins University Press, 1977. Published as a supplement to *Glyph 2, Johns Hopkins Textual Studies.*
'The Age of Hegel.' Trans. Susan Winnett. *Glyph 1,* new series, 1986, pp. 3–43.
  'L'âge de Hegel; La philosophie et ses classes; réponses à *La Nouvelle Critique.*' In *Qui a peur de la philosophie?* Paris, GREPH, Flammarion, 1977.

1978

Titus Carmel. (The pocket size Tlingit Coffin.) Paris, Centre Pompidou, 1978.

The Truth in Painting. Trans. G. Bennington and I. McLeod. Chicago, University of Chicago Press, 1987.

La Vérité en peinture. Paris, Flammarion, 1978.

'Coming Into One's Own.' In Geoffrey Hartman, ed. *Psychoanalysis and the Question of the Text.* Baltimore, Johns Hopkins University Press, 1978.

'Scribble.' Preface to Warburton, *Essai sur les hiéroglyphes.* Paris, Aubier-Flammarion, 1978.

'The Retrait of Metaphor.' Trans. F. Gasdner *et al. Enclitic,* vol. 2, no. 2, 1978, pp. 5–34.

1979

'Living On: Border-lines.' Trans. J. Hulbert. In *Deconstruction and Criticism.* Ed. Harold Bloom *et al.* New York, Seabury Press, 1979.

'La Philosophie des Etats généraux' in *Les Etats généraux de la philosophie.* Paris, Flammarion, 1979.

1980

The Post Card: From Socrates to Freud and Beyond. Trans. Alan Bass. Chicago, Chicago University Press, 1987.

La Carte postale: de Socrate à Freud et au-delà. Paris, Aubier-Flammarion, 1980.

'Ocelle comme pas un.' Preface to Jos Joliet, *L'Enfant au chien assis.* Paris, Galilée, 1980.

'The Law of Genre.' Trans. Avital Ronnell. *Critical Inquiry,* vol. 1, 1980, pp. 55–81. And in *Glyph 7.* Baltimore, Johns Hopkins University Press, 1980.

'La Loi du genre.' Colloque Le Genre. Strassbourg, Université de Strassbourg, 1980.

1981

'The Deaths of Roland Barthes.' Trans. Pascale-Anne Brault and Michael B. Naas. In *Philosophy and Non-Philosophy since Merleau-Ponty.* Hugh J. Silverman, ed. *Continental Philosophy-I.* London and New York, Routledge, 1988.

'Les Morts de Roland Barthes,' *Poétique,* no. 47, 1981, pp. 269–92.

'Télépathie.' *Furor,* no. 2, 1981, pp. 3–41.

'Title (to be announced).' *Substance,* no. 9, 1979, pp. 3–40.

1982

Affranchissement du transfert et de la lettre. Colloquium on Jacques Derrida's *La Carte postale*, April 4 and 5, 1981. Comments by Derrida. Paris, Confrontation, 1982.

The Ear of the Other: Otobiography, Transference, Translation: Texts and Discussions with Jacques Derrida. Trans. Peggy Kamuf. New York, Schocken Books, 1985.

L'Oreille de l'autre: otobiographies, transferts, traductions: textes et débats avec Jacques Derrida. Montreal, VLB, 1982.

'Choreographies.' Interview with Christie V. McDonald. *Diacritics*, vol. 12, 1982, pp. 66–76.

'Interview with Derrida.' In David Wood and Robert Bernasconi, eds, *Derrida and Différance.* Coventry, University of Warwick/Parousia Press, 1985, pp. 107–27. To be republished by Northwestern University Press, 1988. This interview was first published in *Le Nouvel Observateur*, 1982.

'The Time of a Thesis: Punctuations.' In Alan Montefiore, ed., *Philosophy in France Today.* Cambridge, Cambridge University Press, 1982.

1983

'Geschlecht – Sexual Difference, Ontological Difference.' *Research in Phenomenology*, vol. 13, 1983, pp. 68–84.

'La Langue et le discours de la méthode.' *Recherches sur la philosophie et le langage*, no. 3, 1983, pp. 35–51.

'Of an Apocalyptic Tone Recently Adopted in Philosophy,' Trans. John P. Leavey, *Semeia*, vol. 23, 1982, and *Oxford Literary Review*, vol. 6, no. 2, 1984, pp. 3–37.

D'un ton apocalyptique adopté naguère en philosophie. Paris, Galilée, 1983.

'The Principle of Reason: the University in the Eyes of its Pupils.' *Graduate Faculty Philosophy Journal.* (New School for Social Research), no. 10, 1983, pp. 5–45.

1984

Feu la cendre. Firenze, Sansoni, 1984. Paris, Des Femmes, 1987.

Otobiographies: l'enseignement de Nietzsche et la politique du nom propre. Paris, Galilée, 1984.

Signéponge/Signsponge. Trans. Richard Rand. New York, Columbia University Press, 1984. (Parallel French and English translation.)

'Devant la loi.' In A. Phillips Griffiths, ed., *Philosophy and Literature.* Cambridge, Cambridge University Press, 1984.

'Deconstruction and the Other.' Interview with Richard Kearney. In Richard Kearney, ed., *Dialogues with Contemporary Continental Thinkers.* Manchester, Manchester University Press, 1984.

'*Mes Chances*/My Chances.' In Joseph Smith and William Kerrigan, eds, *Taking Chances*. Baltimore, Johns Hopkins University Press, 1984.

'Mochlos ou le conflit des facultés.' *Philosophie*, no. 2, 1984, pp. 7–25.

'No Apocalypse, Not Now.' Trans. Catherine Porter and Philip Lewis. *Diacritics*, vol. 20, 1984, pp. 20–31.

1985

Droits de regards. Photographs by M.F. Plissart with an essay by Jacques Derrida. Paris, Minuit, 1985.

'Des Tours de Babel.' Trans. Joseph F. Graham. In Joseph F. Graham, ed., *Difference in Translation*. Ithaca and London, Cornell University Press, 1985, pp. 165–207. (Also includes French text, pp. 209–48.)

'Des Tours de Babel.' In *L'Art des confins*. Paris, PUF, 1985.

'Les Langages et les institutions de la philosophie.' *Texte*, no. 4, 1985, pp. 9–39.

'Letter to a Japanese Friend.' In David Wood and Robert Bernasconi, eds, *Derrida and Différance*. Coventry, University of Warwick/Parousia Press, 1985, pp. 1–8. Republished by Northwestern University Press, 1988.

'Popularités, du droit à la philosophie du droit,' Preface to *Les Sauvages dans la cité: auto-émancipation de peuple et instruction des proletaires au XIXe siècle*. Seyssel, Champ Vallon, 1985.

'Préjugés – devant la loi.' In *La Faculté de juger*. Paris, Minuit, 1985. (Communications by Jacques Derrida *et al*. Includes six papers presented at Cerisy-la-Salle in July–August 1982.)

'Racism's Last Word.' Trans. Peggy Kamuf. *Critical Theory*, vol. 12, 1985.

1986

'Forcener le subjectile.' Preface to *Dessins et portraits d'Antonin Artaud*. Paris, Gallimard, 1986.

Mémoires: For Paul de Man. Trans. Cecile Lindsay, Jonathan Culler, and Eduardo Cadava. New York, Columbia University Press, 1986.

Parages. Paris, Galilée, 1986.

'Shibboleth' (on Paul Celan). In Geoffrey Hartman and Sanford Budick, eds, *Midrash and Literature*. New Haven, Yale University Press, 1986.

Schibboleth: Pour Paul Celan. Paris, Galilée, 1986.

'Point de folie – maintenant l'architecture.' In B. Tschumi, ed., *La Case vide*. London, Architectural Association, 1986.

1987

De l'esprit: Heidegger et la question. Paris, Galilée, 1987.

For Nelson Mandela. Jacques Derrida and Mustapha Tilli, eds. Trans. Phillip Franklin *et al*. New York, Henry Holt & Co., 1987.

Psyché. Inventions de l'autre. Paris, Gallimard, 1987.
Ulysse gramophone: deux mots pour Joyce. Paris, Galilée, 1987.

II   Selected Bibliography on Derrida and Deconstruction

Books

Allison, David B., ed. *The New Nietzsche.* Cambridge, MIT Press, 1977, 1985.

Altizer, Thomas J.J., *et al. Deconstruction and Theology.* New York, Seabury Crossroads, 1982.

Arac, Jonathan, ed. *The Yale Critics: Deconstruction in America.* Minneapolis, University of Minnesota Press, 1983.

Atkins, Douglas G. *Reading Deconstruction/Deconstructive Reading.* Lexington, University Press of Kentucky, 1983.

Baynes, Kenneth, *et al. After Philosophy: End or Tranformation?* Cambridge, MIT Press, 1987.

Bloom, Harold, *et al. Deconstruction and Criticism.* New York, Seabury/ Continuum, 1979.

Butler, Christopher. *Interpretation, Deconstruction and Ideology: An Introduction to Some Current Issues in Literary Theory.* New York, Oxford University Press, 1984.

Caputo, John D. *Radical Hermeneutics: Repetition, Deconstruction, and the Hermeneutic Project.* Bloomington, Indiana University Press, 1988.

Culler, Jonathan. *The Pursuit of Signs: Semiotics, Literature, Deconstruction.* Ithaca: Cornell University Press, 1981.

Culler, Jonathan. *On Deconstruction: Theory and Criticism After Structuralism.* Ithaca, Cornell University Press, 1982.

Davis, Robert Con, and Schleifer, Ronald, eds. *Rhetoric and Form: Deconstruction at Yale.* Stillwater, University of Oklahoma Press, 1987.

De Man, Paul. *Blindness and Insight: Essays in the Rhetoric of Contemporary Criticism,* second edition. Minneapolis, University of Minnesota Press, and London, Methuen, 1983.

Descombes, Vincent. *Modern French Philosophy.* Trans. L. Scott-Fox and J.M. Harding. Cambridge, Cambridge University Press, 1980.

Eagleton, Terry. *The Function of Criticism from the Spectator to Post-Structuralism.* New York, Schocken, 1984.

Eagleton, Terry. *Literary Theory: An Introduction.* Minneapolis, University of Minnesota Press; Oxford, Basil Blackwell, 1984.

Fekete, John, ed. *The Structural Allegory: Reconstructive Encounters with the New French Thought.* Minneapolis, University of Minnesota Press, 1984.

Felman, Shoshana, ed. *Literature and Psychoanalysis: The Question of Reading – Otherwise*. Baltimore, Johns Hopkins University Press, 1982.

Felperin, Howard. *Beyond Deconstruction: The Uses and Abuses of Literary Theory*. Oxford, Clarendon Press, 1985.

Gasché, Rodolphe. *The Tain of the Mirror: Deconstruction and the Philosophy of Reflection*. Cambridge, Mass., Harvard University Press, 1986.

Hartman, Geoffrey. *Saving the Text: Philosophy/Derrida/Literature*. Baltimore, Johns Hopkins University Press, 1982.

Harvey, Irene E. *Derrida and the Economy of Différance*. Bloomington, Indiana University Press, 1986.

Kearney, Richard. *Dialogues with Contemporary Continental Thinkers. The Phenomenological Heritage*. With P. Ricoeur, E. Levinas, H. Marcuse, S. Breton, J. Derrida. Manchester, Manchester University Press, 1984.

Krupnick, Mark, ed. *Displacement: Derrida and After*. Bloomington, Indiana University Press, 1983.

Leavey, John P. Jr. *Glassary*. Lincoln, University of Nebraska Press, 1987.

Leitch, Vincent B. *Deconstructive Criticism: An Advanced Introduction and Survey*. New York, Columbia University Press, 1982.

Llewelyn, John. *Beyond Metaphysics?* Atlantic Highlands, N.J., Humanities Press, 1985; London, Macmillan, 1985.

Llewelyn, John. *Derrida on the Threshold of Sense*. London, Macmillan, 1986.

Magliola, Robert. *Derrida on the Mend*. West Lafayette, Purdue University Press, 1984.

Melville, Stephen. *Philosophy Besides Itself: On Deconstruction and Modernism*. Minneapolis, Minnesota University Press, 1986.

Merrell, Floyd. *Deconstruction Reframed*. West Lafayette, Purdue University Press, 1985.

Montefiori, Alan, ed. *Philosophy in France Today*. Cambridge, Cambridge University Press, 1982.

Norris, Christopher. *Deconstruction: Theory and Practice*. London, Methuen, 1982.

Norris, Christopher. *The Deconstructive Turn: Essays in the Rhetoric of Philosophy*. London, Metheun, 1983.

Norris, Christopher. *The Contest of Faculties: Philosophy and Theory After Deconstruction*. London, Methuen, 1985.

Norris, Christopher. *Derrida*. London, Fontana Modern Masters, 1987.

Ray, William. *Literary Meaning: From Phenomenology to Deconstruction*. Oxford, Basil Blackwell, 1984.

Ryan, Michael. *Marxism and Deconstruction: A Critical Articulation*. Baltimore, Johns Hopkins University Press, 1982.

Said, Edward. *The World, the Text, and the Critic*. London: Faber & Faber, 1984.

Sallis, John, ed. *Deconstruction and Philosophy: The Texts of Jacques Derrida*. Chicago, University of Chicago Press, 1987.

Salusinsky, Imre. *Criticism in Society: Interviews with Jacques Derrida, Northrop Frye, Harold Bloom, et al*. London, Methuen, 1987.

Silverman, Hugh J. *Inscriptions: Between Phenomenology and Structuralism*. London and New York, Routledge & Kegan Paul, 1987.

Silverman, Hugh J. and Aylesworth, Gary E., eds. *The Textual Sublime: Deconstruction and its Differences*. Albany, SUNY Press, 1989.

Silverman, Hugh J. and Ihde, Don, eds. *Hermeneutics and Deconstruction*. Albany, SUNY Press, 1985.

Silverman, Hugh J. and Welton, Donn, eds. *Postmodernism and Continental Philosophy*. Albany, SUNY Press, 1988.

Smith, Joseph and Kerrigan, William, eds. *Taking Chances: Derrida, Psychoanalysis and Literature*. Baltimore, Johns Hopkins University Press, 1984.

Spanos, William V., ed. *Martin Heidegger and the Question of Literature*. Bloomington, Indiana University Press, 1976.

Staten, Henry. *Wittgenstein and Derrida*. Lincoln, University of Nebraska Press, 1985.

Taylor, Mark C., ed. *Deconstruction in Context: Literature and Philosophy*. Chicago, University of Chicago Press, 1986.

Taylor, Mark C. *Erring: A Postmodern A-Theology*. Chicago, University of Chicago Press, 1984.

Thiher, Allen. *Words in Reflection: Modern Language Theory and Postmodern Fiction*. Chicago, Chicago University Press, 1984.

Ulmer, Gregory L. *Applied Grammatology: Post(e)-Pedagogy from Jacques Derrida to Joseph Beuys*. Baltimore, Johns Hopkins University Press, 1985.

Wood, David. *Deconstruction of Time*. Atlantic Highlands, N.J., Humanities Press International, 1988.

Wood, David and Bernasconi, Robert, eds. *Derrida and Difference*. Coventry, University of Warwick/Parousia Press, 1985; Evanston, Northwestern University Press, 1988.

Articles

Allison, David B. 'Destruction/Deconstruction in the Text of Nietzsche.' *Boundary 2*, vol. 8, no. 1, 1979, pp. 197–222.

Atkins, G. Douglas. 'J. Hillis Miller, Deconstruction, and the Recovery of Transcendence.' *Notre Dame English Journal: A Journal of Religion in Literature*, vol. 13, no. 1, 1980, pp. 51–63.

Atkins, G. Douglas. 'The Sign as a Structure of Difference: Derridean

Deconstruction and Some of Its Implications.' In De George, Richard T., ed., *Semiotic Themes*. Lawrence, University of Kansas, 1981, pp. 133–47.

Atkins, G. Douglas. 'Count It All Joy: The Affirmative Nature of Deconstruction.' *University of Hartford Studies in Literature: A Journal of Interdisciplinary Criticism*, vols 15–16, nos 3–1, 1983–4, pp. 120–8.

Blanchard, Marc E. 'The Sound of Songs: the Voice in the Text.' In *Hermeneutics and Deconstruction*. Albany, SUNY Press, 1985, pp. 122–35.

Blum, Roland P. 'Deconstruction and Creation.' *Philosophy and Phenomenological Research*, no. 46, 1980, pp. 293–306.

Breazeale, Daniel, *et al.* 'Panel Discussion on "Nietzsche Today".' *International Studies in Philosophy*, no. 15, 1983, pp. 105–15.

Brodsky, Gary M. 'Comments on Reading, Writing, Text: Nietzsche's Deconstruction of Author-ity.' *International Studies in Philosophy*, no. 17, 1985, pp. 65–7.

Caputo, John D. 'From the Primordiality of Absence to the Absence of Primordiality.' In *Hermeneutics and Deconstruction*, SUNY, 1985, pp. 191–200.

Caputo, John D. 'From the Deconstruction of Hermeneutics to the Hermeneutics of Deconstruction.' In Hugh J. Silverman, *et al.*, eds. *The Horizons of Continental Philosophy*. Dordrecht, Nijhoff-Kluwer, 1988, pp. 190–202.

Cascardi, A. J. 'Skepticism and Deconstruction.' *Philosophy of Literature*, vol. 8, no. 1, 1984, pp. 1–14.

Casey, Edward S. 'Origin(s) In (Of) Heidegger/Derrida.' *Journal of Philosophy*, vol. 81, 1984, pp. 601–10.

Cousins, Mark. 'The Logic of Deconstruction.' *The Oxford Literary Review*, vol. 3, no. 2, 1978, pp. 70–7.

Culler, Jonathan. 'Jacques Derrida.' In John Sturrock, ed. *Structuralism and Since: From Lévi-Strauss to Derrida*. London, Oxford University Press, 1979, pp. 154–80.

Cumming, Robert Denoon. 'The Odd Couple: Heidegger and Derrida,' *Review of Metaphysics*, vol. 34, 1981, pp. 487–521.

Descombes, Vincent. 'The Fabric of Subjectivity.' In *Hermeneutics and Deconstruction*, SUNY, 1985, pp. 55–65.

Eldridge, Richard. 'Deconstrucion and its Alternatives.' *Man and World*, vol. 18, 1985, pp. 147–70.

Fuller, Steven. 'A French Science (with English Subtitles).' *Philosophy and Literature*, vol. 7, 1983, pp. 1–14.

Gasché, Rodolphe. 'Deconstruction as Criticism.' *Glyph 7*, 1979, pp. 177–216.

Gasché, Rodolphe. 'Quasi-metaphoricity and the Question of Being.' In *Hermeneutics and Deconstruction*, SUNY, 1985, pp. 166–90.

Graff, Gerald. 'Deconstruction as Dogma, or "Come Back to the Raft Ag'in Strether Honey".' *Georgia Review*, vol. 34, 1980, pp. 401–21.

Green, Michael. 'Response to Cynthia Willet-Shoptaw's "A Deconstruction of Wittgenstein".' *Auslegung*, vol. 19, 1983, pp. 82–5.

Hans, James. 'Hermeneutics, Play, Deconstruction.' *Philosophy Today*, vol. 24, 1980, pp. 299–317.

Hartman, Geoffrey. 'Monsieur Texte: On Jacques Derrida, his *Glas*.' *Georgia Review*, vol. 29, no. 4, 1975, pp. 759–97.

Hartman, Geoffrey. 'Monsieur Texte II: Epiphany in Echoland.' *Georgia Review*, vol. 30, no. 1, 1976, pp. 169–204.

Henning, E. M. 'Archaeology, Deconstruction, and Intellectual History.' In LaCapra, Dominick and Kaplan, Steven, eds. *Modern European Intellectual History: Reappraisals and New Perspectives*. Ithaca, Cornell University Press, 1982.

Hobson, Marian. 'Deconstruction, Empiricism, and the Postal Services.' *French Studies*, vol. 36, no. 3, 1982, pp. 290–314.

Holland, Nancy. 'Heidegger and Derrida Redux: A Close Reading.' In *Hermeneutics and Deconstruction*, pp. 219–26.

Hoy, David Couzens. 'Deciding Derrida: On the Work (and Play) of the French Philosopher.' *London Review of Books*, vol. 4, no. 3, 1982, pp. 3–5.

Leavey, John P. 'Four Protocols: Derrida, His Deconstruction.' *Semeia*, vol. 23, 1982, pp. 42–57.

Leavey, John P. 'Jacques Derrida's *Glas*: a Translated Selection and Some Comments on an Absent Colossus.' *Clio*, vol. 11, 1982, pp. 327–37.

Llewelyn, John. 'Derrida: The Origin and End of Philosophy.' In Hugh J. Silverman, ed. *Philosophy and Non-Philosophy since Merleau-Ponty*. *Continental Philosophy-I*. London and New York, Routledge, 1988, pp. 191–210.

Lingis, Alphonso. 'The Pleasure in Postcards.' In *Hermeneutics and Deconstruction*, SUNY, 1985, pp. 152–64.

Liszka, James Jakob. 'Derrida: Philosophy of the Liminal.' *Man and World*, vol. 16, 1983, pp. 233–50.

Loesberg, Jonathan. 'Intentionalism, Reader-Response, and the Place of Deconstruction.' *Reader*, vol. 12, 1984, pp. 21–38.

Lusthaus, Dan. 'Ch'an and Taoist Mirrors: Reflections on Richard Garner's "Deconstruction of the Mirror".' *Journal of Chinese Philosophy*, vol. 12, 1985, pp. 169–78.

Magnus, Bernd. 'The End of "The End of Philosophy".' In *Hermeneutics and Deconstruction*, SUNY, 1985, pp. 2–10.

Margolis, Joseph. 'Deconstruction: Or the Mystery of the Mystery of the Text.' In *Hermeneutics and Deconstruction*, SUNY, 1985, pp. 138–51.

McDonald, Christie V. 'Rereading Deconstruction (Today?).' In *Postmodernism and Continental Philosophy*, SUNY, 1988, pp. 180–92.

Norris, Christopher. 'Names.' *London Review of Books*, vol. 8, no. 3, 1986, pp. 10–12.

Olkowski, Dorothea. 'If the Shoe Fits – Derrida and the Orientation of Thought.' In *Hermeneutics and Deconstruction*, SUNY, 1985, pp. 262–9.

O'Neill, John. 'Deconstructing Fort/Derrida.' In *Postmodernism and Continental Philosophy*, SUNY, 1988, pp. 214–22.

Ormiston, Gayle L. 'Binding Withdrawal.' In *Hermeneutics and Deconstruction*, SUNY, 1985, pp. 247–61.

Pressler, Charles A. 'Redoubled: The Bridging of Derrida and Heidegger.' *Human Studies*, vol. 7, 1984, pp. 325–42.

Rorty, Richard. 'Philosophy as a Kind of Writing.' In *Consequences of Pragmatism*. Minneapolis, University of Minnesota Press, 1982, pp. 89–109.

Rorty, Richard. 'Deconstruction and Circumvention.' *Critical Inquiry*, vol. 11, no. 1, 1984, pp. 1–23.

Rosmarin, Adena. 'Theory and Practice: From Ideally Separated to Pragmatically Joined.' *Journal of Aesthetics and Art Criticism*, vol. 43, 1984, pp. 31–40.

Sallis, John. 'Heidegger/Derrida – Presence.' *Journal of Philosophy*, vol. 81, 1984, pp. 594–601.

Schrag, Calvin O. 'Subjectivity and Praxis at the End of Philosophy.' In *Hermeneutics and Deconstruction*. SUNY, 1985, pp. 24–32.

Schrift, Alan D. 'Language, Metaphor, Rhetoric: Nietzsche's Deconstruction of Epistemology.' *Journal of the History of Philosophy*, vol. 23, 1985, pp. 371–96.

Schrift, Alan D. 'Genealogy and/as Deconstruction: Nietzsche, Derrida, and Foucault on Philosophy as Critique.' In *Postmodernism and Continental Philosophy*. New York, SUNY, 1988, pp. 193–213.

Schrift, Alan D. 'Reading, Writing, Text: Nietzsche's Deconstruction of Authority.' *International Studies in Philosophy*, vol. 17, 1985, pp. 55–64.

Schürmann, Reiner. 'Deconstruction is Not Enough: On Gianni Vattimo's Call for Weak Thinking.' *Graduate Faculty Philosophy Journal*, vol. 10, 1984, pp. 165–77.

Sheehan, Thomas J. 'Derrida and Heidegger.' In *Hermeneutics and Deconstruction*, SUNY, 1985, pp. 201–18.

Silverman, Hugh J. 'Self-Decentering: Derrida Incorporated.' *Research in Phenomenology*, vol. 8, 1978, pp. 45–65.

Silverman, Hugh J. 'Phenomenology.' *Social Research*, vol. 47, no. 4, 1980, pp. 704–20.

Silverman, Hugh J. 'The Limits of Logocentrism (On the Way to Grammatology).' In David Wood, ed. *Heidegger and Language*. Coventry, Warwick/Parousia Press, 1981, pp. 51–70. Reprinted in J.N. Mohanty, ed. *Phenomenology and the Human Sciences*. The Hague, Nijhoff, 1985, pp. 107–19.

Silverman, Hugh J. 'Writing (On Deconstruction) at the Edge of Metaphysics.' *Research in Phenomenology*, vol. 13, 1983, pp. 97–110.

Silverman, Hugh J. 'Phenomenology: From Hermeneutics to Deconstruction.' *Research in Phenomenology*, vol. 14, 1984, pp. 19–34. Reprinted, with 'Afterthoughts,' in Amedeo Giorgi, ed. *Phenomenology: Descriptive or Hermeneutic?* Pittsburgh, Duquesne University Phenomenology Center, 1987, pp. 19–34, 85–92.

Silverman, Hugh J. 'The Autobiographical Textuality of Nietzsche's *Ecce Homo*.' In Daniel O'Hara, ed. *Why Nietzsche Now?* Bloomington, Indiana University Press, 1985, pp. 141–51.

Silverman, Hugh J. 'Interrogation and Deconstruction.' *Phaenomenologische Forschung*, vol. 18. Freiburg, Alber, 1986, pp. 113–27.

Silverman, Hugh J. 'Readings of Texts/Authors of Works.' Session on 'Hermeneutics and Deconstruction.' *Journal of Philosophy*, 1986, pp. 14–15.

Silverman, Hugh J. 'Textuality and the Origin of the Work of Art.' In Hugh J. Silverman *et al*. eds. *The Horizons of Continental Philosophy*. Dordrecht, Nijhoff-Kluwer, 1988, pp. 153–67.

Terdiman, Richard. 'Deconstruction/Mediation: A Dialectical Critique of "Derrideanism".' *The Minnesota Review*, vol. 19, 1985, pp. 103–11.

Wood, David. 'Introduction to Derrida.' In *Radical Philosophy*, Spring 1979, pp. 18–28. Reprinted in R. Edgeley and Osborne, eds. *Radical Philosophy Reader*. London, Verso, 1985.

Wood, David. 'Derrida and the Paradoxes of Reflection.' *Journal of the British Society for Phenomenology*, vol. 11, no. 3, 1980, pp. 225–38.

Wood, David. 'Metametaphysical Textuality.' In David Wood, ed. *Heidegger and Language*. Coventry, University of Warwick/Parousia Press, 1982, pp. 26–45.

Wood, David. 'Heidegger after Derrida.' *Research in Phenomenology*, vol. 17, 1987, pp. 132–49.

Wood, David. 'Beyond Deconstruction?' In A. Phillips Griffiths, ed. *Contemporary French Philosophy*. Cambridge, Cambridge University Press, 1988.

NOTES ON CONTRIBUTORS

Ruben Berezdivin

Ruben Berezdivin received his doctorate from Duquesne University and has taught at Texas Tech University. He now lives in Florida and writes on Nietzsche and deconstruction. He is a contributor to the volume edited by John Sallis and entitled *Deconstruction and Philosophy* (Chicago University Press, 1987).

Rudolf Bernet

Rudolf Bernet teaches at the Catholic University of Leuven (Belgium) and is a member of the Board of Directors of the Husserl-Archives. He has published numerous articles mainly on Husserl, Heidegger, and Derrida and in the areas of psychoanalysis and the history of modern philosophy. He has also edited some of Husserl's writings and translated texts by Derrida.

Walter Brogan

Walter Brogan is Associate Professor of Philosophy at Villanova University. He teaches ancient Greek philosophy and its relation to the continental tradition. His publications include an essay on Derrida and Heidegger entitled 'The Original Difference.' He has also translated Heidegger's study of Aristotle's *Metaphysics* for Indiana University Press.

John D. Caputo

John D. Caputo is Professor of Philosophy at Villanova University and Distinguished Adjunct Professor of Philosophy at Fordham University. He is the author of *The Mystical Element in Heidegger's Thought* (Ohio University Press, 1978), *Heidegger and Aquinas: An Essay on Overcoming Metaphysics* (Fordham University Press, 1982), and *Radical Hermeneutics: Repetition, Deconstruction, and the Hermeneutic Project* (Indiana University Press, 1987).

Deborah Chaffin

Deborah Chaffin is Associate Professor of Philosophy at San Diego State University. She is author of articles on 'Edmund Husserl's *The Apodicticity of Recollection:* An Introduction and Translation,' *Husserl Studies* (1985), 'Passion and the Ethic of Empowerment,' *Cardozo Law Review* (1985), and 'Hegelian Dialectic and the Limits of Representation' in *Postmodernism and Continental Philosophy* (SUNY Press, 1988).

Bernard Flynn

Bernard Flynn teaches at Empire State College (State University of New York). He has published articles on various aspects of contemporary European philosophy and is presently writing a book entitled *Political Philosophy at the Closure of Metaphysics*.

Irene E. Harvey

Irene E. Harvey is Assistant Professor of Philosophy and Director of the Center for Psychoanalytic Studies at Pennsylvania State University. She has written articles on contemporary French thought and various historical figures in philosophy. Her book *Derrida and the Economy of Différance* was published by Indiana University Press in 1986.

Christina Howells

Christina Howells has been a Fellow of Wadham College, Oxford since 1979. She is author of *Sartre's Theory of Literature*

(M.H.R.A. London, 1979) and *Sartre: The Necessity of Freedom* (Cambridge University Press, 1988).

Dalia Judovitz

Dalia Judovitz is Associate Professor at Emory University. She has also taught seventeenth-century French philosophy and literature at the University of Pennsylvania, Duke University, and the University of California at Berkeley. She is author of *Subjectivity and Representation in Descartes: The Origins ᶜᶠ Modernity* (Cambridge University Press, 1987) and articles on philosophy and literature, psychoanalysis, French baroque and classical literature, and post-modernism in the visual arts.

Sarah Kofman

Sarah Kofman teaches philosophy at the University of Paris I, Sorbonne. She has published many books in French on psychology, the visual arts, literature, the Holocaust, and Nietzsche. Those translated into English include *The Enigma of Woman* (Cornell University Press, 1985) and *The Childhood of Art* (Columbia University Press, 1988).

Edith Wyschograd

Edith Wyschograd is Professor of Philosophy at Queens College of the City University of New York. In 1987–8, she was a Fellow of the Woodrow Wilson International Center for Scholars in Washington D.C. She is author of *Emmanuel Levinas: The Problem of Ethical Metaphysics* (Martinus Nijhoff, 1970) and *Spirit in Ashes: Hegel, Heidegger and Man-Made Mass Death* (Yale University Press, 1985).

About the Editor

Hugh J. Silverman is Professor of Philosophy and Comparative Literature at the State University of New York at Stony Brook. He has held visiting teaching posts at the Universities of Warwick and Leeds in England, at the University of Nice in France, and at Stanford University, Duquesne University, and New York University in the United States. Author of *Inscriptions: Between Phenomenology and Structuralism* (Routledge & Kegan Paul, 1987) and more than fifty articles in continental philosophy, philosophical psychology, aesthetics, literary theory, and cultural studies, he is also editor of *Piaget, Philosophy and the Human Sciences* (Humanities/Harvester, 1980), coeditor of *Jean-Paul Sartre: Contemporary Approaches to his Philosophy* (Duquesne/ Harvester, 1980), *Continental Philosophy in America* (Duquesne, 1983), *Descriptions* (SUNY Press, 1985), *Hermeneutics and Deconstruction* (SUNY Press, 1985), *Critical and Dialectical Phenomenology* (SUNY Press, 1987), *The Horizons of Continental Philosophy: Essays on Husserl, Heidegger, and Merleau-Ponty* (Nijhoff/Kluwer, 1988), *Postmodernism and Continental Philosophy* (SUNY Press, 1988), and *The Textual Sublime: Deconstruction and its Differences* (SUNY Press, forthcoming 1989).